REVISE BTEC NATIONAL
Performing Arts

T0346003

REVISION GUIDE

Series Consultant: Harry Smith

Authors: Emma Hindley and Heidi McEntee

While the publishers have made every attempt to ensure that advice on the qualification and its assessment is accurate, the official specification and associated assessment guidance materials are the only authoritative source of information and should always be referred to for definitive guidance.

This qualification is reviewed on a regular basis and may be updated in the future. Any such updates that affect the content of this Revision Guide will be outlined at **www.pearsonfe.co.uk/BTECchanges**. The eBook version of this Revision Guide will also be updated to reflect the latest guidance as soon as possible.

A note from the publisher

In order to ensure that this resource offers high-quality support for the associated Pearson qualification, it has been through a review process by the awarding body. This process confirms that this resource fully covers the teaching and learning content of the specification or part of a specification at which it is aimed. It also confirms that it demonstrates an appropriate balance between the development of subject skills, knowledge and understanding, in addition to preparation for assessment.

Endorsement does not cover any guidance on assessment activities or processes (e.g. practice questions or advice on how to answer assessment questions), included in the resource nor does it prescribe any particular approach to the teaching or delivery of a related course.

Pearson examiners have not contributed to any sections in this resource relevant to examination papers for which they had prior responsibility.

Examiners will not use endorsed resources as a source of material for any assessment set by Pearson.

Endorsement of a resource does not mean that the resource is required to achieve this Pearson qualification, nor does it mean that it is the only suitable material available to support the qualification, and any resource lists produced by the awarding body shall include this and other appropriate resources.

For the full range of Pearson revision titles across KS2, 11+, KS3, GCSE, Functional Skills, AS/A Level and BTEC visit: www.pearsonschools.co.uk/revise

Introduction

Which units should you revise?

This Revision Guide has been designed to support you in preparing for the externally assessed units of your course. Remember that you won't necessarily be studying all the units included here – it will depend on the qualification you are taking.

BTEC National Qualification	Externally assessed units
Certificate	1 Investigating Practitioners' Work
Extended Certificate Foundation Diploma	1 Investigating Practitioners' Work 3 Group Performance Workshop
Diploma	1 Investigating Practitioners' Work 3 Group Performance Workshop 5 Individual Performance Commission
Extended Diploma (General) Extended Diploma (Acting) Extended Diploma (Dance) Extended Diploma (Musical Theatre)	1 Investigating Practitioners' Work 3 Group Performance Workshop 5 Individual Performance Commission 7 Employment Opportunities in the Performing Arts

Your Revision Guide

Each unit in this Revision Guide contains two types of pages, shown below.

Content pages help you revise the essential content you need to know for each unit.

Skills pages help you prepare for your exam or assessed task. Skills pages have a coloured edge and are shaded in the table of contents.

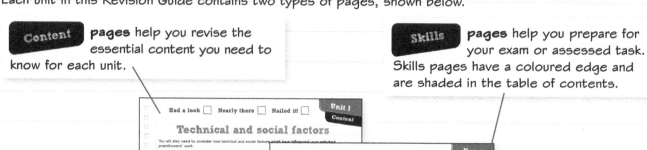

Use the **Now try this** activities on every page to help you test your knowledge and practise the relevant skills.

Look out for the **example student responses** to revision questions or tasks on the skills pages. Post-its will explain their strengths and weaknesses.

Contents

Unit 1 Investigating Practitioners' Work

1   Your Unit 1 set task
2   Task brief
3   Theme and practitioners
4   Assessment outcomes
5   Selecting primary sources
6   Selecting secondary sources
7   Research
8   Different formats
9   Collating information
10 Sources, formats and collating details
11 Documenting research sources
12 Footnotes and your bibliography
13 Historical and cultural factors
14 Economic and political factors
15 Technical and social factors
16 Geographical and physical factors
17 Other influences
18 Themes
19 Intentions, genre and target audiences
20 Influences on others, collaborations and responses
21 Collaborations
22 Critical analysis: getting started
23 Critical analysis: the next stage
24 Making condensed notes
25 Critical analysis skills
26 Further critical analysis skills
27 Performance styles: repertoire
28 Performance styles: the performance
29 Performance styles: relationships
30 Performance styles: production
31 Investigating performance styles
32 Summarising key information
33 Comparisons, conclusions and further research
34 Communicating your key points
35 Presentation of findings
36 Presenting judgements
37 Analysis and presentation

Unit 3 Group Performance Workshop

38 Your Unit 3 set task
39 Task brief
40 Revision stimuli
41 Types of stimulus
42 Theme as stimulus
43 Visual stimulus
44 Text stimulus
45 Aural stimulus
46 Media as stimulus
47 Responding to stimulus
48 Analyse your stimulus
49 What, for whom and how?
50 Where and who?
51 Primary research
52 Secondary research
53 Research and analysis
54 Discussion skills
55 Improvisation
56 Let's experiment!
57 Let's get technical!
58 Thinking about structure
59 Developing physical performance skills
60 Developing vocal performance skills
61 Developing musical performance skills
62 Developing communication skills
63 Develop, shape, create!
64 Developing early stage ideas
65 Developing more early stage ideas
66 Personal management skills
67 Rehearsal skills
68 Teamwork and collaboration
69 Developing mid-stage ideas
70 Continuing to progress
71 Performance preparation
72 Process review
73 Process strengths and developments
74 Performance review
75 Performance strengths and developments
76 Reviewing the process
77 Reviewing the performance

Unit 5 Individual Performance Commission

78 Your Unit 5 set task
79 Task information
80 Task stimuli
81 Understanding commission briefs
82 Commissioning bodies (1)
83 Commissioning bodies (2)
84 Commissioning bodies (3)
85 The purpose of a commission
86 Considering commissioning bodies and their purpose
87 Target audiences
88 Connecting the work to the audience
89 Considering the target audience and context
90 Requirements and constraints
91 Assessing requirements and constraints
92 Generating ideas for performance
93 Working from a thematic stimulus
94 Working from a visual stimulus
95 Working from a textual stimulus
96 Working from a media stimulus
97 Working from an aural stimulus
98 Primary and secondary research
99 Justifying ideas
100 Planning your written proposal
101 Practical exploration of stimulus
102 Establishing links
103 Developing materials and ideas
104 Structure and present action
105 Technical elements
106 Performance skills
107 Individual performance skills
108 Rehearse, practise and review
109 Managing your preparation time
110 Preparing for your solo
111 Evaluation: artistic effectiveness
112 Evaluating artistic effectiveness
113 Evaluation: professional effectiveness
114 Evaluating professional effectiveness
115 Evaluation: meeting requirements
116 Evaluating fulfilment of purpose
117 Evaluating the use of stimulus

Unit 7 Employment Opportunities in the Performing Arts

118 Your Unit 7 set task
119 Task information
120 Planning your preparation time
121 Organisational requirements
122 The purpose of an organisation
123 Vision, mission and values
124 Intended audience and stakeholders
125 Scope
126 Types of legal constitutions
127 Types of organisational structures
128 Advantages and disadvantages of different organisational structures
129 Funding restrictions and opportunities
130 Public sector funding
131 Private sector funding
132 Third sector funding
133 Access to funding: grants and contracts
134 Fundraising and direct selling
135 Marketing, HR and finance
136 Organisational operations
137 Education, creative and technical areas
138 Analysing information
139 Researching the organisation
140 Skills for professional practice
141 Experience for professional practice
142 Effective communication skills
143 Effective written communication skills
144 Pitching ideas
145 What is a promotional portfolio?
146 Alternative portfolio formats
147 Highlighting discipline and skills
148 Highlighting relevant skills
149 Understanding practical work
150 Selecting relevant video footage
151 Promotional intent
152 Are you right for the job?
153 Ensuring professionalism
154 Relating the employment opportunity to your skills
155 Thinking of workshop ideas
156 Your performance skills
157 Writing about your performance skills
158 Your employment skills
159 Your communication skills
160 Planning your written response
161 Planning your digital promotional portfolio
162 Content of your digital promotional portfolio
163 Creating your CV
164 Preparing video evidence
165 Selecting relevant video footage
166 Planning your supervised assessment time

167 Answers

• •

A small bit of small print
Pearson publishes Sample Assessment Material and the Specification on its website. This is the official content and this book should be used in conjunction with it. The questions in *Now try this* have been written to help you test your knowledge and skills. Remember: the real assessment may not look like this.

Your Unit 1 set task

Unit 1 will be assessed through a task, which will be set by Pearson. In this assessed task you will need to research and analyse the work of performing arts practitioners in response to a given brief.

Set task skills

This unit will help you to **revise essential content and skills** that might be needed in your assessed task.

You will practise:

- extending your knowledge and understanding of the contextual factors that influence practitioners' work and creative intentions
- honing your ability to critically analyse practitioners' work and the connections you make to a given theme through communication of independent judgements
- completing a structured piece of writing, investigating contextual influences and critically analysing the work of performing arts practitioners.

You will learn how to structure your writing so that it includes:

- research on selected practitioners
- contextual factors that have influenced and informed the practitioners' work
- critical analysis of their work in relation to a given theme
- critical analysis of at least one piece of repertoire by the practitioners
- clear examples to support your findings, judgements and conclusions
- a comprehensive bibliography of references and research sources.

Assessment checklist

Before any assessment session, make sure you:
- ✓ have double-checked the time and date of your assessment session
- ✓ get a good night's sleep.

Check the Pearson website

The skills pages are designed to demonstrate the skills that might be needed in your assessed task. The details of your actual assessed task may change from year to year so always make sure you are up to date. Check the Pearson website for the most up-to-date **Sample Assessment Material** to get an idea of the structure of your assessed task and what this requires of you.

Now try this

Visit the Pearson website and find the page containing the course materials for BTEC National Performing Arts. Look at the latest Unit 1 Sample Assessment Material for an indication of:

- the structure of your set task, and any preparation time
- what briefing or stimulus material might be provided to you
- any notes you might have to make and whether you are allowed to take selected notes into your supervised assessment
- the activities you are required to complete and the amount of any writing you may need to produce.

Task brief

The revision task below will help you to practise your skills of carrying out research, and writing up your findings, in response to a brief. It follows a similar format to your assessment, but it uses different practitioners and a different theme.

Task

A performing arts evening is being organised. This year, all the performances will be based on the theme of 'Identity' and will include works from Martha Graham and Oscar Hammerstein II.

You have been asked by the organisers to investigate contextual influences and critically analyse the work of either Martha Graham or Oscar Hammerstein. They would also like you to select a second practitioner of your choice, whose work you would recommend to be included in the evening.

The organisers would like you to explore the theme of 'Identity' and justify the inclusion of the work of your two chosen practitioners in relation to the theme.

Before you begin the activity, you are required to complete the following preparatory work.

1   Research the theme: 'Identity'.

2   Select **one** of the following practitioners:
    (a)   Martha Graham
    (b)   Oscar Hammerstein II.

3   Select a second practitioner of your own choice whose work addresses the theme of 'Identity'. For the purposes of this Revision Guide the other practitioner investigated is Kneehigh Theatre Company, in conjunction with Martha Graham or Oscar Hammerstein II.

A practitioner can be an individual or a company with international recognition and an established reputation and presence.

During the investigation of your selected practitioners' work, you will need to:

- research both of your selected practitioners using a range of relevant sources

- select relevant information related to the practitioners' work and the theme

- record information

- collate information

- reference and document your research in the form of a bibliography.

It's always good practice to document your sources while you are researching. If you leave this until you have to write up the bibliography, you will have to go back and try to trace all the references, which is a big job!

Reading a brief

This revision task is used as an example to show the skills you need. The content of a task will be different each year and the format may be different. You will need to refer back to this revision task when completing some of the 'Now try this' activities in your Revision Guide. Read through the information on this page and the next two pages so you are familiar with the theme and practitioners, and also the outcomes.

Theme and practitioners

Below is information about the theme and practitioners in the revision task on the previous page. You might not receive anything like this in your actual assessment, but you can use it to support your investigation and analysis in response to the revision task.

Theme: Identity

Identity in its simplest form is about who a person/group is, or what makes a person/group different from others. At a more complex level, identity is made up of many factors such as nationality, class, ethnicity and gender. Some parts of an identity are ascribed (you have no choice – such as gender, race) whereas others are achieved (you have made choices – such as employment, family life).

Postmodernists believe that identity is now much more complex, and that a new 'hybrid' identity has emerged. This is a combination of different types of identity, and has been influenced by the mass media and globalisation.

Performing arts practitioners and influential companies have always explored the theme of identity in their work, and challenged their audiences to think about identity, whether it be related to gender, race, nationality, sexuality, location or class.

Practitioner 1: Martha Graham (1894–1991)

Martha Graham was a groundbreaking artist of the 20th century. She saw the human body as an instrument of human expression and rebelled against the rigidity of ballet, creating a language of movement based on exhalation and inhalation of breath. Graham believed that the purpose of dance was to illuminate the life and struggles of the human experience. Some of Graham's work relates to national identity, such as *Frontier*. Also, much of her work relates to female identity; Martha Graham moved in a way that was radical for women at the time.

She adopted a psychoanalytical viewpoint on dance, stating that:

'Art is the evocation of man's inner nature. Through art we find man's unconscious – race memory – is the history and psyche of the race brought into focus.'

(Giguere, M., *Beginning Modern Dance*, 1998, Brown, Mindlin & Woodford, p. 50)

Practitioner 2: Oscar Hammerstein II (1895–1960)

Oscar Hammerstein II was a theatrical producer, librettist, lyricist and theatre director of musicals for almost 40 years. He reversed the process of musical writing, writing the lyrics first; his collaborators would then write the score. Hammerstein's most famous collaboration was with Richard Rodgers; together they created numerous popular Broadway musicals. Hammerstein II strongly believed that shows should tell the truth and convey a story. He wanted to communicate real issues, such as racial identity, which is explored in *South Pacific* and *Carmen Jones*. He said:

'I know the world is filled with troubles and many injustices. But reality is as beautiful as it is ugly. I think it is just as important to sing about beautiful mornings as it is to talk about slums. I just couldn't write anything without hope in it.'

(www.brainyquote.com/quotes/authors/o/oscar_hammerstein_ii.html, Brainy Quote, para 3, last accessed 7 April 2016)

Assessment outcomes

Whatever your actual assessed task, you will need to plan the completion of your task, setting yourself clear aims and objectives in relation to the four assessment outcomes. You could use these to help you structure your research and preparation, thinking about what each one involves and how long it will take you to complete.

AO1: Investigating contextual factors

This first outcome is about the investigation process, and covers conducting research from different sources, to collating and recording your information. You will need to show that you:

- carefully identify and select the relevant contextual factors
- know and understand the contextual factors that influence practitioners' work.

🔗 **Links** See pages 13–17 for information on contextual factors.

AO2: The relationship between contextual factors, creative intentions and themes

You will then need to explore the contextual factors that have influenced and informed the work of the selected practitioners. You will need to relate this to the given theme and apply your understanding. You will need to demonstrate that you:

- can apply your knowledge and have an in-depth understanding of contextual factors
- understand how contextual factors deeply influence practitioners' work
- can make insightful connections between the creative intentions of practitioners' work and the theme, using perceptive examples.

AO3: Critical analysis of the work of performing arts practitioners

You will be required to critically analyse the work of both selected practitioners in relation to the given theme. You will need to break down and study the parts (such as a scene/dance number/selection of repertoire from your selected practitioner) and give your own opinion. You will need to show that you:

- can apply critical analysis skills
- can critically analyse practitioners' work
- understand performance, production and repertoire, using perceptive examples to support your work.

AO4: Be able to present conclusions and independent judgements through effective investigation

You will need to show that you can summarise information in a structured fashion, as well as draw your own conclusions from the knowledge you have gained through investigation. You will also need to produce a bibliography to reference your sources effectively. You will need to show that you:

- can select sophisticated sources to fully support and inform your understanding
- can make authoritative independent judgements, justifying your argument with concise reasoning and perceptive use of evidence
- can use sophisticated and accomplished language, structure, tone and subject-specific terminology
- can reference your outcomes comprehensively.

Key questions

It is essential that you set clear aims and objectives:

- ✓ Who are your chosen practitioners?
- ✓ What types of research are you going to undertake?
- ✓ How will you structure your writing?
- ✓ How will you divide your time between research and writing?

Now try this

Look at the revision task on pages 2–3.

1 Write a short time plan for this task.
2 List your aims and objectives for the task.

You may wish to do this as a spider diagram.

Selecting primary sources

You need to select relevant ways to access information relating to the theme and practitioners you will be writing about. One method of research is **primary** research, which involves going out and collecting research yourself.

Interviews

An interview is a direct method of gaining information, although it can be difficult to achieve. Conducting an interview with a practitioner, director, choreographer, playwright, tutor or performer can give you further information about your theme or practitioners.

You must be well prepared, so plan ahead. Write a list of clear and sensible questions, and decide on a system for documenting answers – either by writing them down or recording the interview.

Recording the interview

You could always record the interview and then make notes which can inform your proposal and/or evaluation.

Live performance

If you are able to, watching a live performance is an excellent way of discovering the practitioner's artistic intentions, as well as the factors that influence their work. Make sure that you:

- make notes about the performance, either during the show or soon after the event
- buy a programme.

You might also be able to attend (and record) an after-show talk or discussion which could provide valuable insight into the practitioner and their artistic intentions.

Surveys

Conducting a survey to obtain information is a popular form of primary research. A survey can provide an unbiased approach to decision-making. These are the main things to remember when putting together a survey:

- Why are you sending it? Think about the main reasons so that all of your questions are relevant.
- Pinpoint your demographic: decide who you want to be completing the survey. You may want responses from several different groups.
- Sample size: make sure that you have enough people to complete the survey, so that the results are meaningful.
- Timing: work out which time is convenient for people to answer the survey; for example, at the interval of a performance.

To boost your survey's credibility, you need to consider these points.

You could conduct a survey among your peers, but you will access a much wider audience if you take surveys to a theatre.

Your survey can be online or on paper. Many web companies (such as SurveyMonkey) provide free, customisable survey services – would this be the best way of reaching your target audience?

Now try this

1 Look at the practitioner information on page 3. Create a short survey for a theatre audience at a production of one of Oscar Hammerstein II's musicals.
2 Write down the aim of your survey, and briefly describe how you could carry it out.

If you include vague, open-ended questions, it will be difficult to reach any firm conclusions from your research.

Selecting secondary sources

Secondary sources are pieces of research that already exist and you do not need to create them; for example books, film footage or the internet. These sources are often very useful for finding out more about your theme and chosen practitioners.

Web-based sources

Considerable research is undertaken on the internet, as it is so fast and accessible. You can use search engines to gain access to information, but make sure that you type in key words in order to get the best results. Remember that not all websites are reliable in terms of providing accurate information.

Take a screenshot of useful information you find on the internet, so that you can take notes from it which may contribute to your writing. Don't forget to reference your sources (see pages 11–12).

Print

It is worth making an effort to access print-based sources: visit your local library to consult books, journals, notated dances and musical theatre scores. This might be a more focused form of research, as it is easy to become overwhelmed or distracted when browsing the internet for information.

Using different methods to perform extensive research will impress your examiner.

Archives

You can access information by visiting archives. This might help you to become familiar with different practitioners' work, particularly if you are struggling to find information. Archives contain information documented over a long period of time, so historical factors that no longer exist but influenced practitioners' past work may well be available.

Recorded/digital resources

Recorded or digital footage of a practitioner is an easily accessible secondary source. Watching a performance or an interview with your selected practitioners can support your investigation. You can find videos of productions on the Digital Theatre website, iTunes and YouTube.

Remember to take notes so that you don't forget any vital information!

Case studies

A case study is an account of a person, group or situation that has been studied over time. Looking at case studies of practitioners or performance styles can help you to understand performers' artistic intentions and the characteristics of different styles.

Key theories

Reading key theories of performance could boost your understanding of the principles of dance, acting or musical theatre. Also, historical, political or social theories could be relevant to your research in terms of how they impact on the theme, as well as your selected practitioners' work.

Now try this

1 Perform some brief secondary research on the internet about Kneehigh Theatre Company, related to the theme of identity.

2 Document your findings in note form.

Research

Consider the following tips and guidance in relation to your **research**. You can refer to pages 5 and 6 as a reminder of the skills required.

 **Links** See Unit 3, pages 51–52 for skills advice on primary and secondary research.

Primary research
- Carrying out primary research can be time-consuming, but you will create evidence that no one else will be using.
- In your extended writing you will need to give your own opinion, backed up by evidence; results of your primary research might be used to justify your judgements.

Secondary research
- Spend time looking at different types of secondary research: books, journals, digital archives.
- Internet sources are not always reliable, so make sure that you are accessing professional, trustworthy sites.
- Record your findings accurately, and make sure that you note the correct website address for your bibliography.

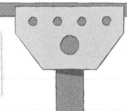

Using a balance of both primary and secondary research will give depth to your writing.

Here is an extract from a learner's writing, explaining the research techniques they used. Read the post-its to understand where they could improve.

Sample response extract

In terms of primary research I was able to see a live performance of Oscar Hammerstein II's work. This helped me to gain more insight into the motivation behind the work, as well as whether this was typical of Hammerstein's work.

 Assume that the reader will know nothing about the practitioners and theme. How did the performance help regarding the motivation behind the work? What is the motivation/intention? Was it typical of the practitioner? What work is typical of the practitioner?

In terms of secondary research I undertook internet research as well as visiting digital archives. I then collated my findings. While participating in internet research, I did extensive searches, making interesting discoveries. Also I found useful information in some books and journals that I found in the library, relating to political and social factors surrounding identity.

 Some valid points made regarding the types of research involved. However, detailed explanation is lacking, such as what discoveries were made. What useful information was found? Why was it useful?

Now try this

Choose one of the practitioners on page 3. Write down **three** types of primary research and **three** types of secondary research you could use to investigate this practitioner.

Different formats

As you collect your research, you can record it in a variety of **different formats**.

Journals and notebooks

You can easily record information in a journal or notebook. You can make notes, create spider diagrams and mind maps or write longer pieces of text.

Photographs

Photographs can be useful in recording research, such as demonstrating a movement or facial expression. They can also provide contextual information such as the historical or social background.

Videos

It might be useful to video some of your research; for example, if you have interviewed someone or watched a performance that you were able to record. You could also record yourself speaking about research you have collected, which you can transfer into note form at a later date.

Blogs

Blogs are a useful way of recording information online in an informal fashion. You can keep updating your blog regularly with relevant information, and might prefer the accessibility of this format.

Now try this

Use the internet to research the Martha Graham Dance Company.

1   Create a spider diagram of key facts about the company.

2   Choose an image which is representative of the company.

3   Write a short blog entry about your findings.

 Try to find at least two different online sources.

Collating information

You will gather a lot of information as you conduct the research and you will need to collate it. You will need to select relevant information and discard irrelevant information. You will then need to organise the information into the format you can use effectively for further work and to help you shape your writing. Read the tips below to help you organise your material.

Selection

You will need to select and organise your findings so that you are left with the most relevant research for the tasks and purpose. You could:

- focus on each of your practitioners using spider diagrams/mind maps
- create files/folders for each practitioner
- use highlighter pens to indicate where most relevant information is located.

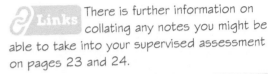 **Links** There is further information on collating any notes you might be able to take into your supervised assessment on pages 23 and 24.

You can keep electronic files or print out information and keep it in separate folders.

Your notes should be well organised and preferably in chronological order, so that you can work through them methodically.

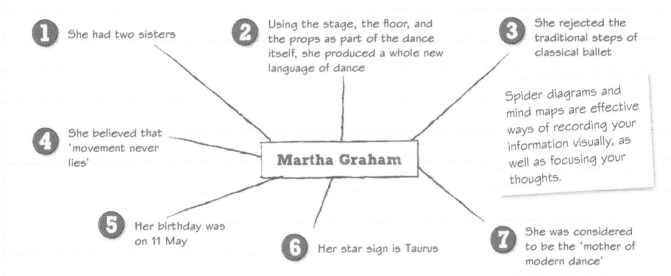

① She had two sisters

② Using the stage, the floor, and the props as part of the dance itself, she produced a whole new language of dance

③ She rejected the traditional steps of classical ballet

④ She believed that 'movement never lies'

Martha Graham

Spider diagrams and mind maps are effective ways of recording your information visually, as well as focusing your thoughts.

⑤ Her birthday was on 11 May

⑥ Her star sign is Taurus

⑦ She was considered to be the 'mother of modern dance'

Rejection

You will need to reject some of your research findings. Make sure that you focus on the **key information** in relation to your theme and selected practitioners. For this set task, you could:

- put to one side any information that does not relate to the theme of identity
- look at each piece of research in terms of how relevant it is to your investigation. For example, Martha Graham's star sign might not be vital information!

Don't automatically delete or throw away rejected information – you may have second thoughts and decide that you need it after all.

How do I organise?

It may be useful to organise your information according to:

✓ contextual factors

✓ the practitioner's creative intentions and themes

✓ performance styles and methods.

 Links See pages 13–17 for information on contextual factors.

Now try this

Look at the spider diagram above. Divide the points into useful and less-useful information – what would you select, and what would you reject?

Give reasons for your choices.

Sources, formats and collating details

Read the extract written by one learner below, along with the accompanying post-it notes. These should help you understand what you should **not** do in your own writing.

Sample response extract

I have used research from one book for my essay, as it provided me with all the material I needed about Martha Graham, Kneehigh Theatre Company and the theme of identity. I found out a lot of extremely relevant information about identity and wrote it all down in my notebook. I also found it interesting to watch Martha Graham's work such as:

Deaths and Entrances (1943)
A prime example of Graham's early psychological works, the dance is inspired by the lives of the three Brontë sisters and the struggle of women to follow their deepest impulses in the face of convention and tradition. Music: Hunter Johnson; Set: Arch Lauterer; Costumes: Graham; Dancers in this clip: Miki Orihara, Katherine Crockett, Virginie Mecene, and members of the Martha Graham Dance Company.

I also enjoyed watching:

Deep Song (1937)
A deeply resonant response to the Spanish Civil War, a cry of anguish, this solo is an embodiment of Graham's fears for a world torn apart by man's inhumanity to man. Music: Henry Cowell; Set: Graham; Costume: Graham; Dancer in this clip: Carrie Ellmore-Tallitsch.

I also watched other works such as 'Dark Meadow' and 'Dance is a Weapon' to gain further understanding of the Martha Graham technique.

 Try to use a variety of sources rather than just relying on one. This will allow you to gather information from different places which will broaden your knowledge and provide a less biased viewpoint.

 The learner has not stated **why** the pieces they watched were relevant and how they relate to the theme. Some of the information included is irrelevant, such as the list of dancers, set designers, etc.

The learner will need to acknowledge the sources in the bibliography, otherwise this could result in plagiarism.

 Remember that each point you make needs to be clear, concise and relevant. It is not a review about why you like a certain practitioner.

To improve this answer, you would need to explore how Martha Graham's technique relates to the theme of identity rather than simply mentioning the names of her other works.

Martha Graham's work – Letter to the World

Now try this

Choose a practitioner you have researched.

1   Describe **one** piece of work you watched as part of this research.
2   Explain why this piece was relevant to your research.

 You could use one of the practitioners on page 3, or another practitioner that you have researched.

Documenting research sources

It is vital that you **document** your **research sources** using citation, referencing and a bibliography.

Citation

Citation means indicating where the information you are using came from so that you give credit to the authors of the source. For example, when you want to use some phrases or words from websites or books, you should let the readers know what kind of sources you used, who created the source and when the source was created. You are therefore giving credit to the authors of the source and avoiding **plagiarism** (effectively 'stealing' ideas from other people).

You will need to use citation throughout your writing for Unit 1. You can cite a work by inserting the author's name and the date of publication in brackets directly after the quoted material in your writing, for example 'Smith, 2010'. This title should then also be listed in the bibliography (see below). Alternatively you can use footnotes to cite sources.

Other useful phrases

'**Paraphrasing**' means taking words or sentences from your sources and putting them into your own words. You still need to mention the original author.

'**Quotation**' means taking words, phrases or sentences directly from the person who created them, putting them inside quotation marks.

Footnotes are used as a way of numerically listing your sources. Insert a footnote reference straight after the quotation. If you are using a word processor such as Word, a number will appear after the quotation and at the bottom of the page. You can then add the relevant source at the bottom of the page. The source will also need to be listed in the bibliography in alphabetical order.

Referencing

Referencing means the format in which you give all the information about a source. There are various systems of referencing, such as 'Harvard referencing'. The approach you will need to take is shown below.

Bibliography

As part of your assessment you may have to write a **bibliography** – a complete alphabetical list of all sources used in your work with the correct referencing format.

Try to organise your bibliography into different sections for books, websites, journals, DVDs and so on, so that it is easy to navigate.

Do not only list sources that you have taken direct quotations from; you also need to write down sources that you have used for background reading, or where you have paraphrased information. This differs from a reference list, where only sources that you have cited/quoted from are listed.

The information you will need for videos or YouTube clips is similar to that for books and websites, requiring the video title or URL as well as key information such as date of recording, publisher/author, location, format and date accessed.

Standard referencing method

For the standard form of referencing, you need to provide this information:

Printed sources
- the author's name (surname then initial)
- title of work
- year it was published
- name of publisher
- page number.

Each detail of a reference is important.

Example: Williams, D. J., 'The Performer on Stage', 2016, Theatre Books, p. 100.

Online sources
- website address (copy and paste this from the browser)
- title of the web page
- paragraph number
- date you last accessed the source.

Web pages change quickly and are sometimes removed, so it is important to date your research.

For example: www.theatrestudies.com, Epic Theatre, para 4, last accessed 1 September 2016.

Now try this

Choose one website and one book that you have used as part of your research. Write a paragraph containing a quote from each source, making sure that you correctly cite or reference the sources.

Footnotes and your bibliography

You will need to document your research sources effectively to avoid plagiarism. Use the tips below to develop your skills in this area.

Sample response extract

I have researched Martha Graham and the theme of identity and I found out that there is a vitality, a life force, an energy, a quickening, that is translated through you into action, and because there is only one of you in all time, this expression is unique which really shows what Martha Graham thought about identity.

The learner has taken a quotation and used it as if the words were their own, which is inappropriate. Anything directly quoted from a source should be in quotation marks. It should then be referenced at the bottom of the page in a footnote and in the bibliography.

Improved response extract

I have researched Martha Graham and the theme of identity, and I found out that 'there is a vitality, a life force, an energy, a quickening, that is translated through you into action, and because there is only one of you in all time, this expression is unique'.1

This quotation gives you some idea about how Martha Graham viewed identity, seeing everyone as expressive individuals.

[1] www.goodreads.com/author/quotes/47790.Martha_Graham, para 2, last accessed 14 June 2016.

The learner has put the quotation in quotation marks, which is correct. A footnote number is also provided which will take the reader to the bottom of the page where they can see the source.

The learner has produced a well-organised bibliography which is split into clear sections and includes references from both websites and books.

Sample response extract

Websites
http://marthagraham.org/about-us/our-history/
Martha Graham Dance Company, para 3, last accessed 10 February 2016.

Books
Thoms, V., 'Martha Graham: Gender & The Haunting of a Dance Pioneer', 2013, University of Chicago Press, p. 31.
Graham, M., 'Blood Memory: An Autobiography', 1993, Sceptre, new edition, pp. 45–48

DVDs
'Martha Graham in Performance', 2002, DVD, California, Kultur Video.

Websites have been referenced effectively, with the title of the website underneath.

The learner has included the author name, book title, publisher and year. This list would be improved by placing the author's surnames in alphabetical order.

DVDs have been referenced effectively.

Now try this

Practise your referencing skills by organising some recent research into a bibliography.

Remember to use sections to organise the type of sources you have used.

Unless you noted all of the information down when you performed the research, you will have to track it down again. Save time by noting down complete references while you work.

Historical and cultural factors

As part of your research you need to look at the context of the work of your selected practitioners. Consider how they were influenced by elements such as historical and cultural factors.

Historical factors: key events

Historical factors: epoch

'Epoch' means a particular period of time in history or a person's life. Researching the epoch of your selected practitioners may help you gain a better understanding of the intentions behind their work. For example, if a practitioner was working within the postmodernist epoch (late 20th century), this may have influenced the kind of work they were creating.

This is a picture of Nelson Mandela and his wife Winnie when he was released from prison in South Africa on 11th February, 1990. Significant events in history such as this one could have impacted on the work of your practitioners. Perform research to discover if this was the case, looking at what key events occurred within their lifetimes, or close to their lifetimes. You may then be able to draw parallels between historical events and the practitioners' creative themes and intentions.

Cultural factors: minority group

Minority groups are people who have less control/power over their lives than the majority or dominant population. If your practitioners belonged to a minority group, this could have impacted on their work and creative intentions.

Cultural factors: world influences

These can be issues, trends and events. World influences are influences caused by anything that affects the whole world. Consider whether your practitioners were affected by world/global influences. If they were, why, and how?

Cultural factors: communities

Cultural factors: other art forms

Other art forms may have influenced the creative outlook of practitioners. For example, an actor/director may be influenced by musicians, dancers or artists from the same era, or a previous one.

Communities are groups of people living in the same place or having a particular characteristic in common. Your selected practitioners may have lived in communities that had a direct impact on the work they were creating.

Now try this

Choose one of the practitioners you have researched. How have historical and cultural factors impacted on their work?

 Try to be specific, listing works or quotations that show the influence of different historical or cultural factors.

Economic and political factors

You also need to investigate how **economic** and **political** factors might have influenced your practitioners' work.

Economic factors: funding conditions

Consider your practitioners' work in relation to what kind of funding was available at the time, and how this may have impacted on the decisions they made. For example, the availability of funds might have affected the scale of their performances or how much they could pay their dancers; these factors would have shaped their work.

Economic factors: financial climate

Your selected practitioners might have been affected by the financial climate – how financially stable the country was at the time of writing/ performing. For example, a recession could mean unemployment and cuts to funding, but alternatively, a financial boom could help to strengthen or develop artistic companies.

Political factors: legislation

This means a law or set of laws made by a government. Legislation exists for most areas of our lives, such as education, health and even the arts. In putting on a performance, practitioners need to observe legislation such as employment laws, or health and safety issues in relation to the venue.

Propaganda is information used to promote a political point of view; it is often of a misleading nature. When artists or practitioners create work that challenges conventions propaganda might be used by their opponents to discourage its popularity. For example in Tennessee Williams' *A Streetcar Named Desire*, law and propaganda were used by the government to discourage the messages and themes of the play.

Political factors: propaganda

Political events: satire

Satire is a genre of literature and performing arts – forms of ridicule such as sarcasm or irony are used to highlight inadequacies or vices. Practitioners may choose to use satire to communicate political messages or intentions, or have been influenced by forms of satire. Modern examples of political satire include the plays of David Hare, or the television programme, *Have I got News for You*.

Political events: current events

The political climate may have an impact on practitioners' work, such as the people in government at the time and their policies. Political events such as elections, referendums, budgets and summits may influence artists, who might choose to communicate to their audiences at a particular point in time.

Now try this

Choose one of the practitioners you have researched. How have economic and political factors impacted on their work?

 It might be helpful to create a spider diagram or mind map to record this information.

Technical and social factors

You will also need to consider how technical and social factors might have influenced your selected practitioners' work.

Technical factors: latest developments

The availability and choice of technology holds many more possibilities for practitioners today compared to previous years. For example, a new role of 'video designer' is becoming popular. Video designers embrace digital technology, bringing it to the stage in terms of 3-D projections, virtual-reality masks and computer animation.

Technical factors: restrictions

In previous years practitioners may have felt restricted by the technical elements available. Recent developments allow practitioners to incorporate more sophisticated sound equipment into their work for example, as well as more complex set designs.

There have also been advancements in the choice and use of lighting. In previous eras, practitioners would have needed to rely more on the content of the work to communicate artistic intentions.

Social factors: fashion

Fashion can relate to clothing, hair, decoration or behaviour. Practitioners could be influenced by fashion in terms of costumes that performers may wear. Popular styles/images could provide inspiration for creating pieces; alternatively, some practitioners may rebel against popular fashion.

Social factors: values

Values are principles or standards of behaviour. Practitioners may wish to reinforce or challenge social values in their work. They may be influenced by standards of behaviour, which are then expressed in their work.

Social factors: media

Media is the main means of mass communication, which includes television, radio, newspapers and the internet. Practitioners can be influenced by what they read, see or hear in the media. This could then translate into the work they create, whether it is news items about earthquakes or television comedies.

Social factors: audience expectations

When watching a performance, an audience would expect to be entertained, first and foremost. Practitioners will strive to do this, although they may also want to communicate serious messages, challenge conventions or invite audience participation.

Now try this

Choose one of the practitioners you have researched. How have technical and social factors impacted on their work?

Geographical and physical factors

You will also need to consider how your selected practitioners were influenced by geographical and physical factors.

Geographical factors: venues

Many different types of venues are possible for performance; for example:

- site-specific such as a beach or castle
- conventional theatre (proscenium arch)
- concert hall
- opera house
- in the round.

Practitioners are influenced by what venues are available and affordable, as well as the particular setting they want for their work. Sometimes work has to be adapted to fit within a type of venue. For dance performances, sprung floors may be a consideration, as well as where the wings are situated. A raked stage may be more suitable for an acting or musical theatre performance.

Outdoor theatres include amphitheatres which are open circular/oval buildings surrounded by tiers for spectators. This structure had an important impact on Ancient Greek drama.

Living in a harsh or beautiful natural environment can influence a practitioner's work.

Physical factors: physical characteristics of a place

Physical characteristics of a place include:

- bodies of water
- climate
- natural vegetation
- animal life.

A practitioner's work could be influenced by the natural environment in which they grew up. Also this might stimulate them to create work about places where they lived / aspired to live / disliked living.

Now try this

Choose one of the practitioners you have researched, and consider how geographical and physical factors have impacted on their work.

Other influences

You will need to consider influences such as other practitioners, performers and educators, for example teachers and mentors.

Influences from other practitioners and performers

Your chosen practitioner might have been influenced by other practitioners or performers in their field. In fact, it would be difficult for practitioners not to be influenced by what they have watched as they are growing up or when they are developing as artists.

Alternatively practitioners could rebel against popular practitioners or performers and instead try to create new works that may challenge conventions, such as the way in which Oscar Hammerstein reversed the process of writing musicals (lyrics before music).

Lloyd Newson created a new form of dance theatre with his company DV8: Physical Theatre.

Influences from education, teachers and mentors

A practitioner's outlook and knowledge of the field will be shaped by where they received their training. This in turn could have an impact on their work.

Some practitioners attribute much of their success to their education, whether it is the institution itself, specific teachers or mentors. Practitioners could also be influenced by friends or family members.

Martha Graham was influenced by her father who used physical movement to remedy nervous disorders.

Now try this

Choose one of the practitioners you have researched.

1 Describe the influences of other practitioners and performers on their work.
2 Describe how their education impacted their work.

Themes

As part of your investigation you will need to consider the themes behind your selected practitioners' work.

War

War is a common theme in performance. This ranges from showing conflict between people in the form of a physical theatre group piece, to musical theatre performances or plays taking the theme of war or based on a particular war.

War enables conflict to be explored and shown, creating tension and taking the audience on an emotional journey, often to demonstrate the futility of war.

Many anti-war plays were created in response to the First and Second World Wars – for example, *Oh! What a Lovely War*.

Some dance styles are associated with war/combat. For example, capoeira combines martial arts and dance, and originated in Brazil. It is viewed as a fighting method and a means of self-defence as well as being performed for entertainment.

The Punch and Judy puppet show is based on morality: Punch is both the hero and the villain

Morality

Morality is about the extent to which something is right or wrong. It can be communicated through all disciplines, but is most famously demonstrated in 'morality' plays. Here, the hero is faced with choices of good and evil; he meets characters who symbolise abstract qualities such as vice or virtue. Morality plays were popular in Europe during the 15th and 16th centuries. The purpose of these plays was to teach a moral lesson.

Romance

Love and romance is an ever-popular theme in performance. From musical theatre performances such as **West Side Story**, telling the tale of forbidden love, to Shakespeare's 'romance plays' such as **The Tempest**, this age-old theme is frequently used. Practitioners seek new ways to convey this universal theme, which often include an obstacle such as unrequited or unreciprocated love.

A new spin on the theme of love and romance by the physical theatre company Frantic Assembly in *Lovesong*.

Now try this

Choose one of the practitioners you have researched. Identify a theme that they have explored and describe how they have interpreted this theme through their work.

Have they successfully reworked an old message, or defied convention and presented the audience with something totally new?

Intentions, genre and target audiences

When investigating your practitioners, you will need to consider their creative intentions, genre and intended target audiences.

Creative ideas and intentions

An intention or creative idea relates to what the practitioner is trying to express or communicate in performance. This could be a serious topic, or perhaps is purely for entertainment. For each of your practitioners think about these questions:

- Are there recurring themes/intentions in their pieces?
- Are the practitioners successful in conveying their intentions?
- How do they achieve this?

Kneehigh Theatre Company's themes have been described as 'universal and local, domestic and epic'. In their production of the legend *The Umbrellas of Cherbourg*, love and endurance are the main themes.

Hammerstein and Rodgers continued to merge the styles of operetta and musical comedy into a completely new genre known as the musical play. This became the most consistently successful partnership in American musical theatre.

Genre

Genre means style, which in performing arts involves a particular set of characteristics. Examples of genre are: comedy, tragedy, fantasy, realism.

Some practitioners choose to rebel against the conventions of a genre. For each of your practitioners, think about these questions:

- What genre does their work sit in?
- Is it typical of the genre?
- Why?

Target audiences and intended effect

The target audience is a particular group at which a performance is aimed. When choreographing or directing, a practitioner will have a target audience in mind, as well as an intended 'effect' on the audience, whether this is to shock or entertain. For each of your practitioners think about these questions:

- What was their usual target audience?
- What was the intended 'effect' on the audience, and does this fluctuate between pieces?
- Why does it fluctuate?

Martha Graham's work intended to have a 'visceral' effect on the audience, connecting to their feelings rather than their intellect.

Now try this

Give **one** example of how creative intentions, genre or target audience could be affected by:

(a) historical factors

(b) economic or political factors

(c) social or technical factors

(d) geographical factors.

Links Look at pages 13–17 for more on these contextual factors.

Influences on others, collaborations and responses

When investigating your practitioners, you will also need to think about how they influenced others, who they have collaborated with and how the audience responded to their work.

How practitioners' work has influenced others

As well as your selected practitioners being influenced by others, they have the capacity to have an impact on their audiences and other practitioners. In relation to your practitioners, think about these questions:

- Have they influenced others?
- Who have they influenced?
- How has this been expressed?

For example, Martha Graham was influenced by Ruth St. Denis and Ted Shawn. She then went on to influence many other dancers including Alvin Ailey, Merce Cunningham and Twyla Tharp whom she taught.

> No practitioner works in a vacuum – each influences and is influenced by other practitioners, past and present.

Ruth St. Denis

Martha Graham

Twyla Tharp

Collaboration with other practitioners

Practitioners often collaborate with other practitioners in the creation of work. This allows a combination of ideas to take place, with practitioners pooling their thoughts and drawing on each other's particular skills. In relation to your practitioners, think about these questions:

- Have they collaborated with anyone?
- Who?
- How has this affected their work?

For example, Martha Graham collaborated with some of the foremost artists of her time, including the composer Aaron Copland and the sculptor Isamu Noguchi.

Public and critical responses to their work

Practitioners may receive mixed responses to their work, whether from the general public who pay to watch their performances, or the critics who are paid to write about them. In relation to your practitioners, think about these questions:

- How has their work been received by the public and critics?
- What are the reasons for this?
- Has this affected them when developing further material?

Now try this

Choose a practitioner you have researched. Briefly describe:

(a) how their work has influenced others

(b) the public and critical responses to their work.

 Use the questions above to help you.

Collaborations

Here are some extracts from learners' writing who decided to talk about the influence of collaboration on their chosen practitioners. Read the extracts and post-its to understand how to write an effective response about the influence of contextual factors on practitioners.

Sample response extract

Oscar Hammerstein II famously collaborated with Richard Rodgers, with Rodgers creating the melodies and Hammerstein II writing the words. Together they wrote 11 musicals between 1943 and 1959. Six of these were huge successes and Oklahoma, which was their first collaboration, ran for an impressive five years. Rodgers and Hammerstein II focused on meaningful story lines; no longer was the music just for decoration – music had to be rooted in character and plot.

Good example of how a practitioner collaborates and creates material. Has he collaborated with other practitioners?

Good use of facts to demonstrate the success of their collaboration. A reference would need to be provided to acknowledge the source.

Could any of the above information be linked to the theme of identity? For example some of Hammerstein II's work relates to social/political/cultural identity.

An example of a direct influence has been provided here.

You could also use direct quotations to justify any statements you make. If you do, remember to state their source in your bibliography.

Effective link to identity.

Sample response extract

Kneehigh Theatre Company were influenced by 'Footsbarn Theatre' who were also based in Cornwall. (It's believed that Footsbarn also led to the creation of Complicite and Told by an Idiot: these companies like to reach out to their audience and incorporate elements of circus and clowning into their work.) This demonstrates that geographical identity is important to Kneehigh.

The public's response to Kneehigh's work is sometimes very interactive. For example, at performances of 'Tristan and Yseult' the audience act more like fans, blowing up white balloons in the wedding scene and dancing through the interval. This demonstrates a physical and emotional response.

Good example of audience reaction.

Remember to reference any information you use in your bibliography.

Here is the Kneehigh Theatre Company on location at Hayle in Cornwall.

Now try this

Choose one of the practitioners from page 3, or another practitioner that you have researched. Create approximately half a page of notes on the contextual factors that have affected that practitioner.

Making concise notes is an important skill.

Critical analysis: getting started

You need to critically analyse practitioners' work in relation to the theme.

Analysing contextual factors that have influenced the work

Having collated research about contextual factors, you will need to analyse your information. This will include thinking about these questions:

- **How** have contextual factors influenced the work of your practitioners?
- What are your **opinions** about this?
- How do your findings relate to the **theme**?

For your assessment you will need to critically analyse at least one scene/dance number/ selection of repertoire from a piece of work by your own choice of practitioner.

Oklahoma provided escapism from the harsh realities of the Second World War. However, it was more than just comedy and romance; there was a strong storyline which was based on *Green Grow the Lilacs*.

Critical analysis involves not only breaking down and studying the parts, but also providing a subjective opinion.

Exploration and understanding of alternative viewpoints

Your exploration should be wide-ranging; at this stage you should be able to collate varied viewpoints and appreciate different schools of thought relating to the practitioners and theme. Think about:

- critics' and reviewers' opinions
- audience responses
- how this may have impacted on the practitioners and the work they create.

It is beneficial to consider a range of viewpoints before stating your own opinion. You may share someone else's views or have entirely different ones.

To access a variety of viewpoints you will need to ensure that your research and exploration is extensive, collecting information from different sources.

Interpreting the information collected

Once you have all your research in front of you, begin to **interpret** it; in other words, explain what it means.

It may seem daunting to try and interpret your information; be patient and work through it methodically, focusing on the different elements one at a time.

Asking yourself 'why' in relation to each piece of information is a good idea. Otherwise you are in danger of merely 'describing' rather than 'explaining' or 'analysing'.

Think about:

- how this has impacted on the work of the practitioners
- how this relates to the theme.

How important is this piece of information?

How do I interpret the information?

What impact did this have on the practitioner?

How does it relate to the theme?

The interpretation process

Now try this

Choose a practitioner you have researched. Analyse the impact of **two** factors on your selected practitioner's work (use the questions above to get you started).

You might find it helpful to create your analysis in note form, spider diagrams, flow charts or mind maps.

Bear in mind the process of interpretation illustrated above.

Critical analysis: the next stage

You will also need to consider prioritising and evaluating information, as well as making independent judgements.

Prioritising the information collected

It is important to cover all of the elements listed in the specification in your written essay.

This will mean prioritising the information: selecting the most significant material in relation to the two practitioners and theme. When you have collated your information, think about selecting your best pieces. If some of your information does not shed any light on the practitioners' work, it probably should not be included in your essay.

If you have conducted extensive research, you will probably need to discard some of the information. Think of this as a necessary filtering process in order to refine your findings.

Keep discarded information (and sources) in a safe place, in case you change your mind or the focus of your analysis alters.

Evaluating the information collected

Evaluating means judging the significance of something. Once you have sorted through your research and prioritised information of value, it is now time to state why it is significant. You can refer to its strengths as well as weaknesses in relation to a practitioner's work.

You may have experience of evaluating your own work. Apply these evaluation skills to the work of others. Think about what stands out, and what could be developed.

Making independent judgements

Having considered the opinions of others about the practitioner's work, you will be expected to make your own judgements. You may form an entirely different opinion from other critics, or share a viewpoint. The important thing is to be clear about **what** your opinion is and **why**.

Be confident in expressing your own opinion. As long as you clearly explain how you have reached that decision and show that you have taken on board the opinions of others, it doesn't matter what viewpoint you take.

It is difficult not to be heavily influenced by a review of a practitioner's work, but it is important to make up your own mind.

Carousel

Best Show Ever!' '5 stars'. ★★★★★

Now try this

Look at some of your own research notes.

1 Highlight the most important pieces of information.
2 Identify at least **two** less important pieces of information which you could leave out.

If you find that lots of your information is not relevant, perhaps you need to improve your research skills so that in future you can quickly identify the important information to support your essay.

Making condensed notes

Being able to make concise notes can help you to revise. You may also be able to take some notes into your assessment. This page shows you how to generate useful notes.

Sample notes extract

I am focusing on the work of 'South Pacific' to explore in more detail. The work premiered on Broadway in 1949 and ran for 1925 performances. The aim of the collaborators was to make money and send out a message about racism. The plot is about an American nurse who is working on an island in the South Pacific during the Second World War. She falls for an expat French plantation owner, but finds it hard to accept his mixed-race children. A sub plot (another romance), between an American lieutenant and a young Tonkinese woman, explores his fears of the social consequences if he were to wed his Asian sweetheart. Racial prejudice is explored throughout the musical, epitomised in the song 'You've Got to Be Carefully Taught'.

This learner has written out their response to their writing in full. If you format your notes for the supervised assessment in this way, it will take too long and you won't have time to do enough research. Instead, you need to use bullets or diagrams to summarise the information you have collected, analysed and prioritised during your preparation. What are the most significant pieces of information in this paragraph? It may help to present this in the form of a diagram.

Improved notes extract

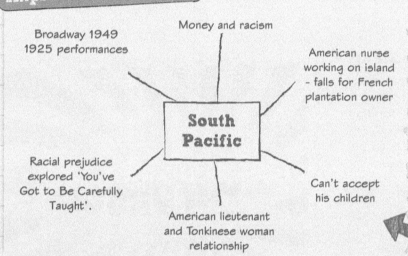

Broadway 1949
1925 performances

Money and racism

American nurse working on island – falls for French plantation owner

South Pacific

Racial prejudice explored 'You've Got to Be Carefully Taught'.

Can't accept his children

American lieutenant and Tonkinese woman relationship

Preparatory notes

You may be allowed to take some of your preparatory notes into your supervised assessment time. If so, there may be restrictions on the length and type of notes that are allowed. Check with your tutor or look at the most up-to-date Sample Assessment Material on the Pearson website for details.

This learner has created better notes by presenting the same information in the form of a mind map. It would be a good idea to further condense this type of information. Discard some of the words/phrases so that you are left with the key points only.

Improved notes extract

South Pacific:

- Broadway 1949
- Message of racism: 'You've Got to Be Carefully Taught'
- Relationship 1 – American nurse and French plantation owner
- Relationship 2 – Tonkinese lady and American Lieutenant

This learner has made the most concise effective notes which will enable them to access information easily. This will help them to prepare a piece of writing.

Now try this

Choose a section of your own research notes which is written in full. Rewrite this information in bullet point form.

Remember you can do this in stages, going from the full version to a mind map/ spider diagram and then bullet points.

Critical analysis skills

In your assessment you will need to use critical analysis skills to explain how a practitioner has been effective in communicating the chosen theme. You will need to draw on evidence from the research you have carried out and use this as a basis to make your own independent judgements. Read the sample response extracts with post-it notes below to understand how you might do this.

Sample response extract

I think that Rodgers and Hammerstein II's 'South Pacific' has many strengths, including its modern and mature approach. The songs and stories seem to fuse together fluently and there are elements of tragedy, comedy, romance, fantasy and reality throughout. There are also examples of the pair communicating messages through the storyline, which are subtle and effective. For example, the character Joe confronts his own prejudices in the song 'Carefully Taught' and also expresses his feelings about racial barriers. This shows that Rodgers and Hammerstein II like to communicate messages relating to the social and cultural/political climate of the time. It also illustrates their handling of identity relating to visual appearance and race.

 Effective subjective opinion including relevant observations.

 How does he confront his own prejudices? More detail could be provided here.

 Successful link to theme of identity.

A still from *South Pacific*

Independent judgement made here regarding the choice of repertoire in relation to locality.

Could this be linked to the theme of identity perhaps?

Sample response extract

Kneehigh Theatre Company have clearly been influenced by geographical, historical, cultural and social factors, drawing inspiration from the people, landscape, culture and history of Cornwall. This probably links to their selection and interpretation of the Cornish legend 'Tristan and Yseult'. They often performed outdoors in unusual locations such as cliff-tops and quarries, where local people could access their work. Now they tour both the UK and internationally, but are still intent on making their work accessible to the community. Kneehigh say that they want to reach people who might not be able to see their work because they are restricted, for example by a lack of money.

Whenever you can, use direct quotes, making sure you reference them by giving the full source in the bibliography.

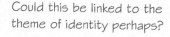

Now try this

Choose one of the practitioners listed on page 3. Write a paragraph about their treatment of identity. Remember to prioritise and evaluate your information, and make an independent judgement of the work.

25

Further critical analysis skills

These additional sample learner responses should help you to see what you need to do when drawing conclusions, making comparisons and exploring opportunities for further research.

Sample response extract

Oscar Hammerstein II was influenced by family members who had a background in the theatre. His father was the manager of a famous Vaudeville theatre and his uncle was a well-known producer. Hammerstein II went on to surpass them with his talents. He also had a massive influence on other musical theatre practitioners, for example Stephen Sondheim. Sondheim wrote lyrics for shows such as 'West Side Story' and 'Sweeney Todd' and put his success down partly to Hammerstein II who had guided and influenced him from an early age. When Hammerstein II died, he left behind him three children: William, Alice and James.

Example of how Hammerstein II has influenced others.

This last sentence of information is not relevant and could be omitted.

Stephen Sondheim

Sample response extract

Comparisons between practitioners with specific examples provided.

Could any of this information be linked to the theme of identity?

Potential for further investigation identified.

There are similarities between the work of Footsbarn Theatre Company and Kneehigh which relate to their use of puppetry. In Footsbarn's 'Cuckoo's Nest' and Kneehigh's 'Dead Dog in a Suitcase' puppets are used to dramatic effect. Puppetry also has links with the work of Martha Graham. She choreographed a piece called 'Punch and the Judy' which is a comic ballet about marital discord. However puppetry is not the main performance method for any of the above practitioners.

It would be interesting to further investigate the key performance methods for both Kneehigh and Martha Graham, in order to gauge whether there are other links in addition to puppetry, such as use of costume and set.

This information will need to be sourced effectively in the bibliography even though there are no direct quotes.

Now try this

Look at the two sample response extracts above. For each one, write a paragraph either supporting their arguments, or presenting an opposite view. Give evidence from your own research to support your points.

Remember to find source details for all quotations and background information and include them in the correct referencing style in the bibliography.

Performance styles: repertoire

As part of your investigation you will need to look at a practitioner's repertoire – this means the collection of performances that a practitioner produces.

Investigating a practitioner's repertoire

For each of the six elements shown in this diagram, you will need to carefully consider:

- how it is significant to the practitioner's work
- whether it is typical of the practitioner's work
- how it is used to communicate meaning.

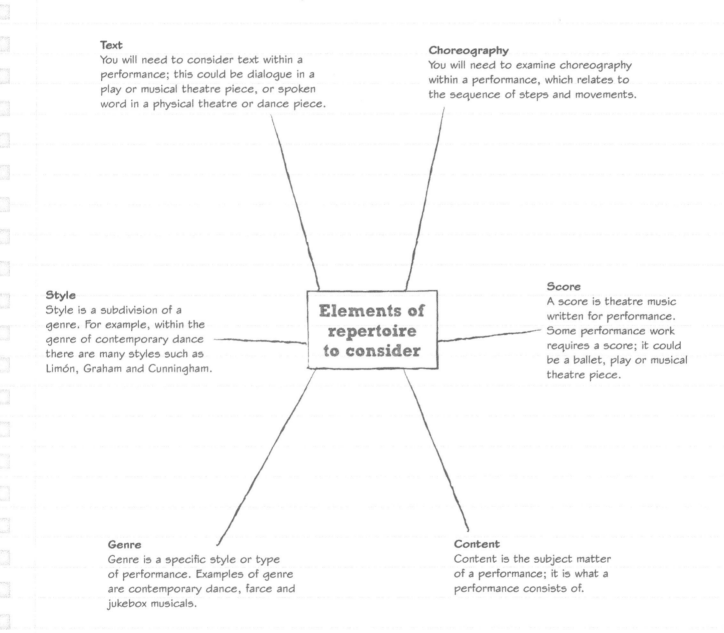

Text
You will need to consider text within a performance; this could be dialogue in a play or musical theatre piece, or spoken word in a physical theatre or dance piece.

Choreography
You will need to examine choreography within a performance, which relates to the sequence of steps and movements.

Style
Style is a subdivision of a genre. For example, within the genre of contemporary dance there are many styles such as Limón, Graham and Cunningham.

Elements of repertoire to consider

Score
A score is theatre music written for performance. Some performance work requires a score; it could be a ballet, play or musical theatre piece.

Genre
Genre is a specific style or type of performance. Examples of genre are contemporary dance, farce and jukebox musicals.

Content
Content is the subject matter of a performance; it is what a performance consists of.

Now try this

Choose one of the practitioners listed on page 3, or select another practitioner you have researched. Create a spider diagram with notes on the six elements of repertoire listed above.

Performance styles: the performance

You will also need to look at elements of performance such as pace, timing and dynamics when writing about how a practitioner has communicated the chosen theme. Think about the **specific ways** in which practitioners use these elements to communicate meaning, and give examples from their work wherever possible.

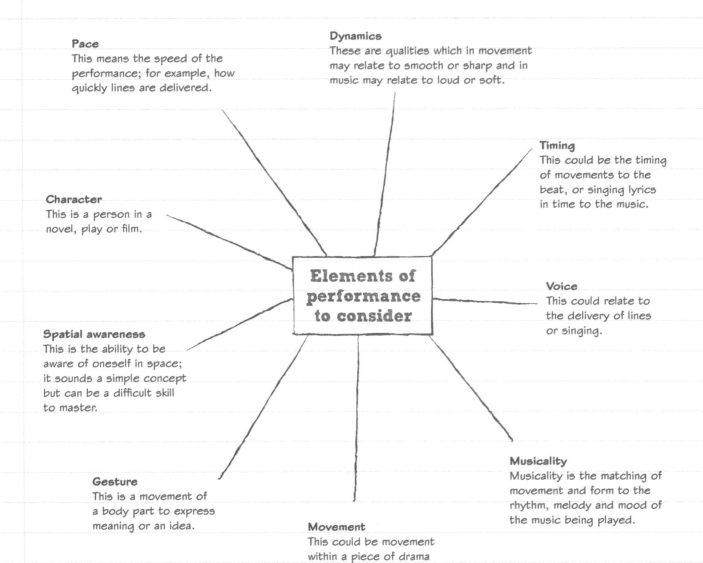

Dynamics
These are qualities which in movement may relate to smooth or sharp and in music may relate to loud or soft.

Pace
This means the speed of the performance; for example, how quickly lines are delivered.

Timing
This could be the timing of movements to the beat, or singing lyrics in time to the music.

Character
This is a person in a novel, play or film.

Elements of performance to consider

Voice
This could relate to the delivery of lines or singing.

Spatial awareness
This is the ability to be aware of oneself in space; it sounds a simple concept but can be a difficult skill to master.

Gesture
This is a movement of a body part to express meaning or an idea.

Movement
This could be movement within a piece of drama or dance movement.

Musicality
Musicality is the matching of movement and form to the rhythm, melody and mood of the music being played.

Now try this

Choose five elements of performance shown here, and create a spider diagram relating to how Martha Graham or Kneehigh Theatre Company use these to create meaning.

Performance styles: relationships

A practitioner creates many relationships during performances. You need to investigate how they do this, and how these relationships link with the chosen theme.

Performer to performer

During a performance, performers most often have a relationship with each other. For example, the characters may literally be related within a plot, or a theme of anger could be communicated by the relationship between dancers.

Practitioners might use dialogue or song to communicate relationships, or devices such as question/answer or action/reaction in movement and dance.

Simply sharing the same space means that spatial relationships are evident such as side to side or back to back.

Contact work

Contact work is often used to demonstrate relationships between performers. For example:

- In physical theatre, dance or contact improvisation, performers may use lifts, falls and other weight-bearing movements to demonstrate relationships.

- In acting, performers may participate in stage combat (a technique designed to give the illusion of physical combat) to demonstrate an aggressive relationship.

Contact between performers can help to establish the type of relationship that the practitioner wishes to communicate.

Performer to space

A performer has a relationship with the space in which he or she is performing. For example:

- Using a particular part of the space or travelling across a certain pathway can communicate a message to the audience.

- Using levels in space (such as the floor) can also help to establish a mood or create meaning.

- Body shape in the space can signify emotion (a curved, closed position would suggest an introverted emotion).

Performer to audience

Performers have a relationship with the audience. Usually it is expected that performers will entertain their audience, who will sit and watch, responding with applause.

In some types of theatre work, such as Forum theatre, the audience play a more active part, and are able to stop and start the action.

Playwright and director Bertolt Brecht wanted to alienate his characters from the audience by using distancing techniques, with actors sometimes stepping out of character.

Performer to accompaniment

Accompaniment (such as music or sound effects) is often used in performance to create a mood, help to establish characters or imply a scene or era. Performers have a relationship with the accompaniment in that they may sing/dance in time with the music, react to musical/sound cues, or move in a certain manner in response to the music.

Placement and role of audience

Performers use strategies to target a particular audience and make them feel that the work has been created just for them. Sometimes the audience may play a role such as becoming involved in the performance through audience participation, for example with Augusto Boal's Forum theatre where the audience are invited to alter the outcomes of the play.

Now try this

Choose a practitioner that you have researched. Create a spider diagram with the name of your practitioner in the centre, and six arms representing the six categories listed above. Make notes on each arm to describe the relationships your practitioner develops.

Performance styles: production

You will also need to consider production, design and technical elements such as set, costume and sound. These can help practitioners to communicate meaning. Some practitioners are renowned for their collaborations with technicians or costume designers.

Set
Practitioners may use set to establish an environment or era, or to create a mood. Martha Graham and the sculptor-designer Isamu Noguchi famously collaborated on *Appalachian Spring* – Noguchi created stunning sets including a sculpture that can be used as a chair

Make-up
Make-up can transform a performer and is often used to exaggerate facial features or establish a character

In *The Lion King*, make-up is used to dramatic effect.

Costume
Practitioners may use costume to visually enhance a performance and communicate meaning, or establish character or environment. Léon Bakst was a famous painter and designer of scenery and costumes. He designed richly coloured sets and costumes for the Ballets Russes

Puppetry
Puppetry is a form of theatre/ performance that involves the manipulation of puppets. It is an ancient art form, believed to have originated around five thousand years ago

The life-size horse puppet in the stage adaptation of Michael Morpurgo's novel 'War Horse' is a good example.

Multimedia
This is performance in which different forms, such as speech, song, dance, film or video, are mixed together. For example, projections and AV (audio/ video) can be used creatively, with performers interacting with visuals, such as in the work of *Le Théâtre du Corps*.

Production, design and technical elements

Lighting
Lighting can enhance a performance by creating visual effects as well as mood or atmosphere. Durham Marenghi is a lighting designer who has created lighting design for plays in London's West End as well as Royal and Olympic events

Sound
Sound design can impact on the success of a performance. Gareth Fry is a sound designer who worked on Complicite's *The Encounter*, developing a wired headphone system that enables the audience to listen to sound through individual headphones

Special effects
Lighting, video and special effects are used in theatre to create moments of magic. They can have a significant impact on the mood of a piece of theatre; for example the use of pyrotechnics (fireworks)

Mask
Masks can also transform a performer. Some of the oldest theatre masks are from Ancient Greek theatre.

Topeng Dance which comes from Indonesia uses masks to relate the tales of Balinese and Javanese ancestors returning temporarily to inhabit the mask.

Now try this

Choose a practitioner you have researched. How have they used production, design and technical elements to communicate meaning and style?

Use bullet points to make clear and focused notes.

Investigating performance styles

These learner responses should help you to see what you need to do when discussing performance styles and methods in your writing.

Sample response extract

Martha Graham's collaborations with set designer Isamu Noguchi were particularly successful:

'Noticing a need to have stage sets that were as innovative as her dances, she started collaborating with Noguchi to design these sets to compliment her performances.'[2]

Noguchi created the set for Graham's first piece, 'Frontier', which had an American theme; this relates to the theme of 'Identity' of new settlers in a new land. The setting helps to create the vastness of the American landscape.

Graham also uses her movement style and choreography to create meaning in her works. For example, in 'Lamentation' (which is about mourning), her movements include rocking, writhing and twisting to express grief. The costume is also used to help communicate the meaning of the piece. Graham wears a tube-like shroud which restricts her movement and emphasises the introverted mood. This also links to female identity, presenting a strong image of a woman grieving, which is achieved through repetition of movement and musical motifs. The use of set and space further enhances the isolation of the lone figure, who performs seated on a bench, as if unable to escape.

[2] http://www.carnegiehall.org/BlogPost. aspx?id=4294974067, Carnegie Hall, para 2, last accessed 9 April 2016.

> Good example of link between meaning and set design.

> Quotation backs up earlier point made.

> Footnote with reference provided.

> Effective link to the theme.

> Example of how the set is effective.

> Link between movement, choreography, costume and meaning.

> Examples of movements provided to back up earlier point.

> Explanation of how costume, set, music and movement add to the piece and reinforce the intention, as well as how they link to the theme.

Sample response extract

Oscar Hammerstein II uses songs to further the plot and communicate messages. He writes the lyrics and his collaborator Richard Rodgers writes the music. Their relationship was successful for many years: 'Their musical theatre writing partnership has been called the greatest of the 20th century.'[3] Rodgers and Hammerstein also used what is referred to as the 'formula musical.' This means that it may have a predictable plot, but it will also have a strong baritone lead, a dainty soprano lead, a supporting lead tenor and a supporting alto lead.

[3] https://en.wikipedia.org/wiki/Rodgers_and_Hammerstein, Wikipedia, para 2, last accessed 7 July 2016.

> Good example of use of songs to communicate meaning. What meaning is being communicated? Some specific examples could be provided.

> Effective use of quotation to back up point.

> Good example of how Rodgers and Hammerstein structured their work.

Now try this

Choose a practitioner you have researched. Create half a page of bullet point notes on how your selected practitioner communicates style and meaning through repertoire, performance, relationships and production.

> Look at pages 27–30 for help with these aspects.

Summarising key information

You will need to be able to summarise key information you have collected during your research, both in any notes you prepare, and in your writing. This page summarises the key areas to think about when pulling together your notes, as per advice given throughout this unit.

Consider validity of material collected

You will need to consider whether your material has been collected from reliable sources. Remember that not everything that you read is true!

There are some websites where anyone can contribute information, so be wary of these. Check to see who has written or provided the information. Reviews from the main broadsheet newspapers are examples of reliable sources.

Analyse selected material

You will need to read, digest and then analyse your material. Examine the information in detail so that you gain a better understanding of it, and can interpret it effectively.

For each piece of information, think about why it is important:
What does it mean, and how is it significant?

Consider alternative viewpoints

Remember to look at information from different viewpoints, so that you are not just providing one opinion. You can present a range of opinions and then state where your opinion lies, backing up your opinion with examples or logical reasoning.

Considering alternative viewpoints will help to provide a broad outlook that demonstrates thorough research.

Refer to contextual influences on practitioners

Remember to make reference to contextual influences such as historical, political and social factors. This is one of the main areas for investigation. Go through the list of contextual influences methodically for each of your selected practitioners, making notes as you work. You can then refer back to these at a later date.

Make connections and links between theme(s), creative intentions and influences

Another main area of investigation is making links, whether they relate to collaborations with other practitioners or connections between themes and how they are communicated.

Go through the list of all the factors that need consideration in relation to your selected practitioners, making organised notes throughout the process.

Consider genre and style

Remember to consider genre and style as part of your investigation. Think about how each practitioner communicates meaning and what methods they employ. How might they be the same or different from the standard genres or styles? Consider repertoire, performance, relationships and production elements in connection with how creative intentions are communicated.

Are the practitioners typical of their genre, or do they challenge the conventions of the genre?

Now try this

Choose a practitioner you have researched. Look through your research notes and identify **two** areas where you could improve your notes or find additional material.

Comparisons, conclusions and further research

You will need to establish links, draw conclusions and ideally make reference to any opportunities for further research within your writing.

Establishing links and comparisons

You will also need to establish links and comparisons to the work of other practitioners. This may be in terms of similarities between contextual factors, creative intentions or performance methods that you have detected during the research process. You may also notice differences.

You may also establish links and comparisons in connection to the theme.

 Make sure you have solid grounds for making links and comparisons; try not to force similarities that are tenuous.

 Contrasts between practitioners' work are also worth mentioning.

 How does each practitioner explore the theme of 'Identity', and how much does their own identity influence their work?

Drawing conclusions

As part of your writing you will be required to reach conclusions about the information you have collected. This will mean forming opinions based on different sources of research, as well as contributing your own thoughts.

The conclusions may relate to contextual factors, creative intentions or performance methods.

 Don't rush to make conclusions; take your time and ensure that you have collected all the information and read through it carefully. Only then should you go ahead and make informed decisions.

Opportunities for further research

You can comment on the potential for further investigation. For example, you may find that there are areas of your research which would benefit from further exploration. This does not mean that you have to carry this out, but you will improve the quality of your answer by commenting on what could be further explored and for what purpose(s). This demonstrates that you are looking beyond the work which you have produced.

 There is only so much information that you can provide within the time constraints of the assessment. Therefore, you will need to be selective in your analysis.

 Try to identify at least one opportunity for further investigation.

Now try this

Make a list of links you could make between the work of Martha Graham and Kneehigh Theatre Company.

 Are there similarities in contextual factors, creative intentions or performance methods?

Communicating your key points

These learner responses should help you to see what you need to do when summarising information you have collected to support your independent judgements and conclusions.

Sample response extract

Rodgers and Hammerstein's work has been labelled as sentimental: 'if you are a diabetic who craves sweet things, take along some extra insulin, and you will not fail to thrill to The Sound of Music.' However, others argue that this is not the case, and indeed the pair confront themes such as death in 'Carousel' and 'Oklahoma', and racial intolerance in 'South Pacific'. Although the fact that they were 'formula musicals', which meant that plot and casting could be seen as predictable, Rodgers and Hammerstein succeeded in bringing a new twist to the musical, using songs to further the plot, communicating age-old themes with a modern approach.

 Different viewpoints provided with specific examples.

 Quotation will require footnote/source.

 Ability to analyse and come to a conclusion. However, different research sources could be included, for example quoting from different reviews.

Contextual factors mentioned although this could be expanded.

Sample response extract

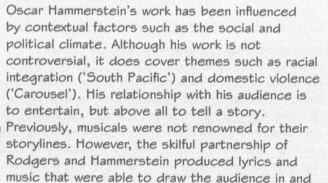

Specific examples of performances to support points raised.

Target audience and relationship with the audience.

Genre and style discussed, with reference to stylistic elements.

Oscar Hammerstein's work has been influenced by contextual factors such as the social and political climate. Although his work is not controversial, it does cover themes such as racial integration ('South Pacific') and domestic violence ('Carousel'). His relationship with his audience is to entertain, but above all to tell a story. Previously, musicals were not renowned for their storylines. However, the skilful partnership of Rodgers and Hammerstein produced lyrics and music that were able to draw the audience in and take them on a journey.

Now try this

Choose a short section of your own research notes. Practise writing these notes up into a response. Imagine your response will be read by someone else, so make sure you write clearly and use accurate spelling, punctuation and grammar.

 You may be able to refer to some notes in your real assessment. Ask your tutor or check the Sample Assessment Material on the Pearson website for details.

Presentation of findings

It is crucial that you present your findings effectively. Consider these factors when planning your writing. See pages 11 and 12 for guidance on how to create your bibliography.

Format and structure

When you put together a piece of writing, it is important that you consider the following:

- Introduction – this will help to shape your structure; state what you will be covering in your investigation.
- Conclusion – use this to sum up your information.
- Paragraphs – try to broach different subjects/areas of discussion in separate paragraphs.
- The narrative should flow and your structure should be logical and coherent.

Tone

The tone of your writing should be formal and serious rather than conversational; you need to express your ideas in a professional manner. Remember to do the following:

- Use appropriate terminology (see below) and give all practitioners their correct names.
- Don't use informal vocabulary, abbreviations or 'text speak' such as 'btw'.
- Assume your reader knows nothing about the subject. Ensure you explain in logical sentences and provide direct examples wherever possible.
- Do not just describe; go beyond this, with focused analysis and opinions backed up by justifications.

Language

Think about the language you are using. Be clear and concise – don't ramble! Remember to:

- check your spelling
- check your grammar; for example, sentences should be complete and not too long
- proofread your work to minimise errors.

Subject-specific terminology

It is important that you use terminology which is appropriate for the subject. For example, each performing arts sector will have certain terms and language that relate to skills and styles.

✓ You need to use subject-specific terminology, so research any terms you do not recognise.

✓ Wherever possible, use the correct term rather than the layman's term. For example, 'choreography' is the accurate term for the sequence of steps and movements, rather than 'making up dances'.

Now try this

Read the brief for the writing part of the revision task on page 2. Write a short plan of your written response. Use headings for each of your main points, and identify which section of your research notes will be useful for each heading.

 You should always write a plan before beginning a piece of writing.

Presenting judgements

You will need to consider how you present your judgements, including the use of critical analysis. Use the guidance below to help enhance your investigative skills.

Use of critical analysis

Although the word 'critical' sounds negative, critical analysis is a positive process, where you are given the opportunity to explain, interpret, evaluate and analyse. It differs from descriptive writing in that it involves developing an argument, weighing up the evidence and arguments of others and contributing your own conclusion. You will need to:

- be confident in your delivery
- provide more than one opinion
- include positive and negative aspects that you can comment on
- consider the quality of the evidence you have found
- assess the usefulness of information
- draw your own conclusion.

Explaining views and interpretations

You will need to explain views and interpretations within your investigation. Explanation helps to make information clearer. For example, a critic's viewpoint about the influence of contextual factors on a practitioner may be complex; explanation can clarify and even summarise this information. Sometimes viewpoints, quotes or indeed performance material can be interpreted in different ways. Therefore, an explanation of the meaning or meanings may be required. You are entitled to voice your opinion relating to interpretation, as long as you can support your judgement(s) effectively.

You may still need to include some description within your writing, in order to set the context for example.

Presenting structured arguments, conclusions and judgements

Your arguments, conclusions and judgements will need to be clear and well structured. Remember to think about how you can incorporate evidence into the argument you are developing. Also, try to be consistent and consider how you structure your line or lines of argument throughout. This will mean thinking about the ordering of your paragraphs.

For each paragraph it may help to consider:
- ✓ introducing the point
- ✓ making the point (with supporting evidence)
- ✓ reflecting critically on the point.

Use of relevant examples to support arguments, conclusions and judgements

Backing up your arguments with examples is vital in order to validate your opinions. Examples can be drawn from a multitude of sources such as reviews, text, digital archives or books. You may refer to particular works you have seen on YouTube. The important point is that your examples need to be relevant to the argument, conclusion or judgement you are making. Explaining why your examples are relevant actually contributes to the critical element of your writing. Don't assume that the reader will automatically follow your train of thought; it needs explaining.

Try not to string too many quotes together at once in order to strengthen your argument. Take time to explain the relevance of each one before moving on to the next.

Now try this

Choose a practitioner that you have researched.

1 Jot down a short sentence that summarises your opinion of the work of your selected practitioner.
2 Write a paragraph explaining that opinion in detail, and justifying your opinion with evidence from your research notes.

Analysis and presentation

This page gives further advice on how to improve the way in which you present your findings and your independent judgements.

Clear, concise and effective structure. Introduction presents a structured argument, explaining what will be achieved during the investigation.

Sample response extract

For my investigation I am going to be focusing on two practitioners: Martha Graham and Kneehigh Theatre Company. I will be analysing their work in relation to the theme of identity. During the investigation the main areas I will be exploring are contextual factors, creative intentions and performance styles and methods. I will be using primary and secondary research, investigating a range of sources.

Firstly I am going to explore contextual factors in relation to Martha Graham. Graham was influenced by the era in which she was creating work, as well as by her father who was a physician. She reacted against the balletic movements of the time, in search of an expressive movement vocabulary that could convey human emotions more realistically. She developed movements such as cupped hands and flexed feet, as well as the use of contraction and release. Having watched her father deal with nervous disorders, she was influenced by his belief that the body could express its inner senses. It could be said that she created a new identity of expression.

 Accurate coverage of areas of investigation.

 Good use of language and structure of paragraphs.

 Contextual factors are explained in connection with her background and era.

 Examples of movement vocabulary to support independent judgement.

Response is well thought out and links to theme of identity. Evidence of effective critical analysis in the form of the learner's own opinion.

References will need to be provided in the bibliography for the sources of this information.

Clear structured start to paragraph with the focus identified.

Could examples of pieces be provided here to support the statement?

Sample response extract

Another part of my investigation is based on creative intentions and themes. Graham often created work that was based on social, psychological and political themes. In her choreography she created something timeless, which entertained generations of audiences. Kneehigh Theatre Company's themes are diverse, and repertoire is often based on mythological tales for example 'The Red Shoes' by Hans Christian Andersen with their main purpose being to entertain.

A main difference between the two practitioners is that Graham created a unique movement vocabulary based on contraction and release. Kneehigh, on the other hand, work across many disciplines, incorporating elements such as puppetry, live music and visual imagery.

Good example of a creative intention here, with effective use of language and a specific example.

Link between the two practitioners.

References will need to be provided in the bibliography for the sources of this information.

Now try this

Look at the brief for the writing part of the revision task on page 2. Write a 200-word introduction for your own piece of writing.

 Remember to consider format, structure, tone, language and subject-specific terminology.

Your Unit 3 set task

Unit 3 will be assessed through a task, which will be set by Pearson. In this assessed task you will need to devise and develop a group performance piece in response to a brief.

Set task skills

Your assessed task could cover any of the essential content in the unit. You can revise the unit content in this Revision Guide. The skills pages are designed to **revise skills** that might be needed in your assessed task. They use selected content and outcomes to provide an example of ways of applying your skills.

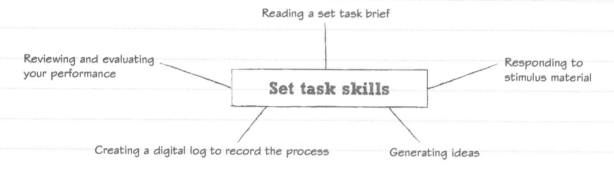

Reading a set task brief

Reviewing and evaluating your performance

Set task skills

Responding to stimulus material

Creating a digital log to record the process

Generating ideas

Workflow

The process of creating a group performance piece might follow these steps:
- ✓ Review the brief.
- ✓ Brainstorm likely ideas.
- ✓ Use workshops to devise a performance.
- ✓ Log ideas and reflect on the process.
- ✓ Perform and record a performance piece.
- ✓ Reflect on and review how you created and performed your piece.

Check the Pearson website

The skills pages are designed to demonstrate the skills that might be needed in your assessed task. The details of your actual assessed task may change from year to year so always make sure you are up to date. Check the Pearson website for the most up-to-date **Sample Assessment Material** to get an idea of the structure of your assessed task and what this requires of you.

Now try this

Visit the Pearson website and find the page containing the course materials for BTEC National Performing Arts. Look at the latest Unit 3 Sample Assessment Material for an indication of:
- the structure of your set task, and whether it is divided into separate parts
- what briefing or stimulus material might be provided to you
- how much time it is suggested you spend on each section of the task
- the activities you are required to complete and how to format your responses.

Task brief

This Revision Guide provides a revision task for you to practise and revise your skills (see below). It follows a similar format as your assessment, but uses a different stimulus. See the possible options on the next page.

Task

You have been asked to work as part of a small performance company of three to seven performers to create an original piece of work that you will present as an informal performance to an invited audience.

You are required to use a stimulus as a basis for developing the piece.

The performance piece needs to be between 10 and 20 minutes long.

The audience will want to see an original piece created in response to the stimulus. Your performance company will need to work creatively together, drawing on all your strengths to create an imaginative and innovative piece of work.

Throughout the task you are required to complete a digital process log, under supervised conditions.

The digital process log will capture your contribution to the development and rehearsal process.

You must demonstrate your personal contributions to artistic decisions made within the group context in response to:

- planning and interpretation of the stimulus
- development and realisation of creative ideas
- review and reflection of the workshop performance.

The log may include embedded digital photographs, video and audio files in one or more of the entries.

You will need to refer back to this revision task when completing some of the 'Now try this' activities in your Revision Guide. Read through the information on this page and the next two pages so you are familiar with the activities and stimuli.

Revision stimuli

There are many types of stimuli you need to be prepared to use when you are responding to a brief and preparing a performance (see next page). For the purposes of this unit of the Revision Guide, you will be provided with five sample stimuli you can use to practise generating performance ideas. Note that the Skills pages in this Revision Guide will focus on the visual stimulus below and the Acting (Physical Theatre) performance strand.

Theme

This example **theme** as stimulus is 'The Civil Rights Movement'.

This is the stimulus which will be used as the basis for examples of work in this unit.

Visual

This example **visual** stimulus is *Bird in flight* by Eadweard Muybridge.

Text

This example **text** as stimulus is Charlie Chaplin's quote below.

> **Mirror is my Best friend, Because When I Cry It Never Laughs**

Aural

This example **aural** stimulus is Chase and Status's track entitled 'Eastern Jam'.

Search online to listen to this track.

Media

This example media stimulus is part of an *Independent* news story.

Refugee crisis: Greek governor calls for state of emergency over thousands of people stranded on border

Upcoming summit will attempt to tackle the humanitarian crisis on the Greek border.

Ahead of a summit on 7 March aimed at trying to find a solution to the migration crisis engulfing Europe, a Greek governor has made an urgent call for help, asking his government to declare a "state of emergency" over the thousands of people stranded on the Greece-Macedonia border.

Some 13,000 to 14,000 people are trapped in the area surrounding the Idomeni border crossing, while another 6,000 to 7,000 are being housed in refugee camps around the region, said Apostolos Tzitzikostas, governor of the Greek region of Central Macedonia. That means the area handles about 60 per cent of the total number of migrants in the country.

Types of stimulus

Your performance will be based on a stimulus. This is a jumping-off point for your own creativity and ideas. Your stimulus will fall into one of the five following categories. Whatever stimulus you are given, you will need to research and explore it thoroughly in order to inform the planning and development of your performance piece and write about it in your digital log. Use the following pages to help you understand the areas to think about for any type of stimulus.

1 Theme
A social, cultural, historical or ethical theme could form the basis for your performance. You might need to do research on your theme.

A wedding celebration is an example of a cultural theme.

2 Visual
You might have to respond to a photo, painting, sculpture, graphic or found object. Think about what thoughts, feelings and associations the stimulus produces.

A found object

Stimulus

5 Media
Your project might be based on a newspaper, magazine, documentary or video. Think about the key message of the media you are given, and how you can respond to it.

A documentary could form the basis for a performance.

3 Text
Your stimulus might be a poem, short story, quotation or lyric. You could use this text in your presentation, or just use it as inspiration.

4 Aural
A song, sound or piece of music can be very evocative. You might choose to integrate it into your piece, or just respond to its rhythms or the atmosphere it evokes.

Now try this

Which kinds of social, historical, ethical or cultural themes can you think of? Make a list of possible themes, noting the challenges and opportunities which each one would offer.

Try to choose examples which would give you a broad scope for your research and performance.

Theme as stimulus

You may be given a theme as a stimulus for your performance. Themes are divided into four main categories.

Social

Social themes relate to society, for example:

- gender inequality
- poverty
- crime.

A stimulus reflecting poverty could provoke strong emotions for your performance.

Cultural

Cultural themes relate to customs, traditions and values such as:

- celebrations
- spirituality/religion
- tradition.

A celebration could be a specific occasion or a general concept.

Historical

Historical themes relate to past events such as:

- Second World War
- the Industrial Revolution
- Civil Rights Movement.

War is a powerful stimulus for performance.

Ethical

Ethical themes relate to morality/what is right and wrong, for example:

- euthanasia
- abortion
- the death penalty.

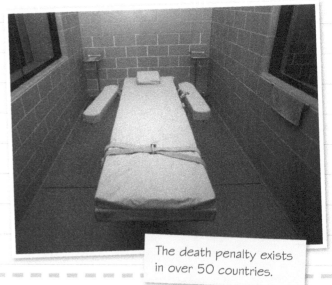

The death penalty exists in over 50 countries.

Now try this

Choose one of the themes above. Use the internet to identify **five** key words based on that theme which could form the basis of a dramatic or movement improvisation.

Visual stimulus

You might be given a visual stimulus for your performance. Visual stimuli are divided into five main categories.

Photograph

A photograph could be taken of a:

- landscape
- object
- person
- animal.

This photograph combines all of these elements. You can use any or all of these elements for inspiration.

Painting

A painting could be:

- historical
- still life
- everyday scene
- landscape.

Landscape

Object

Person

Animal

Sculpture

Sculptures are three-dimensional works of art, made by one of these processes:

- carving
- modelling
- casting
- constructing.

Graphic

Graphic art is two-dimensional and includes:

- printmaking
- computer graphics
- calligraphy
- drawing.

Found object

A 'found object' is an object that has been created for a purpose other than art, for example:

- a piece of furniture
- an item of clothing
- a tool
- food.

Objects in your performance

Objects are often used in performances as they can provide an extra dimension, add interest or create a scene. They are referred to as 'props'. When you are planning and developing your performance and preparing your digital log, you may want to think about what props you could use, even if your stimulus was not an object.

Now try this

1   Look at the visual stimulus on page 40. Write down the first **ten** words that come to mind based on this image.
2   Underline **five** of these words that you think would be a good starting point for devising material.

Text stimulus

You may be given text as a stimulus for your performance. Texts are divided into four main categories.

Poem

Poetry is a form of literary expression and is often rhythmical, which makes it distinct from other texts. A poem could be:

* a Shakespearean sonnet
* a limerick
* blank verse.

Blank verse does not rhyme, but includes a regular metrical rhythm. You could explore the rhythm in movement terms, to create a motif.

It's
raining again!
So, what shall we do?
Let's go out and play, just me and you.
We can put on our wellies and jump and splash.
It's
fun
in
the
rain.
Just
me
and
just
you.

A shape poem is the same shape as the object it is describing.

Short story

In most cases, a short story is significantly shorter than a novel. It has five main components:

* character
* setting
* plot
* theme
* conflict.

As with performance, a short story has to portray conflict in an efficient way for maximum impact.

Quotation

A quotation is a short piece of text taken, for example, from a book or a speech. A quotation is written in quotation marks. It could be something that a famous person has said, or simply information taken directly from a document.

Songs often have verses and a repeating chorus. There are similarities to this in performing arts, where a motif can occur repeatedly to reinforce a theme or help to weave together a plot.

Lyrics

Lyrics are often referred to as the words of a popular song. Performance can be inspired by melody or lyrics, or a combination of the two.

The lyrics to 'Space Oddity' by David Bowie are about an astronaut deep in space. The repetition of the question in the song creates tension. This could form the inspiration for material based on being lost (in space or otherwise).

Now try this

Look at the text stimulus on page 40. Write some notes on how you could transform the text into dialogue, vocals and/or movement.

What ideas does the text give you, and how can you explore these?

Aural stimulus

You may be given an aural stimulus for your performance. Aural stimuli fall into two categories: music and sound.

Music

There are many types of music that may be provided as a stimulus to be used for inspiration for your performance. For example:

- classical
- electronic (UK garage, house music and ambient)
- rock
- jazz
- popular
- country
- Latin (such as salsa, tango and merengue)
- metal
- punk
- rap
- grime
- reggae
- R&B.

Music in your performance

When you are compiling your digital log, you will need to consider any music involved. Even if music is not the stimulus for your performance, you may decide to incorporate music to enhance your piece.

Think about why you are choosing a particular type of music and what it does to improve the piece. It may create an atmosphere, provide a regular beat, set a scene or add an extra dimension. Or it may do a combination of these things at different points within the performance.

Some of the equipment used to make electronic music and sounds.

Sound

You may get some form of sound as a stimulus for your performance. This could be an electronic sound, a sound from everyday life, or a 'found sound'.

Sound in performance

Sound can be used in a variety of ways in performance. Abstract sounds can form a backdrop for dance and movement.

In a play or musical theatre performance, sound effects may be employed in order to simulate reality, create illusion or convey a mood. For example, in a stage 'brawl' an imaginary bottle may be broken over someone's head. The bottle is fake but it becomes real when the sound editor adds the 'crash' made by the glass bottle. Can you think of examples?

Found sound

Have you ever heard of 'found sound'? This is when everyday noises or sounds are incorporated into music. It is often created using whatever material is available at the time, and/or body parts (body percussion) such as creating rhythms by clapping, slapping thighs or tapping fingers on a table.

Now try this

1 Using the 'Eastern Jam' stimulus on page 40 as your inspiration, create a rhythmical motif.
2 Record the rhythmical motif.

Think about how this could be developed to create a soundscape for performance.

You could record sound using your smartphone, tablet or laptop.

Media as stimulus

You may be given a media stimulus for your performance. Media stimuli fall into four categories.

Newspapers and magazines

A newspaper or magazine headline, image or article could be provided as inspiration for performance.

Sir Bradley Wiggins and Mark Cavendish win world Madison championships

- Pair repeat 2008 Manchester triumph despite late crash.
- Cavendish seals third world title at the discipline.

Headline

Victory as a theme for inspiration for motifs

Image

A newspaper article may have various features that could inspire you.

Things to consider

Consider the main message that is being put across. How could this be translated into acting, dance or musical theatre? Think about the different considerations that would need to take place. For example, to portray a news item about an earthquake you could create a script, develop motifs or use lyrics to communicate the message, depending on the genre of performance.

Documentaries and videos

A television documentary or video could be the subject matter for your performance.

Theme tune and other sounds or music.

Setting

Narrative

Title graphics

Main characters

You could be inspired by the different elements of a television programme.

The main message

What is the main message or subject matter being communicated in the documentary or video? Remember you may need to condense your ideas, as a documentary or video may be lengthy and your performance time could be limited. Capturing the main idea(s) is essential.

Now try this

Using the extract from a newspaper article on page 40, create a spider diagram of words that connect with the main theme of the article. Think about how the words could be translated into material for performance.

Responding to stimulus

As part of your log you may need to write about how you responded to and interpreted your stimulus. Below are extracts from digital logs in which learners have written about how they responded to the visual stimulus on page 40. Use these to understand what you will need to do in your assessment.

Sample response extract

Assume that the reader knows nothing about the process; it is down to you to explain what happened in detail.

Planning and interpretation of stimulus

Entry Date
4 May

Entry

Using the Eadweard Muybridge image, we decided that 'flight' was evident in the image. There happened to be a shopping trolley in the studio, so we explored ways of using the trolley to demonstrate flight.

We rode inside it, pushed and pulled it, balanced on it, leaned on it. We also considered the sounds that it made. All the time we thought about how the trolley travelled like a bird, and how we could capture this without moving, for example using still tableaux. I suggested using some of the lines and curves in the image as the basis for a motif.

We used the trolley to help create visually exciting shapes in space. I suggested each choosing a body part to explore the trolley with. We did this and it helped us to produce some visually exciting material.

You could improve this answer with further explanation about what the tableaux were, what shapes were created, what body parts were used and what was produced.

We experimented with balances

We explored levels for example by doing leaps.

The answer could be improved by providing annotated photographs to accompany the writing. You could also embed a video clip of how you experimented with the props.

Ideas for musical theatre

For musical theatre, ideas could be explored and developed to produce songs, dialogue and movement/dance. For example, the concepts of 'open' and 'closed' could be explored. Two separate groups (one representing 'open' and the other 'closed') could form contrasting characters or moods, or even be in competition with each other.

To improve the answer, the learner could explain what **level** their partner used as well as how they travelled around the room.

Sample response extract

Planning and interpretation of stimulus

Entry Date
4 May

Entry

We decided to create some duologues based on the Muybridge image. I suggested that one person could be a leader, and the other a follower to echo the flight of the birds in the image. Initially we brainstormed the idea to produce key points to cover. The words were then used as the inspiration for the duologues. In addition to the text, we thought about how our posture would help to show our status. As the follower I decided to mimic my partner's posture, but on a different level. We then experimented by travelling round the room with each of us alternating between being the leader and the follower.

Now try this

1   Using the visual stimulus on page 40, spend 5–10 minutes walking around the room using your voice and body to communicate your initial responses.

2   Make some quick key-word notes about what you discovered.

Analyse your stimulus

You need to understand your stimulus properly, which will involve some analysis. To do this, you will need to discuss, brainstorm and explore your stimulus through improvisations and other techniques.

Discussion

It is important to discuss your ideas with your group. Remember to respect other people's opinions and allow your peers sufficient time to voice their thoughts.

It may be a good idea to take turns to speak, with someone elected to take notes ('minutes').

For your digital log it will be useful to record discussions so that you can then refer to them later.

Don't be afraid to put across your ideas, even if they might seem a bit wacky! It is good to use your imagination and let your mind run riot.

Improvisation and practical responsive techniques

Improvisation involves responding to a stimulus spontaneously. It is particularly helpful for generating performance material.

Try immediately improvising a response to a stimulus. Alternatively, brainstorm the stimulus, select key words and then use them as the basis for a more structured improvisation.

Here are some tips when improvising:

• Be bold

• Trust yourself

• Respond to others where possible, perhaps using contact

• Stay focused

Hot seating

This is a responsive technique used in Performing Arts whereby a selected person sits in the 'hot seat', having taken on a character. The audience asks this person questions and the person must respond, staying in character. This is a useful way of developing roles for performance.

Now try this

Select an item of clothing. Improvise with the item of clothing. See what happens and how much you can think 'outside of the box'.

 When you are improvising, try not to over-think it; just relax and explore your stimulus without feeling inhibited.

What, for whom and how?

Three important aspects to consider when creating a performance piece are: what are you trying to communicate, for whom are you performing and how are you going to do this? You'll need to think about all three of these when planning your performance, but you'll also need to keep sense-checking them throughout the course of your assessment period.

Artistic intention

Artistic intention is about what you are trying to convey or express in performance. You need to be as clear as you can when communicating your intention.

It is a good idea to check whether your intention is clear in each entry in your digital log. Check your intention is shown clearly in all of the following:

- dialogue
- movement/dance
- lyrics/songs
- music
- set
- props.

If you find that there are elements that are not required, reject these sections/phrases/scenes.

Target audience

You need to identify your target audience when creating material for performance. Here are some examples:

- children (for example a Theatre in Education (TIE) performance)
- adults
- learners
- families
- a combination of the above.

Your target audience will determine the content of your material. For example, for children the language and complexity of the content would need to be suitable. The target audience will also influence the way you pitch the material so that it is at the correct level to be engaging.

Form and style of the performance

You may be performing a piece of drama, dance or musical theatre. Within each of these genres there are numerous forms and styles.

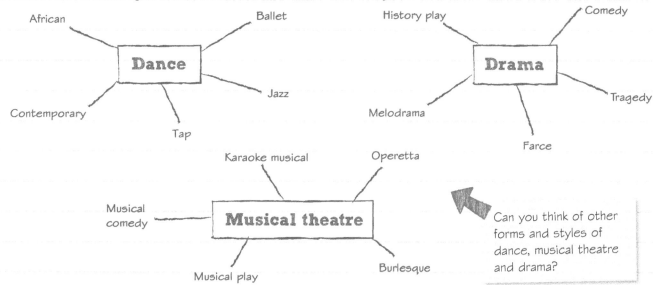

Now try this

1 Taking the theme of 'The Civil Rights Movement' as your stimulus, select a performance pathway (acting, dance or musical theatre).

2 Make a list of:

(a) what you are trying to convey (main message) and your means of doing this (such as dialogue or movement)

(b) who you will be performing to

(c) what style(s) or form(s) this might take.

Where and who?

Two other important aspects to consider when creating a performance piece are the staging possibilities for your performance and who will be selected for the roles.

Creative and staging possibilities

It is likely that you will perform your piece at school or college, or perhaps in a local theatre. Think about how you can be creative with what is available. Can you transform the space by using a set or a backdrop? Or even adapt it by considering where the audience are sitting?

Costumes and props

Don't just use costume or props for the sake of it. Think about what they are adding. Does a costume help to establish a character or create spectacle? Does a prop help to set a scene or help to develop a storyline? Remember that you are the main communicator of your intention, so don't rely on props and costumes to do your hard work! Try to rehearse with props and costume so that you can get used to how they feel and how they might affect your performance.

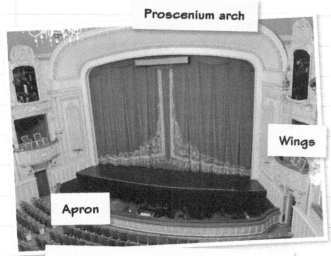

Proscenium arch

Wings

Apron

Many performances take place in traditional proscenium arch theatres where the audience face the performers.

Stage

Some theatres are more unusual, such as theatre in the round. You could recreate a 'theatre in the round' by placing your audience around the centre of the space.

Developing performance roles and casting

You will need to allocate roles for your performance. It makes sense to base choices on people's individual skills. You could ask each member of the group to make a skills audit: a list of the skills they currently possess and their areas for improvement. The skills can then be matched to the requirements of each role.

Growing into your role

Your performance roles will evolve as the creative process unfolds. Try to ensure that even if the roles are not exactly equal in terms of time duration on stage, they should be fairly similar. The important element is being able to showcase your skills within the given time frame (which, for the purposes of this revision task, is 10–20 minutes). If you are struggling with executing particular skills within your role, share this with your group. Roles can be adapted and negotiated as long as they are agreed in advance of the rehearsal period.

Now try this

1 For one of the performance pathways (drama, dance or musical theatre), list **five** of your strongest individual skills and five areas of improvement.

2 Write down **two** ways in which you could develop each area of improvement.

Primary research

You will need to carry out research about your stimulus. Research can be categorised into two different types: primary and secondary. Primary research involves going out and collecting research yourself, such as making observations or conducting interviews. This research should inform the decisions you make for your own performance.

Existing performance works

You could watch a performance of a play that may have similar artistic intentions to your own. You can gain information about the company, style of performance and intention of the choreographer/director. You will gain first-hand experience of the components that make the performance unique, and the experience might stimulate your own creative ideas.

Practitioners

Listening to a practitioner speaking about their work or a particular performance is a good opportunity for primary research. It may provide you with valuable insight regarding the performance piece, as well as useful tips for your performance.

Existing performance texts

You may be able to access scripts, plays and notation of dance works, in order to enhance your understanding of a particular performance, style of performance or choreographer/playwright.

It is useful to look at existing scripts to see how they are structured. For example, if you are creating your own script, it is useful to see how the action and dialogue are written.

Interviews

You may be able to interview a practitioner, director, choreographer or playwright to gain further information about your stimulus or performance pathway. Make sure that you:

- decide exactly what you want to know
- provide clear questions
- write down the answers.

It is important to record the interview, for accuracy and so that you can include it in your digital process log if you want to.

Now try this

Imagine you are interviewing a choreographer or playwright in your chosen pathway (acting, dance, musical theatre) about a recent performance. Write down **five** questions to ask.

Secondary research

It is likely that it will also be useful to carry out secondary research about your stimulus. Secondary research involves gathering existing research, for example by using the internet, printed publications or digital archives.

Internet

Much research is undertaken on the internet, as it is so fast and accessible. Use search engines to help you gain access to information, ensuring that you type in relevant key words in order to get the best results. Remember that not all websites are reliable in terms of providing accurate information.

> You can always provide a screenshot of useful information that you find on the internet. This can be incorporated into your digital process log, or you can provide the weblink.

Printed publication

Books and journal articles that analyse and comment on a performance piece will be a good springboard for building your own ideas.

Showing that you have performed extensive research via different methods will demonstrate a thorough approach. You can access printed publications at school, college or your local library.

DISCOVER

Don't just see a play, discover it.

Get closer to our work through Discover events that run alongside our in house and visiting productions. A great opportunity to learn more about how a play comes to life or to pose your questions to the cast and creative teams.

DISCOVER DAYS

The Gaul - Saturday 15 October
10.30am – 12.30pm
Ticket £17.50 (includes Discover Day workshop, matinee ticket and post-show Q&A)

Digital archives

You can access performance material by visiting digital archives either in a library or via the internet. Watching past performances will help to familiarise yourself with a certain style of dance, theatrical form or genre of musical theatre.

After watching a performance, note the key components of the style, and consider how these elements can be transferred to your own performance piece.

Plagiarism

It is essential that you acknowledge all of your sources when you are taking information from the internet, printed publications or digital archives. As advised on page 2, make sure you write down websites and publishing/recording details as you conduct your research, otherwise you will forget where you found your information.

Remember to put quotations in quotation marks.

Now try this

1. Taking the newspaper article on page 40 as your stimulus, carry out some internet research about the topic and make notes as you work.

2. Trim the information so that you are left with only the key points that will be useful inspiration for a performance piece.

 Remember to make a list of all websites visited.

Research and analysis

You will need to demonstrate how you researched and analysed your stimulus in your log. Use these extracts from other learners' logs to help you understand how you might do this.

Sample response extract

Planning and interpretation of stimulus

Entry Date
4 May

Entry

We took it in turns to contribute to the discussion by passing a pretend 'mike' around, so that only one person could be heard at a time.

We allocated research responsibilities. For example, I volunteered to research the origin of the stimulus, as well as suggesting ways in which it could be explored.

Having completed the research, we collated our findings and then began to analyse them. We talked about how the stimulus could be explored by brainstorming the image and creating a mind map. We considered any problems that might occur such as the image being a bit abstract which made it open to interpretation. I suggested using the key words from the mind map as the basis for forming a motif, which could then be developed.

You could improve this answer by describing the specific problems, and suggested solutions, in more detail.

Digital process log checklist

You must plan and develop a group performance based on your interpretation of the stimulus. In your digital process log you need to show that you have considered:

☑ what form and style the performance will take

☑ who the target audience is

☑ how you will communicate your artistic aims and intentions

☑ what practical performance skills you and your company can apply to the performance piece

☑ time and resources.

You could be assessed on your individual contribution to the interpretation of the stimulus, planning and the generation of ideas.

The learner has referred to their individual contribution, which is important because you may be assessed on your **individual contribution** to the interpretation, planning and generation of ideas.

Be aware of plagiarism. Remember to acknowledge your sources as you work, referencing all websites that you take information from.

Always try to justify your decisions. For each decision, explain **why** you reached it. You could improve this answer by explaining **why**, for example, you decided to explore the idea of patterns in more detail.

Sample response extract

Planning and interpretation of stimulus

Entry Date
4 May

Entry

I decided to carry out secondary research into the stimulus, *Bird in flight* by Eadweard Muybridge. By searching on the internet I discovered that Eadweard Muybridge's photography of animals captured minute, split-second movements in a way that had never been done before, through the use of camera timers. https://blogs.loc.gov/picturethis/2014/04/eadweard-muybridge-birth-of-a-photographic-pioneer/

I thought about the motion of the birds and the patterns created and how this could be translated into performance. Working with my partner we looked at bird flight and experimented with sound and travelling. We played around with using mime as a means of communicating our intention. We tried our best to bring the picture to life.

Now try this

1. Research the aural stimulus on page 40.
2. Make notes on your findings, and draw up a list of references for the sources you found, including websites, books, journals and magazines.

Discussion skills

Following the planning stage, you will embark on the creative process. Developing and realising creative ideas will involve lots of discussion.

Remember to use different methods to aid the creative process. These might be:

- **brainstorming** – collecting all your initial ideas about a topic as a group
- **debate** – a formal discussion where points of view can be aired by everyone equally. Remember to take some notes.

You could record some of your early creative discussions using your smartphone and embed an audio file into your digital log. Remember you'll need to write about what you have discussed as well.

Brainstorm through to mind map

Once you have discussed and gathered your ideas, organise your ideas into a mind map that shows the relationships between them. This will help you to streamline the ideas you have and work out what you will take forward in your creative process.

Sample notes extract

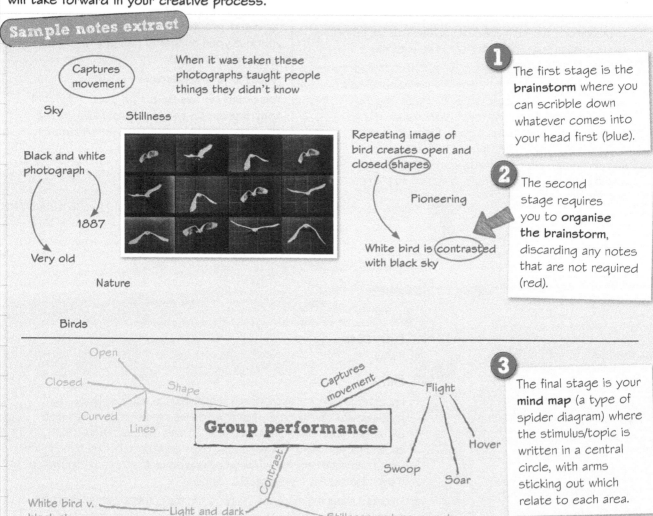

1. The first stage is the **brainstorm** where you can scribble down whatever comes into your head first (blue).

2. The second stage requires you to **organise the brainstorm**, discarding any notes that are not required (red).

3. The final stage is your **mind map** (a type of spider diagram) where the stimulus/topic is written in a central circle, with arms sticking out which relate to each area.

Now try this

Choose a stimulus you have researched.

1 Brainstorm your thoughts and initial ideas about this topic.
2 Condense your brainstorm into a mind map.

 You could use one of the stimuli on page 40.

Improvisation

Improvisation is an excellent means of generating material for your performance. It involves spontaneity; in other words, it requires no preparation.

Exercises

It is important to be relaxed around your peers when improvising. It is a good idea to participate in exercises such as icebreakers or trust exercises before improvising. Try walking around the room, guiding your partner while they have their eyes closed. Steer them carefully by their shoulders, so that they don't bump into anyone else. Then swap over.

Looking for openings

This involves being perceptive and seeing when there are opportunities to respond or engage with others during improvisation. Using stillness and pauses is important, as although you don't want to be stopping and thinking about every decision, it sometimes makes sense to have a moment of reflection before continuing your improvisation.

Contact improvisation

Contact improvisation involves a physical dialogue between performers. Different points of contact can be made using parts of the body. Selecting a body part such as the elbow could be the basis for an improvisational task. You could set up a task with a partner where one person leads by performing an action, and the other person then reacts to this.

Using each other's weight is also useful in contact improvisation, which can be developed through trust exercises.

Choreographic tool

Although improvisation is by its nature spontaneous, it can also be used as a choreographic tool. It may be useful to film your improvisations. You can then watch them back and select material that you may want to develop further.

You could create text spontaneously by using a popular task called 'word a minute'. This involves creating a story by adding one word at a time. Recording this would also enable you to select specific material to develop.

Taking risks

Staying in character/maintaining technique

As an actor it may be necessary to perform an improvisation 'in character', which will mean maintaining your physical and vocal identity. For dance you will be required to sustain your technical skills throughout.

The more risks you can take in an improvisation, the more exciting your results will be! Try to think 'outside the box' and use your imagination as much as possible.

Now try this

1 Using the visual stimulus on page 40, perform a movement/vocal improvisation for one minute only.
2 Record the improvisation, using your smartphone, laptop or tablet, and watch it back.
3 Select the main movements/vocals that could form the basis of a motif/scene.

Let's experiment!

Experimenting with your stimulus is a useful way of generating exciting and original material. This may be through physical or aural exploration, or by using established techniques and methods of known practitioners.

Physical

This may involve exploring a character or dance technique, but the essential ingredient here is a physical response to a set stimulus. Responding to a stimulus physically may involve direct contact/exploration of a stimulus (such as exploring the dimensions of a table). Alternatively it could include experimenting with the physicality of a character, for example exploring the movements of a young child. It may be a combination of the two!

Aural

This could involve exploration of dialogue in acting, songs in musical theatre or incorporating sound into dance material. It may include experimentation with:

- melody/harmony
- pitch
- accent
- rhythm
- tone
- projection
- volume.

Techniques and methods of known practitioners

You can call on techniques and methods of known practitioners when experimenting in order to develop material.

Dancers could use the work of Merce Cunningham to instigate development of abstract movement. Or you could have a go at a technique called 'chance dance': an action/dynamic/pathway is attributed to each number on the dice and motifs are formed and developed by rolling the dice.

Actors could explore the work of practitioners such as Bertolt Brecht, who pioneered the alienation technique. This is designed to distance the audience from what they are watching by reminding them of the artificial environment of the theatre performance. It is referred to as 'breaking the fourth wall' – the invisible barrier between the stage and the audience.

Musical theatre performers could explore the techniques of Busby Berkeley, a choreographer in the 1930s who created kaleidoscopic effects by using clever camera techniques, inventive costumes and extensive use of formation and pathways.

Busby Berkeley, a Hollywood movie director, often captured his musical sequences from above to show the geometric patterns he created.

Now try this

Select a stimulus that you have researched or thought about.

1 Use key words based on that stimulus to experiment physically or aurally. Try to create as many different effects as possible.

2 Write a short digital log entry about your experiment.

Links Look at pages 53 and 65 for more on creating a digital log entry.

Let's get technical!

You will need to consider a number of staging and performance techniques that might help you to communicate with your audience. You will need to be able to record your decisions effectively when you write up your log. Here are some possible ways of doing this.

Staging techniques

You will need to consider the following aspects when staging your performance. Consider what is available as well as how much time you can devote to this aspect of performance. You can transform the space, however limited it may be, by using the following:

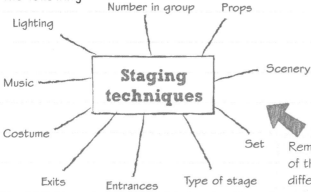

Remember that different parts of the stage can be used for different locations.

Performance techniques

There are some performance techniques that are generic such as projecting, being expressive and stepping into the light in order to be seen. Communicating to the audience is also important for all performance pathways. Some techniques may be more specific and involve mastery of a particular way of singing, acting or dancing. For example, when acting you may wish to include slow motion, soliloquy or freeze-frames.

Projecting is vital in order to communicate artistic intentions to the audience.

Documenting your exploration

When you explore a particular genre or style of acting, dance or musical theatre in preparation for your performance, you will need to document your creative process. As well as recording footage via video/audio, there are other possibilities such as:

• visual/graphic notation such as dance notation

• script writing
• story boarding.

What is story boarding?

Story boarding is a means of showing how your performance will unfold, providing images in sequence. For the purposes of your digital process log, you can annotate the images to provide further detail.

Labanotation

Labanotation is a famous system for recording and analysing movement. Abstract symbols are used to show the direction, body part, duration and dynamic of the movement.

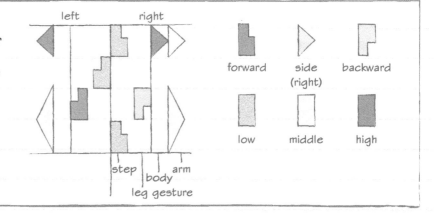

Now try this

1 Taking your chosen pathway, consider five staging or performance techniques that could be used for your performance piece.

2 Write down how each of these will be used and for what purpose.

Thinking about structure

Structure is an important consideration when planning your performance.

Structural elements

Within the various performance genres there are specific structural elements.

In acting you may come across the following structures:

- Naturalistic: the impression that real life is presented on stage
- Classical: three acts (beginning, middle and end)
- Surreal: the play isn't staged in a 'real' time or place
- Episodic: several short scenes linked by the same character, place/theme.

Structure in musical theatre

In musical theatre there isn't always a set structure, but musicals are highly structured, with songs and scenes that are cleverly interlinked. They are often influenced by all types of theatre. **Songs** can help to establish a character, move the plot along, create tension, establish a setting or provide turning points in the story. Some musical theatre does make use of the **three-act convention**. Songs can also be interchanged with spoken dialogue, or they can take you away from the plot and serve as light relief!

Compositional structures and devices

Compositional structures relate to how dance/movement is organised. For example, a dance could tell a story and would therefore have a narrative structure. The structures also relate to music and therefore could be applied to the development of musical theatre.

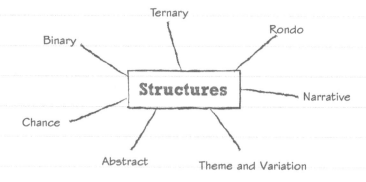

Devices are the ways in which dance/movement material can be shaped. For example a narrative dance based on loneliness would include motifs developed to convey that. A simple motif could be augmented (developed or used more often), inverted (flipped around) or fragmented (broken up) to make the movement more varied.

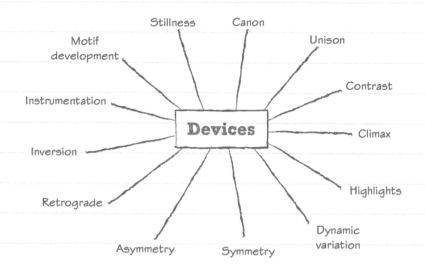

Now try this

1 Carry out research and create a brief description of each of the structures and devices listed.

2 Give examples of when you have used these structures and devices and why.

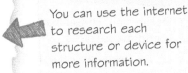
You can use the internet to research each structure or device for more information.

Developing physical performance skills

Physical skills are an essential requirement of acting, dance and musical theatre.

Physical performance skills

In your performance you will be required to exercise a range of physical skills. Some examples are:

- balance
- coordination
- posture
- spatial awareness
- eye contact
- strength
- flexibility
- control
- rhythm
- awareness of and relationship to other performers
- use of tension.

Find definitions for all of the terms listed. You will then be able to use the correct terminology in your digital process log.

Movement and technique classes

In order to be able to use these skills effectively, you will need to participate in regular movement/technique classes. Make sure that you warm up carefully before undertaking any strenuous exercise, as well as taking part in a cool-down at the end of the class.

Warm-ups should include pulse-raising exercises as well as movements to mobilise and stretch the muscles. Cool-downs should include slower exercises which bring the heart rate back down to its usual pace. They can also include relaxation techniques and stretches.

Dance forms such as ballet require body discipline and control.

The whole body is important for communicating meaning – the face, arms and posture.

Now try this

1 List the physical skills that were required for a scene/dance/song in which you have recently participated.
2 Choose one physical skill and explain why it was necessary for your interpretation of the role or piece.

Developing vocal performance skills

Vocal skills are an essential element of acting and musical theatre; they may also be incorporated into dance/movement.

Vocal performance skills

In your performance you will be required to exercise a range of vocal skills.
For example:

- Application of breathing techniques
- Control
- Range
- Tone
- Pitch
- Intonation

- Pace
- Balance
- Poise
- Dynamics
- Projection
- Pause
- Body and facial relaxation

- Intonation
- Modulation
- Inflection
- Articulation
- Resonation

> Find definitions for all of the terms listed. You will then be able to use the correct terminology in your digital process log.

> Being able to read from a vocal score could be a requirement.

an - cto   Spi - ri - tu   in   glo - ri - a De - i   Pa - tris,

> Use of good posture is an important vocal skill.

Warming up and cooling down

Ensure that you participate in regular vocal warm-ups and cool-downs as part of your safe practice. Warm-ups could include some general physical stretches as well as vocal exercises. One example is taking the first five notes of a five-tone scale and performing the notes using different vowel sounds and then introducing lip trills/humming. You may also wish to perform exercises which will help you to relax, such as massaging the forehead, cheeks and jaw area or performing facial yoga! This involves mobilising and stretching exercises for your face, neck and throat. Cool-downs should include gentler exercises to slow the pace after a vocal workout.

Now try this

Randomly select five of the vocal skills above and brainstorm how you could use them in your performance. Undertake internet research to support your learning.

> How can these skills enhance your performance, and what exercises could you do to improve them?

Developing musical performance skills

An understanding and appreciation of music is important in many genres of performance.

Musical performance skills

In your performance it may be useful to exercise skills relating to music. The diagram shows some examples.

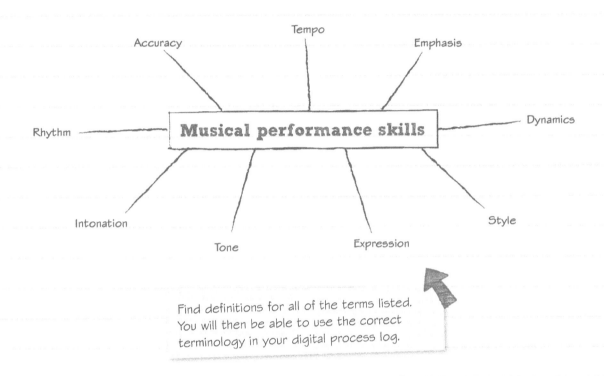

Find definitions for all of the terms listed. You will then be able to use the correct terminology in your digital process log.

Matching music skills to your pathway

If musical theatre is your chosen genre, you will need to reproduce songs effectively using skills such as pitch, tone, intonation and vocal expression. In addition, you may need to participate in dance numbers demonstrating the relevant musical skills.

If dance is your chosen genre, you will need to keep in time with the music, respond to dynamic and rhythmic changes, and express the style/emotion.

If acting is your chosen genre, you might need to develop the skills shown above if participating in any dance/movement numbers, or physical theatre. You may also be required to respond to musical cues so skills such as rhythm will be important.

Most music terminology is written in Italian, and includes words such as 'piano' (which means quiet) and 'staccato' (which means detached). If you are reading a music score, it will be much clearer if you are familiar with Italian terms.

Now try this

1   Make notes on how musical performance skills are important for your performance.
2   List **five** ways in which you could improve aspects of your musical skills.

Developing communication skills

Communication skills are vital for performers, whether this means conveying a message or expressing an emotion. On stage, you will need to communicate with other performers and also with the audience.

Communication skills

In your performance you will be required to exercise a range of communication skills. See below for some examples.

- Communication of mood
- Communication of emotion
- Interpretation of stimulus
- Communication of intention
- Communication of style/form
- Communication with other performers
- Communication with the audience

In your group performance you will need to interact with others to communicate your intention effectively. You may also need to communicate with the audience, for example by drawing them in or alienating them, whatever your chosen intention.

Performance skills that you can use to communicate

You can use some or all of the following performance skills to communicate with your audience:

- Awareness of other performance elements (lighting, costume, set)
- Focus
- Control
- Projection
- Expression

- Characterisation
- Phrasing
- Musicality
- Vocalisation
- Conceptualisation
- Physical/vocal embodiment of a role

- Use of stillness
- Use of gesture
- Dynamics
- Breathing
- Timing
- Emphasis

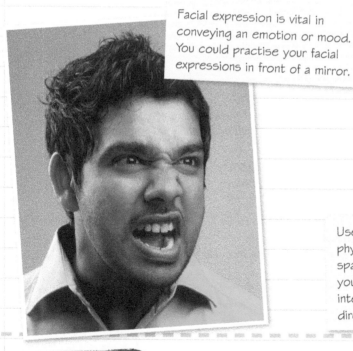

Facial expression is vital in conveying an emotion or mood. You could practise your facial expressions in front of a mirror.

Use of space is important when thinking about physical embodiment of a role. As well as being spatially aware so that you don't bump into your peers, you also need to use the space in interesting ways, for example by exploring levels, directions, dimensions and pathways.

Now try this

Choose five of the performance skills listed above. For each skill:

1 Give a specific example of when you have used that skill in a performance.
2 Describe the effect created by your use of that skill and what it communicated to the audience.

Develop, shape, create!

The creative process involves careful consideration of the following elements.

Selection and rejection of ideas and material

You may have generated a vast amount of material through improvisation and choreographic tasks. You will want to keep some of the material and get rid of some, which will involve thoughtful decision-making.

Choices

When making your choices, think about whether the material is contributing to the overall performance. For example, does it enhance the piece by helping to tell the story, establish a character, create a mood, express an emotion or set a scene?

Responding to feedback

During the creative process you may receive feedback from your peers. It is a good idea to jot down the comments that are provided. Take time to consider the feedback you have been given, and do your best to make the necessary changes.

Comments	Achieved?	How?
I don't believe in your character. Develop your character so that it is more credible	Yes	I have written a 'role on the wall' diagram for my character and thought about how they speak, behave, dress and move. I have practised vocal and movement skills to help me be in character at home. I have practised in front of a mirror and memorised how I look and move, and recorded myself to watch back.

You could create a table that lists each comment and states whether and how you have responded to it.

Shaping and refining material

Structuring your material will involve putting it into an order as well as making tweaks and adjustments to improve your performance. Recording your work and watching it back will enable you to see where any shortcomings are evident. You can then make the necessary changes.

If you are struggling, think back to what your performance is about and its main intention(s).

Refining performance skills through rehearsal

The rehearsal process is valuable for not only memorising material but also for practising and refining your performance skills. Consider the following during rehearsal:

- repetition of material
- using mirrors
- recording yourself and watching it back
- watching each other in groups and providing peer feedback.

Explaining and justifying your creative decisions

If you keep a log you will need to explain and justify your creative decisions.

For every example you provide of a creative decision, you will need to support this by stating **why** you made that choice. Why, for example, you have kept one thing and discarded another? Keep in mind the intention(s) of the piece, so that you can comment on what relevance your choices have on the overall performance.

Remember!

If you keep a log, assume that the reader has no prior knowledge of the process and outcome. Be clear and concise, and document your choices in a logical order.

Now try this

Think about some feedback you have recently been given by your peers or tutor. Record the feedback in a table like the one above, showing how you responded to it and whether you have improved as a result.

Developing early stage ideas

You can use your log to demonstrate how you developed your creative ideas at an early stage.

Digital process log checklist

In your digital process log you need to show that you have considered:

☑ the duration of the piece (for the purposes of this revision task it is 10–20 minutes)

☑ performance skills of the group

☑ performance form and structure.

You will be assessed on your exploratory techniques, ideas for form and content, selection and development of performance skills, personal management and collaborative skills.

Documenting evidence

There are many ways you can record evidence of your creative process for your digital process log. For example, you could incorporate:

> Presenting evidence in a variety of ways is ideal. Don't rely too heavily on one method of documentation.

- still images
- audio recordings of, for example, discussions
- video clips
- scans of notes, including rehearsal notes, diagrams, sketches, brainstorms and mind maps
- minutes of meetings.

> Notes from brainstorms and mind maps are useful ways of showing how your ideas have developed.

Make sure you explain what each item shows, and how the activity contributed to your planning and interpretation.

> This might seem complicated, but it's nothing you don't already do on social media. Just remember to keep a back-up of your files, just in case you lose or break your phone.

Sample response extract

Development of creative ideas: early stage review

Entry Date
18 May

Entry

Annotated stills

Based on the same stimulus, I explored the idea of contrast shown in the image by developing a character with a split personality. I explored the character through movement, turning my head in different directions and moving about the performance space frequently.

I also explored the potential of communicating my intention through a rap. I wrote lyrics that relate to 'flight' which is a main feature in the Muybridge photograph.

In this image I am using the Muybridge photograph stimulus to explore emotion. I am exploring the contrasting emotions of happiness and sadness to reflect the open and closed shapes in the photograph.

Now try this

Use your phone or a digital camera to take photographs of an exploration or improvisation. Create a digital log entry using these photographs.

> Make sure you annotate the photographs to describe the creative processes involved.

Developing more early stage ideas

You can use your log to demonstrate how you developed your creative ideas at an early stage.

Sample response extract

Development of creative ideas: early stage review

Entry Date
18 May

Entry

We decided to explore the theme of flight images and contrast, linked to the Muybridge photograph theme, by improvising with partners. We selected three gestures and then used levels, space and pathways to vary our movements.

In the photograph I am exploring negative emotions, using posture and facial expression to intimidate my partner. We then went on to explore relationships such as face to face, back to back, action and reaction. Lastly we added spoken word to enhance the motif, for example by shouting/whispering phrases such as 'Get off!' or 'Leave me alone!'

You will be assessed on your exploratory techniques, ideas for form and content, selection and development of performance skills.

Think about the key qualities to show:
- accomplished use of exploratory techniques
- sophisticated ideas for form and content
- confident and justified use of performance skills in refining of material.

Sample response extract

Development of creative ideas: early stage review

Entry Date
18 May

Entry

Having explored in pairs, we then shared some of our material to create a quartet section. I demonstrated effective co-operation skills, negotiating which material to keep and which to discard. I managed my time wisely by making decisions without any delay, but with adequate consideration. I decided to draw some pathways to help us use the space effectively. Here are some of the pathways we used. We performed the material travelling through the three different pathways, pausing in still positions at certain points.

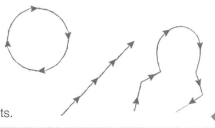

This learner was clearly engaging in discussion and showing initiative by suggesting ideas. Other skills shown are good teamwork and cooperation. The learner could improve their answer by explaining **why** they paused in still positions at certain points. The learner has embedded diagrams which are an effective way of illustrating the creative process.

Now try this

Think about a recent exploration or improvisation you have carried out. Write a short digital log entry detailing:
- any performance skills you demonstrated
- the ways in which those skills could be developed and improved.

If you have a video of a recent exploration you could watch that before writing your entry.

Personal management skills

As a performer you will need to exercise a high standard of personal management skills.

Attendance

You will be expected to attend classes and workshops regularly. If your performance is in a group, it is vital that you do not let your peers down by missing classes. Absence slows down the creative and rehearsal processes, and may compromise the role(s) that you are given.

As well as attending regularly you will be expected to show commitment and enthusiasm throughout the process, as well as showing respect for your tutor and peers.

Your attire is also important, as well as being mentally prepared. For dance, acting or musical theatre the requirements may be quite specific, such as wearing clothing that you can easily move in, isn't too baggy and shows your line. For dance/movement within any performance pathway, you should wear your hair tied back and have bare feet unless specific dance shoes are needed. Chewing gum and wearing socks are strictly prohibited!

Punctuality

Punctuality is an important factor during the planning and preparation stages. Being late can:

- show a lack of self-discipline
- be potentially dangerous as you may miss a warm-up
- mean you miss valuable discussion/creative tasks/rehearsal
- impair your role within the performance if you get sidelined.

You need to be prepared for the professional performance world. Lateness would not be tolerated and you would be at risk of getting sacked.

Meeting group and individual deadlines

Meeting deadlines is crucial. The performance process is lengthy and requires careful planning. If everyone plays their part there is a much better chance of everyone being successful. If you miss deadlines you could potentially:

- slow down the creative process
- affect your own achievement and that of others in your group
- hinder the quality of the performance outcome by delaying the different stages of the process (planning-creation-rehearsal-performance).

Also remember that the impression you make is important – you never know who you might meet during the process. It could be your future agent!

Now try this

Create a check list of everything you need to do to prepare for a rehearsal.

 For more information about rehearsal skills, see page 67.

Rehearsal skills

Rehearsal skills are an essential element of the performance process. You will be required to rehearse your group piece using the following skills.

Learning and absorbing material

Whatever your discipline, you will be required to learn and absorb material. This may mean memorising lines, movements, songs or any combination of the three. Different techniques are involved in memorising material.

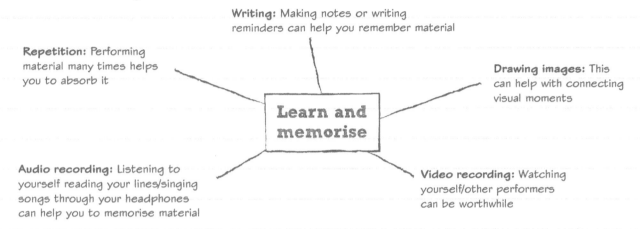

Writing: Making notes or writing reminders can help you remember material

Repetition: Performing material many times helps you to absorb it

Drawing images: This can help with connecting visual moments

Learn and memorise

Audio recording: Listening to yourself reading your lines/singing songs through your headphones can help you to memorise material

Video recording: Watching yourself/other performers can be worthwhile

Applying, developing and refining performance skills

Now you are in the rehearsal phase, you will need to think about how to apply, develop and refine your performance skills. You will need to be familiar with the material before you can do this effectively. Consider your role(s) and what is required in terms of performance skills. Are you portraying a character, are you part of a chorus line or communicating a theme through dance?

Refer back to the lists of physical, musical, vocal and performance skills. Take each skill and think about how you can apply, develop and refine it. Take dynamics for example – are they clear within your performance? Could you improve your dynamic range by showing contrast more effectively? What rehearsal skills will you employ to achieve this?

Listen to your group

Remember, when you are in the process of learning material it is important to listen very carefully to your group members.

Feedback from your peers can also help you with skills development.

Now try this

Think about some material you have recently learned. Make a list of the techniques you used to help you learn and memorise it.

How can you improve your memory skills?

Teamwork and collaboration

As you will be working in a group, teamworking skills are extremely important. You will need to demonstrate the skills explained below during the performance process.

Giving and taking instruction and direction

You will need to both give and take instruction and direction during the rehearsal process. Remember the following advice to improve in this area:

- Be clear
- Be concise
- Be heard
- Listen

> If you find it hard to remember instructions, you can always write them down or record them.

Trust and cooperation

In group performance it is important to trust and be trusted by your fellow performers, as well as cooperating effectively. You need to feel comfortable when you are in close physical proximity for example, such as during physical combat scenes. Trusting your peers will enable you to take more risks and feel at ease. Trust exercises and icebreakers can help to achieve this.

A trust exercise

Contributing ideas

Part of the devising and rehearsal process is about sharing your own ideas to create original material. Consider the following:

- Be brave.
- Allow others to speak without interruption.
- Let each member of the group have an equal turn in contributing their ideas.

> Remember that contributing ideas will enhance your achievement, and you will have more to refer to in your digital log. Ideas can always be jotted down and put into a hat, so that they are anonymous.

Receptiveness and responsiveness to the ideas of others

Allowing others to feel comfortable in group situations is important, as it is only when this occurs that the creative juices can flow! Consider the following:

- Be open-minded.
- Respect others' opinions.
- Try out others' ideas; give them a chance.

> Remember to be positive and enthusiastic! This will rub off on your fellow performers and you will be helping to create an enjoyable and productive environment.

Now try this

1 Describe a trust exercise or icebreaker that you could teach your group.
2 Make a list of the skills that are involved in this exercise. Which ones are the most challenging to master?

Developing mid-stage ideas

You can use your log to demonstrate how you developed your creative ideas halfway through the creative process. Some of the things you will be assessed on are your **personal management and collaborative skills**.

Digital log checklist

In your digital log you need to show that you have considered:

☑ the duration of the piece (10–20 minutes for the purposes of this revision task)

☑ performance skills of the group

☑ performance form and structure.

You will be assessed on your exploratory techniques, ideas for form and content, selection and development of performance skills, personal management and collaborative skills.

Sample response extract

Development of creative ideas: mid-stage review

Entry Date
4 June

Entry

In the fifth group workshop activity I demonstrated initiative by contributing the idea of developing our flight motif in pairs, using our stimulus. I led a discussion with my group, addressing how the motif could be developed, such as through exploration of pathways, dynamics, travelling and canon. I then provided clear instructions, allocating two kinds of motif development to each pair.

When each pair had completed their task, we watched each other's work and recorded it. It was interesting to see how different the material that had been created was. We are going to develop this material further by combining our findings.

There is clear identification of the individual part played in developing material for the group performance. Although it is acceptable to use 'we', also aim to use 'I', as this demonstrates what you have done as an individual.

Sample response extract

The learner has effectively addressed elements of the specification such as attendance, punctuality, meeting deadlines, contributing ideas, giving instruction and cooperation. Examples of the adjustments made could be provided to improve the answer.

Development of creative ideas: mid-stage review

Entry Date
4 June

Entry

I arrived early to rehearsal wearing the appropriate kit, so that I could practise my lines. I performed my dialogue to the group, which meant I had fulfilled my individual deadline effectively.

We then practised the material created so far, noting down where changes could be made. I suggested refining some of the leading and following section, as I felt there was some material that was less relevant to the piece as a whole. The group agreed so we then went through each scene, making the necessary adjustments. I suggested different formations that we could stand in to deliver the lines, such as a triangle or a diagonal line.

Now try this

Write a short digital log entry about how well you participated in a recent rehearsal, workshop or class.

Continuing to progress

You can use your log to show that you have refined and developed material since you last made an entry in it. In this way, you can demonstrate your progression.

Sample response extract

Development of creative ideas: mid-stage review

Entry Date
4 June

Entry

I am really pleased with how the material is developing since my last log entry. We have been busy extending and shaping material, as well as refining it. Whereas before, we were in the exploratory stages, we are now further on in the process, selecting the best material and discarding material that is less relevant, as well as thinking of ways of enhancing the structure and our performance skills. I decided that there is one section where the intention is not as clear as it could be. So to address this I suggested listing reasons why it is not clear and each of us providing a solution. This really helped and we got to the bottom of why it wasn't clear, as well as how this could be rectified.

The learner sees the progression they have made and explains this clearly. The learner outlines some of the activities that have taken place and provides reasons for this.

To improve the answer, the learner could have listed the reasons why the piece was not as clear as it could have been, as well as providing the solutions.

Sample response extract

Development of creative ideas: mid-stage review

Entry Date
4 June

Entry

I thought it would be a good idea to perform some of the material to our peers to get some feedback. We did this and it was constructive, as they provided some suggestions regarding what needed improvement. We listened carefully to their advice and made notes. One of the improvements was the tableaux section, which is meant to show the difference between stillness and motion through the use of lines and curves. The transitions between each tableau weren't effective, and needed to be more expressive and visually interesting. I thought it would be interesting to try moving between each tableau with a different dynamic, such as 'heavy' or 'fast' or 'slow.'

We also worked on exaggerating our facial expressions whilst in the tableau, to demonstrate contrasting emotions such as sadness and happiness

Peer observations and sharing of ideas are effective ways of improving material. They involve cooperation, listening skills and negotiation. The learner has stated that the tableaux section wasn't working, providing specific ways to improve it.

The learner could improve this answer by explaining exactly why the tableaux section wasn't working. In addition, further information could be provided about what each tableau represents and why contrasting emotions are being shown.

Now try this

Choose a performance skill or technique that you have developed or improved.

1 Describe the tasks or activities you carried out to work on this skill or technique.
2 Explain how this skill or technique has improved.

Performance preparation

When you are required to perform your piece, it will be important to clearly demonstrate all the skills, production elements and techniques that you have been exploring during your preparation period.

Work in progress

During your performance you will need to show that you have:

- performed confidently and fluently to communicate ideas, meaning and style
- demonstrated responsiveness and sensitivity to other performers in order to contribute to the group
- applied consistent focus, engagement and strong technical command, in a way that is appropriate to the creative intention.

Don't forget what it's all about!

It is important to remember that you will be performing a work in progress.

Production elements of the work, such as costumes, lighting and sound may still be undecided or unfinished. Remember to consider audience feedback, allowing you to gauge audience responses and receive constructive criticism in order to develop the work further.

Here are some things to think about when you are preparing for your performance:

Preparing for your performance

1. Make sure you have rehearsed in full costume and with other production elements in place.

2. Memorise your material effectively so that you know it off by heart.

3. Think about all the possible things that could go wrong and find solutions.

4. Make sure that you have packed everything that you will need on the day.

5. Think about how you are going to gather feedback from the audience and prepare questions/questionnaires in advance (see page 5 for more information).

6. Consider potential health and safety issues such as wearing socks, jewellery or chewing gum.

7. Communicate effectively with your group so that you are clear about individual roles and responsibilities.

8. Put any distractions to one side and enjoy your time on stage.

Performing your piece

You will perform your piece under supervised conditions at a time confirmed by your teacher. Your teacher will record your performance, so it can be submitted for assessment. At the start of the recording you will need to identify yourself and your teacher will give you guidance on this.

Audience

You and your teacher should invite an audience to come and watch your performance. It is a good idea to prepare an audience feedback form so that you can gather their ideas and suggestions. They will be a crucial element of your log entry.

Now try this

Write a checklist of things to consider:

(a) in the week before your performance

(b) the day before your performance

(c) on the morning of your performance.

Process review

The final part of your digital process log should be written after you have performed. You will need to reflect on the working process leading up to your performance and the performance itself. You will need to consider the following elements about the overall process.

Interpretation of stimulus and ideas

Consider how well you have interpreted your stimulus and ideas. Consult any notes you have taken during the process, as well as recorded clips. Think about the following points:

- Is your intention clear?
- Are there parts that could have been clearer?
- How could they have been made clearer?
- Did you use costume(s)/prop(s) to enhance your piece? Why?
- What initial research did you do about your stimulus in order to generate ideas?
- What structure/form did you use?
- What genre/style(s) did you incorporate, and why?

Use of exploratory techniques

Think about how well you have employed exploratory techniques such as improvisation in order to generate material. Consider the following:

- What exploratory techniques did you use?
- Were they successful?
- Did you find some techniques more effective than others?
- What were the benefits of improvisation?
- How did you record/document your exploratory tasks?
- Did you work individually or in groups?
- What skills would you like to develop for future exploratory tasks?

Own development and contribution of ideas

Think about how your skills have developed during the process, taking into account the following points:

- What ideas did you contribute?
- Were they successful?
- Did you find it easy/difficult to communicate your ideas to your group?
- If you were to repeat the process, would you make any changes to your contribution?
- How do you think you have developed as a performer?

Using performance skills to develop and shape performance material

As well as improving your performance skills, you will also have honed your creative skills during the process. Think about what skills you used when developing and shaping material.

You will have been involved in decision-making, negotiation and pushing your creative boundaries. What decisions did you make, and how did this affect the process? Would you go back and do anything differently if you could?

Now try this

Write a paragraph about why each of the four categories above is an important part of evaluating the working process.

Process strengths and developments

In order to evaluate the working process effectively, you will need to consider your strong points as well as areas you can improve.

Identifying your strengths and areas for improvement

Look back at your notes, recorded footage, feedback from peers and your tutor, and your log entries. Consider your strengths and areas for improvement.

You may wish to include any skills audits and/or footage that demonstrate progression.

 Remember, at this stage you are thinking solely about the working **process**. You'll evaluate your actual performance next.

What to cover

Consider the following when addressing your strengths and areas for improvement:

- physical skills such as balance, coordination, alignment, flexibility, posture, stamina
- vocal skills such as use of pitch, tone, range, intonation, articulation, projection
- musical skills such as use of dynamics, expression, emphasis, timing, rhythm
- use of constituent features such as costume or props
- contribution of ideas
- shaping of material
- participation in group tasks
- response to feedback
- rehearsal skills
- attitude and commitment to the project.

Opportunity for honesty

Remember not to be shy about your strengths – this is not showing off! Everyone has strengths and this is your chance to comment on your best achievements during the process leading up to performance. Equally, don't be embarrassed about any shortcomings you have; it is valuable to consider your weaknesses and how far you have progressed during the preparation period.

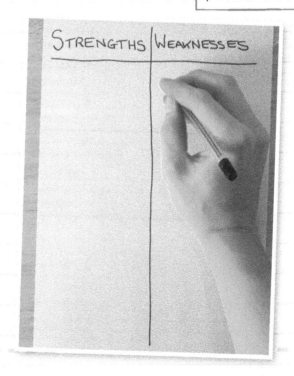

Now try this

Read through the list above and write down your main strengths and areas of improvement for each point.

Performance review

The final part of your digital process log involves reflecting on the performance. You will need to consider the following elements.

Effectiveness of the performance in realising the creative intention

Consider how well you interpreted your stimulus and ideas in performance. Consult any notes you have taken since the performance, as well as watching the performance itself. Think about the following:

- Is your intention clear?
- Are there parts that could have been clearer?
- How could they have been made clearer?
- Did you use costume(s)/prop(s) to enhance your piece? Why?
- What structure/form did you use?
- What genre/style(s) did you incorporate and why?
- If you were to revisit this project, what would you do differently regarding creative intention?

Effectiveness of your performance skills in realising the creative intention

Consider how well you employed performance skills in performance. Think about the following points:

- What performance skills did you use?
- Were they successful?
- Did you find that you were better at some performance skills than others?
- Why?
- Which skills would you try to develop for future performances?
- How would they enhance the performance?

Development of the material

Think about how you would have developed the material further in terms of staging and production elements if this were to be realised as a fully resourced production. Consider the following:

- Would you have incorporated costume and props differently/to any greater extent?
- Why?
- Would you have made changes regarding music and lighting?
- Why?

Development of your performance skills

If the performance was to be realised as a fully resourced production, how would you need to develop your performance skills? Consider the following, for example:

- Would performing in a larger venue mean developing your vocal projection?
- Would physicality, movement and facial expressions need to be exaggerated further so that they are clearer on a larger stage?
- How would you need to adapt staging and production elements? Would there be more lighting and sound equipment? How would a bigger performance space affect the set and staging?

Now try this

Write a paragraph about why each of the four categories above is an important part of evaluating your performance.

Performance strengths and developments

In order to evaluate your performance effectively, you will need to consider your strong points as well as the areas you can improve.

Identifying your strengths and areas for improvement

Look back at your notes and recorded footage of the performance. Think about any feedback received, including the audience's reaction. Use this information to help you consider your strengths and areas for improvement.

You are thinking about the **performance**. This is where your audience feedback sheet and any discussions you had with your audience will be useful.

Considering your strengths and areas for improvement

Consider the following when addressing your strengths and areas for improvement:

- physical skills such as balance, coordination, alignment, flexibility, posture, stamina
- vocal skills such as use of pitch, tone, range, intonation, articulation, projection
- musical skills such as use of dynamics, expression, emphasis, timing, rhythm
- performance skills
- use of constituent features such as costume or props
- attitude and commitment during performance.

Progression of skills

It is useful at this stage to consider how your skills have progressed from when you first started the creative process, up to and including the performance. Do you have any footage that demonstrates your skills at the outset, which you can compare to your skills during the performance? What differences can you see?

Your development as a performer and how this has taken place is a valuable point for discussion in your digital process log.

Audience reaction

Following the performance the audience will engage in a feedback session. You will need to ask the audience targeted questions to help you write a final log entry.

The questions could include the following:

- Was the intention of the performance clear?
- Was this due to the structure, performance, skills, costume and props, or a combination of these factors?
- Could anything have been done to improve the performance?
- What else should we do if the performance was professional?
- What were the strengths and weaknesses of the performance?

Now try this

Read through the list of possible areas for improvement above, and write down your own main strengths and areas of improvement for each point.

Reviewing the process

You will need to review, and reflect on, the creative working process in your digital process log.

Working process

It is important for you to reflect on the effectiveness of the working process. This includes a review of your personal management and collaborative skills and the impact of your own contribution and that of others. Your entry in your digital process log needs to demonstrate:

- perceptive, justified judgements
- sophisticated, creative ideas for further development of the performance material
- insightful and thorough evaluation.

This is a clear and concise review which includes specific examples of how personal management and collaborative skills have been employed during the process. To improve the quality of the response, the learner could have elaborated on **how** they collaborated with their group.

Sample response extract

Review and reflection

Entry Date
18 June

Entry

During the creative tasks with my group, I exercised high levels of self-discipline, always arriving early and warming up appropriately. If there were any absentees I worked quickly to confront the issue and resolved it by making the necessary adjustments. For example, when my partner was absent I directed the pair section instead, alternating between the learners present to demonstrate material.

I collaborated with my group in rehearsal. We watched each other and provided feedback, such as what was strong and what required improvement. It was necessary for me to exercise trust and cooperation, for example when we practised the contact section. As some of the contact was quite risky, it was important that I developed trust in my partner and that initially involved trust games and exercises.

Skills audit

A skills audit is a good way of documenting your strengths and weaknesses, as well as how you can address any issues. Try to include all of the aspects on which you are being assessed in your audit. Also aim to make regular entries/updates to show progression over a period of time.

Sample response extract

Review and reflection

Entry Date
18 June

Entry

Name and date:		
Required skill	Personal rating	Evidence
Balance	1 **2** 3 4 5	I can only balance for a short length of time on one leg
Coordination	1 2 3 4 **5**	I am able to perform complex sequences using my arms and legs in a coordinated manner
Flexibility	1 2 3 4 **5**	I am fairly flexible, for example I can do the splits
Vocal projection	1 2 3 4 **5**	I am very good at projecting my voice on stage
Facial expression	1 **2** 3 4 5	I am not very good at using my facial muscles effectively
Articulation	1 2 **3** 4 5	I am fairly good at articulating when delivering lines
Characterisation	1 **2** 3 4 5	I am not very good at getting into character

Key: 1 = weakest and 5 = strongest

Now try this

1. Use a table like the one on the right to create your own skills audit.
2. Add a column stating how you could improve each element of the skills audit.

Reviewing the performance

It is important that you review, and reflect on, your performance in your log.

Digital process log checklist

In your digital process log you will need to consider the:

☑ feedback and response from your invited audience

☑ recording of the performance.

You will be assessed on your reflection on the effectiveness of the performance. This includes a review of your own contribution and that of others and your ideas for further development of the performance.

Language and writing style

Remember to include appropriate technical terms in your digital process log, to show that you are familiar with and have considered these. Also remember to justify your decisions as you work. Provide clear examples to back up your ideas.

Sample response extract

> **Review and reflection**
>
> **Entry Date**
> 18 June
>
> **Entry**
>
> Having watched the recording of the performance, I thought we made the intention very clear. As a group I think we achieved this by employing effective team work, trust and excellent negotiation skills. Also the performance skills used were of a high standard.
>
> In the recording I noticed that my use of facial expression was really effective in communicating the relationship between myself and Dan. Also my physical embodiment of the role helped to create tension in the penultimate scene where I am cowering in fear. My vocal projection was fairly strong throughout; however, I could further develop this by improving my posture and slowing down the pace of some of my lines.
>
> There was positive audience feedback on my idea of using the broom as a prop, which I quickly held up in front of me to create a barrier between myself and Dan. They said that this really helped to communicate the sense of the sudden division between us.

The text refers to the recording of the performance, as well as individual strengths and weaknesses. Specific examples are provided. The comments refer to relevant skills such as teamwork, trust, negotiation, physical and vocal skills.

To further develop this written work, further evaluation of the audience feedback should be incorporated. For example, it could include discussion about whether the audience enjoyed it, and how they could see it being developed for a professional performance.

Now try this

Think about some recent audience feedback you have received and write a paragraph about how the feedback will affect the decisions you make when developing the performance further.

The audience could just consist of your peers; it doesn't have to be an invited audience.

Your Unit 5 set task

Unit 5 will be assessed through a task, which will be set by Pearson. In this assessed task you will need to devise and develop an individual performance piece in response to a commission.

Set task skills

Your assessed task could cover any of the essential content in the unit. You can revise the unit content in this Revision Guide.

The skills pages are designed to **revise skills** that might be needed in your assessed task. They use selected content and outcomes to provide an example of ways of applying your skills.

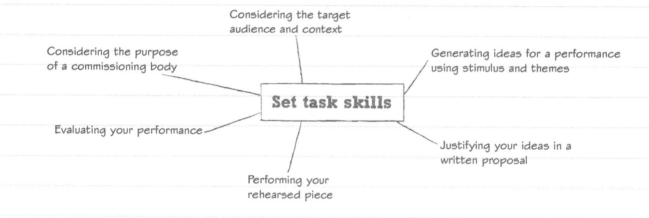

Considering the target audience and context

Considering the purpose of a commissioning body

Generating ideas for a performance using stimulus and themes

Set task skills

Evaluating your performance

Justifying your ideas in a written proposal

Performing your rehearsed piece

Workflow

The process of creating an individual performance piece might follow these steps:

- ✓ Review the commission brief, stimulus and theme.
- ✓ Generate performance ideas.
- ✓ Justify your ideas in a written proposal.
- ✓ Rehearse and record your performance piece.
- ✓ Evaluate your performance.

Check the Pearson website

The skills pages are designed to demonstrate the skills that might be needed in your assessed task. The details of your actual assessed task may change from year to year so always make sure you are up to date. Check the Pearson website for the most up-to-date **Sample Assessment Material** to get an idea of the structure of your assessed task and what this requires of you.

Now try this

Visit the Pearson website and find the page containing the course materials for BTEC National Performing Arts. Look at the latest Unit 5 Sample Assessment Material for an indication of:

- the structure of your set task, and whether it is divided into separate parts
- any notes you might have to make and how long you might have to prepare in advance of the assessment
- what briefing or stimulus material might be provided to you
- how much time you are allowed for each section of the task
- the activities you are required to complete and how to format your responses.

Task information

Below is a revision task which is similar to the format of your real assessment. However, the task information and stimuli are different, and are provided so that you can practise the required skills for the activities you will need to complete.

Task information

This page gives information on the commissioning body and the commission. You have a choice of stimulus that must be used when developing the proposal and creating your final performance.

The commissioning body

Artsworth City Council is a local authority wishing to promote the performing arts and make them more accessible to residents living in the area. It regularly commissions performing arts work, and this year it would like to celebrate the upcoming Olympic Games by organising a broader programme of events. The aim is to combine sport and the performing arts to engage the widest possible audience.

The commission

Artsworth City Council is now commissioning new work for this summer's programme of events. This year the council wishes to celebrate sport and the community through a series of different performing arts disciplines. It wants to provide entertaining and stimulating experiences for its audience.

Performances may include acting, dance, musical theatre or another performance discipline such as circus skills, variety or stand-up comedy.

The work may be **devised by the performer** and/or **developed** from existing material such as a script, score or choreographic instruction, in order to meet the requirements of the commissioning body.

Target audience

Your performance work should appeal to an audience of all ages, from toddlers to the elderly.

Length of performance

- The performance should run for five to eight minutes in total.
- It could comprise of a single continuous performance piece or several shorter pieces linked together.

Logistics

- This must be a solo performance.
- The performance should use only a minimum amount of technical resources, for example basic lighting, sound and costume.
- It should be suitable for a small indoor performance space, e.g. drama/dance studio, community hall, small theatre.

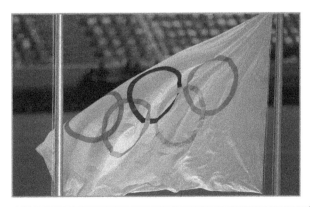

Task stimuli

For the purposes of this unit of the Revision Guide, you will be provided with five sample stimuli of different types. You will use them as a starting point for your performance.

Theme

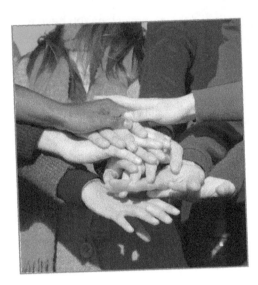

Your sample theme as stimulus is 'Unity'.

Visual

Your sample visual stimulus is Banksy's *There's always hope.*

Text

Your sample text as stimulus is the following quote by the late South African President, Nelson Mandela:

'Sport has the power to change the world. It has the power to inspire. It has the power to unite people in a way that little else does. It speaks to youth in a language they understand. Sport can create hope where once there was only despair. It is more powerful than government in breaking down racial barriers.'

Aural

Your sample aural stimulus is David Bowie's track 'Heroes'.

Search online to listen to this track.

Media

Your example media stimulus is an *Independent* article entitled 'How trail running "helps to boost physical and mental health"'. Use your phone or tablet to scan this QR code and read the full article or view the article online (http://activetea.ch/2mA2us7).

Read the article

Understanding commission briefs

In order to **understand** the commission brief it is important to consider the context. This means looking at the circumstances and facts that surround the commission.

The purpose of the commission

Think about what the commission is aiming to achieve.

* Does it have one main objective, or are there several?
* How can you put this objective into the material you create?
* How can it be communicated?

You will need to keep coming back to the objective(s) during the creative process.

Links The purpose of a commission could be to both entertain and educate. See page 85 for more information about possible purposes of a commission.

You will need to consider how to communicate your purpose(s). This could be through the particular form/style, characters, dialogue, dance, song, costume, music, set and so on.

The type of commissioning body

The type of commissioning body will affect the performance material you create. You will need to consider the following points:

* Is it a charity, arts council, local authority, commercial company, museum, art gallery or tourist board?
* What makes each of these commissioning bodies different in terms of expectations, regulations and requirements?

Links See pages 82–84 for more information on types of commissioning body.

Addressing the requirements of a commissioning body gives your performance its overall direction.

Make sure you research the different types of commissioning bodies, and in particular the one you are allocated for your assessment.

Differences between commissioning bodies

Each type of commissioning body differs in its outlook, and it might have its own particular way of working. Within each type there will also be differences. For example, the mission statement for one charity will not be the same as any other, even if there are similarities.

Links to previous or planned future projects

You may be given information in your commission brief regarding previous projects that took place prior to your commission, or plans for more events to take place in the future. This allows you to see the commission in context in terms of a timeline, providing a framework for your performance.

This information could help to inform your material, as it gives it more perspective. For example, if you know that previous large-scale performances have taken place but now the commissioning body want to focus more on smaller-scale events, you can be sensitive to the changes and thus help to implement them more effectively.

Now try this

Using the commission brief on page 79, consider the three elements above. Jot down the key points regarding the purpose of the commission, the type of commissioning body and any information you may have been given about previous or planned future projects.

Commissioning bodies (1)

'Commissioning' means formally choosing an individual or group to do a specific piece of work. The following pages cover two types of organisation that might commission performing arts work and what values and goals they might have in doing so. You will need to consider the commissioning body when developing your performance for Unit 5.

1 Charities

Charities might commission work in order to:

- benefit a specific group of people
- raise awareness of an issue
- raise money for a cause or campaign.

If you are producing work that has been commissioned by a charity, it is important to make sure that the work matches the values and goals of that charity. You can do this by:

- reading the charity's mission statement
- talking to charity workers, or members of the communities served by the charity
- researching the work that the charity carries out.

Bristol-based artist Dan Canham produced this work for Dance Umbrella, a charity that supports the evolution of dance and provides opportunities for upcoming artists. Setting the work in a car park reflected Dance Umbrella's commitment to innovative work.

2 Arts Council England

Arts Council England is a governmental body that supervises public funding of the arts in England. There are also similar arts councils in Wales (Arts Council of Wales), Scotland (Scottish Arts Council) and Northern Ireland (Arts Council of Northern Ireland).

Arts Council England frequently commissions new work to:

- bring arts and culture to everyone
- promote specific types of performance work.

Arts Councils usually seek applications for funding from performance artists. If you are creating a commissioned work for an Arts Council it is important to state clearly in your proposal how the work will reach and benefit a wide range of people. Arts Council projects often include educational elements, and should reflect the diversity of their target audiences.

The Arts Council England's Creative People and Places fund focuses on parts of the country where involvement in the arts is substantially lower than the national average. This image shows part of its Luton Creates project, which gives a voice to local people and organisations. Artists involved in the project had to engage with members of the local community to help them tell their stories.

 Links There is more about target audiences on pages 87 and 88.

Now try this

1 Visit Arts Council England's Creative People and Places website at www.creativepeopleplaces.org.uk.

2 Use the 'Our Projects' page to identify a project near you. Describe two ways in which it meets the needs of that particular area, and how it helps residents to engage with the arts.

Don't forget to acknowledge your sources when performing internet research. See page 11 in Unit 1 for more information on how to do this.

Commissioning bodies (2)

A commission can also come from a local authority or commercial company.

3 Local authorities

Local authorities may commission performing arts work in order to:

- support local projects/events
- celebrate the diversity of communities
- commemorate local historical events.

Local authority commissions are often closely related to locality and community. They often draw on the skills of local arts groups, companies, schools, colleges and businesses.

Academy of Northern Ballet Centre for Advanced Training students perform *Small Steps* at Leeds Town Hall.

Leeds City Council organised a Holocaust Memorial Day where various local groups performed a programme of events to commemorate the Holocaust, Nazi persecution, and subsequent genocides in Cambodia, Rwanda, Bosnia and Darfur. In this instance the focus is on the local authority commissioning work to commemorate a worldwide historical event, rather than a local historical event.

4 Commercial companies

Commercial companies may commission performing arts work in order to:

- promote products
- raise awareness of their brand
- sell tickets to events.

As many commercial companies reach large audiences, particularly through broadcasting, this is an ideal way to access large numbers of people.

A flash mob is a powerful way for companies to market product or deliver a strong message about its ethos and aims. This is particularly true if it is filmed and uploaded to the internet. Search for T-Mobile Dance on YouTube.

Now try this

1 Use the internet to research performances recently commissioned by a local authority or commercial company.

2 Write some notes on whether the performance achieved the aims of the commission.

 Would a different performance discipline have been more successful? In what way?

Commissioning bodies (3)

A commission can also come from a museum, art gallery or tourist board.

5 Museums and art galleries

These bodies may commission performing arts works in order to:

- promote/launch events and exhibitions
- celebrate the work of specific practitioners/ artists.
- present an idea/concept/theme through a range of art forms
- offer visitors a diverse cultural experience.

Programming performing arts within museums and galleries engages existing visitors in different ways, as well as broadening the audience. For example, commissioning a street dancer to perform in a museum could bring in a younger and more diverse audience.

To hand, by Siobhan Davies and Matthias Sperling, photo by Pari Naderi.

Choreographers Siobhan Davies and Matthias Sperling were invited to create a new work for the Whitechapel Gallery in 2011. The work was performed within Claire Barclay's exhibition Shadow Spans and was informed by Davies' and Sperling's engagement with Barclay's installation and the ideas behind her work.

6 Tourist boards

A tourist board may commission performing arts works in order to promote local areas of interest and attractions to ensure people visit.

This could be in the form of a site-specific performance that will bring the audience to a specific locality. Alternatively a performance may take place in a stage space but relate to an area of interest/attraction in terms of performance content.

Sometimes inviting famous performers to appear in a television advertisement or on social media to promote an area is enough, rather than requiring a full performance. Chris Hemsworth has been a popular choice for global ambassador for Tourism Australia's new aquatic and coastal experiences campaign, #SeeAustralia.

Now try this

Think of either a local museum, art gallery or tourist board that you know.

Think of **five** possible commissions they might give, using different performing arts disciplines. What would be the commissioning body's goals or values behind each of these commissions?

Think about the profile of the commissioning body you have chosen, and why the specific performing arts discipline would be the most relevant.

The purpose of a commission

When you create your performance for Unit 5, you will not only need to think about the overarching values and goals of the commissioning body, but also the specific stated purpose of the commission you have been given. Note that a commission might have more than one purpose.

Entertainment

A commission may be purely for the purposes of entertainment or this could be just one of its purposes. You can often use entertainment to inform, educate and raise awareness of specific issues.

When preparing an entertaining performance you will need to consider elements such as the target age of the audience and and ensure the type of entertainment is suitable for them.

Education

A commission may have the primary purpose of education; this could be targeted at children, teenagers or adults. It could target a specific topic as part of the school curriculum. Theatre in Education (TIE) companies are a good example of performers commissioned to educate.

In this instance your message is extremely important to your performance. You will need to consider the key points to be communicated, and how to convey them in an interesting and original manner, using the appropriate tone.

In Saltmine's production of **Escape**, issues such as cyberbullying and internet safety are covered.

Informing

A commission may be for the purposes of informing an audience. Informing is similar in purpose to education in providing information, but may take more of a commercial or promotional slant. For example, a mobile phone company might commission a flash dance to inform people about their new service for making video calls.

The focus of your performance will be imparting the relevant facts and information to your target audience.

Celebration

A commission may be for the purposes of celebration. This could mean celebrating a particular festival, landmark or personality.

You will need to focus on the relevant type of celebration, for example religious or cultural, and ensure the content and tone of your performance is appropriate.

Commemoration

A commission may be for the purposes of commemoration. This could mean commemorating an event or person(s), such as a war, national event or person of national significance.

Being sensitive to your subject matter is an important consideration here. The performance will need to be tasteful and relevant, and you will need to undertake research to gain background knowledge.

Raising awareness of an issue or topic

Raising awareness of an issue or topic is related to educating and informing but may be less about imparting specific information or facts, and more about making an impression on the audience to ensure they go away and think about the issue further.

You will need to focus on communicating your main objective clearly, probably in a very memorable way that will have a long-term impact on your audience.

Now try this

Taking into account the purposes of the commission brief on page 79, and using the thematic stimulus of 'Unity' on page 80, describe some possible features of a performance piece in your relevant discipline that would meet the purpose of the commission.

Consider how your commission might differ depending on its purpose.

Considering commissioning bodies and their purpose

You need to be able to write a proposal for your performance in response to the commission you have been given. In the proposal you will need to include discussion of the commissioning body and the purpose of the commission.

Here are some sample extracts from other learners' performance proposals. They are writing about how their proposal meets the commissioning body's aims/values and the purpose of the commission on page 79.

> **Keep focused!**
>
> When planning and then writing up your proposal, try to really think about the **type** of commissioning body and what the main **purpose** of the commission is. Consider what requirements and constraints different types of commissioning bodies may have to follow, as well as what the commission is aiming to do.

Try to **explain** the type of commissioning body. What is unique about it and how may this affect the performance?

Sample response extract

Because the commissioning body is a local authority, it will want to make links with the local community and enable everyone local to become involved in the event. As a local myself, I am uniquely qualified to know about location issues and concerns and be able to engage with the likely target audience. I am going to make my performance more relevant to the locality by incorporating dialogue and lyrics relating to the area. For example I aim to perform a monologue about sport which includes names of local sports centres and teams, such as the Artsworth Sports Centre and the Artsworth Football Club.

Good use of examples of how they will take into account the commissioning body's aims/values here.

Sample response extract

The main purpose of the commission brief is celebration. In order to celebrate the upcoming Olympic Games, I performed research so that I firstly had knowledge about the Olympic Games and the type of sports that it included. I discovered that golf and rugby sevens are the two new sports that will be included in the Games. I have therefore decided to base some of my movement vocabulary around these two sports, keeping the purpose of celebration in mind. I will improvise around the two sports and how winning each one would be celebrated, which links to both sport and celebration effectively. I will also incorporate some dialogue which includes references to local golfing and rugby heroes.

Good example of research being performed which then informs decisions.

Could give more detail about the improvisations such as using key words or actions. Was the improvisation filmed/refined/shaped? Try to include as much explanation as possible.

Example(s) of dialogue could be included to justify the decision.

> **Now try this**
>
> Look at the commission brief on page 79 and the aural stimulus on page 80. Make notes on a proposal you might make for a performance taking into account the type of commissioning body and purpose of the commission.

Target audiences

You will need to consider your target audience when writing your proposal and developing your performance. There are many factors that define different types of target audience, and they are listed below.

Type

What **type** of audience is it? This could be very broad, or it could be very specialist. It could consist of:

- the general public
- families
- a local community
- a specialist group.

Identifying the target audience

The commission brief will not always explicitly state the target audience. You may need to think about the commissioning body or commission purpose to identify this. For example if a commissioning body is a company that produces expensive cars, their target audience will be people who typically earn over a certain amount of money. They may also (but not exclusively) be in an older age bracket and be male.

Age

What **age** is your audience? This affects your performance quite dramatically. For example, the audience could consist of:

- children aged under five
- children aged between 5 and 16
- young adults
- older adults
- elderly people.

The message and narrative of a performance needs to be very clear for children aged under five.

It's important that the performance is age appropriate. The requirements for an audience of children aged under five compared to an audience of young adults would be considerably different.

Try to think about what appeals to each age group, as well as methods of communication that are appropriate. The language you use may differ between the age groups too.

Gender

What **gender** are your audience?

- Female
- Male
- Mixed

A mixed audience

Although most subjects and means of communication appeal to both genders, a particular commission may be more geared towards one gender than another; for example, raising awareness of breast or prostate cancer.

Now try this

Look at the commission on page 79. Describe your target audience. Make reference to type, age and gender.

Connecting the work to the audience

It is important that the performance you are proposing, and will then go on to develop, meets the needs of the target audience. There are four key factors to consider when planning your performance proposal.

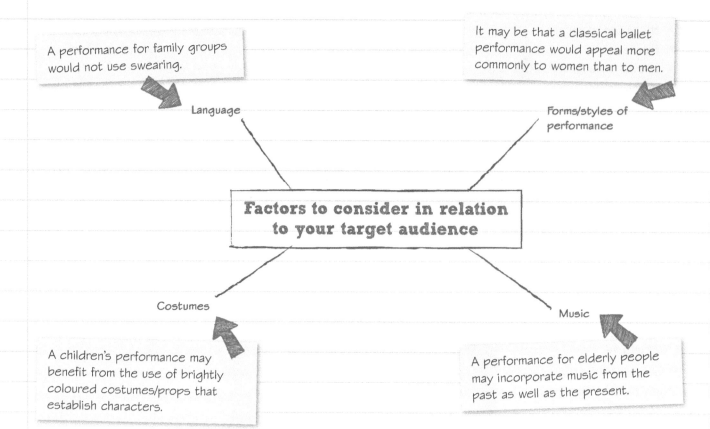

A performance for family groups would not use swearing.

It may be that a classical ballet performance would appeal more commonly to women than to men.

Language

Forms/styles of performance

Factors to consider in relation to your target audience

Costumes

Music

A children's performance may benefit from the use of brightly coloured costumes/props that establish characters.

A performance for elderly people may incorporate music from the past as well as the present.

Being aware of potential social and cultural issues

This is another significant element. Being sensitive about these issues may mean carrying out research so that you gain further knowledge which can help to inform your decisions. For example, if you are creating a performance based on a cultural festival, you will need to be aware of the traditions as well as the confines of that particular culture.

Social issues also may be relevant, such as tailoring content so that it is inclusive and respectful of the target audience.

What does your audience want to see?

Try to put yourself in the position of the target audience. Think about your likes and dislikes, your beliefs and values, and what you find acceptable or offensive. This is a way of 'getting into character' and putting yourself on the receiving end of the performance.

Exploring these requirements and undertaking research can help you to understand your target audience properly.

Now try this

Focusing on the commission on page 79, make notes on how you will ensure the performance is appropriate for the target audience and that potential social and cultural issues are handled sensitively.

Considering the target audience and context

In your written proposal you will need to include discussion of the target audience and the context of the commission brief.

Read the sample extracts from learners' proposals below, which are based on the commission brief and stimuli on pages 79 and 80. They will help you understand how you need to discuss target audience and context of the commission brief in your proposal.

Engaging with your audience

In your proposal, try to make suggestions about **how** you will engage your particular audience. Consider elements such as production values, form and structure, style, language, space and performance skills in relation to the requirements of the commission brief and stimulus.

This is true, but try to be more **specific** in identifying what performance styles and type of music you will use. Why do these appeal to your wide target audience?

This is not the best tone for your proposal. Try to be positive in your outlook. A lot of entertainment appeals to both young and old, male and female so try to identify these here.

Sample response extract

With the target audience type spanning across families, the general public and the local community I feel that I need to produce material which appeals to all. Also the age and gender are all-inclusive, confirming that the performance will need to be far-reaching and appeal to children, teenagers, adults and the elderly, both male and female. This will mean considering performance styles, language, music and other production elements such as costume.

It is quite a difficult task, so I plan to research the different audiences that the commission covers to gain some insight. I think that my performance will not necessarily appeal to all, but hopefully it will appeal to some, which is all I can hope for.

Sample response extract

The main purpose of the commission brief is to celebrate sport through the performing arts. I hope to do this by creating a performance that embraces sport and its different benefits, whether for health, confidence or sense of community. My aim is to engage the audience by combining musical theatre sequences that all communicate the same message. My stimulus (the article from the *Independent* under 'Media') will be interpreted by taking the audience on a journey, moving through different parts of the space (as if on a trail run) for different sequences.

The type of commissioning body is the local authority, which I have researched. The council has previously commissioned performing arts work but not on this scale. This should not impact too much on my performance.

Context of the commission

When looking at context, try to look at the reason for the commission, as well as the type of commissioning body and how any previous or future plans may impact on this.

Good explanation with reference to a specific example.

Explain what discoveries you made through research. What requirements and constraints have been typical of a local councilin the past? How will your performance be different?

Now try this

Look at the commission brief on page 79 and the text stimulus on page 80. Write notes on how you could create a performance to meet the objectives and purpose of the brief, which also takes into account the target audience and commission brief context.

Requirements and constraints

There will be various requirements and constraints relating to your performance, over and above the commissioning body, commission brief, purpose and target audience. You will need to plan for the restrictions on time, resources and space when writing your proposal.

Working to timescales and deadlines

You will need to work to a timescale and meet deadlines effectively, as would any professional performer working to a commission brief. You will need to plan and manage your time accordingly.

Read your commission brief, choose your stimulus, and research and plan your proposal. Divide this time up carefully so you know you have considered all the elements required.

You need to spend plenty of time developing your ideas and rehearsing your performance before you actually perform. Make sure you participate in any group exercises that might be organised, as well as rehearsing your solo performance.

It might help to take some notes about your performance as you develop it, so as to jog your memory before you write the evaluation.

Check the Pearson website for the most up-to-date **Sample Assessment Material** to get an idea of the timescales for your assessed tasks.

You will then write up your proposal.

For the purposes of this revision task, your performance should be 5–8 minutes long.

Finally, you need to write your evaluation.

Supervised assessments

Your supervised assessment slot is dictated by Pearson. You cannot choose an alternative slot! ALWAYS make sure you attend when you have supervised assessments.

Working with available resources

The resources available might be basic. It is essential to communicate your intention(s) clearly and think of the additional elements such as costume, set and lighting as only existing to enhance your performance. Imagine that you have no resources at all when creating your piece; any additions can then be considered a bonus.

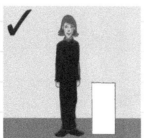

Remember not to rely on costume, set and lighting to communicate the message for you.

Working with available performance space

You will only have a small indoor space in which to perform your solo piece. There may not be much scope for a lot of movement and you can't perform outside. Think about how you will still effectively meet the commission brief with this requirement.

Managing constraints

As any professional would, you may need to do some creative thinking to help you to overcome limitations that you feel may affect your performance. This might be making your own props where possible, using an extra level to increase your performance space, or using mime to 'create' props or objects which you can't obtain.

Now try this

Think about some recent material that you have created and then performed. Describe how you managed your time during this project and ensured that deadlines were met.

Time management skills are difficult to master. How could you improve your skills?

Assessing requirements and constraints

In any written proposal, you need to be able to consider what skills are required to address the requirements and constraints of the commission brief.

As the theme of the commission is sport, with the objective being to promote it to a wider audience, I want to make sure that my performance is accessible. I want sport to appeal to people who may not have previously engaged in it, and make everyone feel like they can get involved. To do this I will perform several different monologues but with varying levels of audience participation.

As I have minimum resources, I will ask audience members to come up and be my props, such as being a hurdle or a football. This will help to engage them from the outset, as this is my opening piece. It will also meet the purpose of entertaining and follow through on the theme of 'Unity' and will also appeal to audience members of all ages. However, I will need to have just one audience member up on stage with me at a time because of the tight performance space I have and because I don't want people distracting me from my performance in case I run over the 8 minutes maximum time.

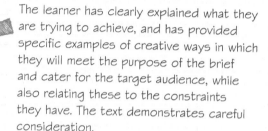

The learner has clearly explained what they are trying to achieve, and has provided specific examples of creative ways in which they will meet the purpose of the brief and cater for the target audience, while also relating these to the constraints they have. The text demonstrates careful consideration.

Check the Pearson website for the most up-to-date **Sample Assessment Material** to make sure it's OK to ask other people to get involved in your assessed performance.

A positive attitude is displayed, with suggestions for how to work with the props available in a creative way.

Making your own prop(s) or painting a piece of set could enhance your solo performance without taking up too much time.

In terms of available resources, I am happy to work within the constraints, such as making my own costume for my opening monologue and using a torch as lighting to 'spotlight' myself when I am pretending to be the winner of the hurdles race, as well as using a cloth over the torch to create a mystical lighting effect when I am recalling my memories of the previous Olympic Games. I understand the need to create a solo performance that can stand alone and will not rely on production values heavily. I am going to hum and/or sing my own theme music to my sports events at various points, which will also fulfil the key purpose of entertaining my audience.

Now try this

Look at the commission brief on page 79 and the visual stimulus on page 80. Make notes on the requirements and constraints that would need to be considered. Come up with some basic suggestions on how you could creatively overcome them while meeting the commission brief.

Generating ideas for performance

As part of a written proposal, you need to be able to consider what skills are required to respond to the brief and stimulus and how you will employ them. Read the extracts from these learners' proposals to understand how to do this.

Sample response extract

In order to meet the commission brief I will need to work imaginatively to generate innovative material. I plan on doing this by setting myself creative tasks such as improvisations. I will structure the improvisations so that they show effective response to the stimulus. For example, I will use key words and different starting points for exploration. In addition, my research can help to inform my improvisations and experimental tasks.

In order to refine my material successfully I will listen to peer feedback as well as selecting and rejecting material where necessary. I will try to 'think outside the box' by not always choosing the first ideas that spring to mind.

You can improve your answer by being specific about **how** your research informed your improvisations and experimental tasks. Give some examples and explain how they are linked to your specific stimulus.

Effective ways of working creatively are listed here, with specific examples, but the learner needs to explain what their research focused on and what decisions they have made as a result.

Generating ideas

You may wish to initially make lists of what ideas the stimulus and commission brief generate. As the creative process develops you can then make notes regarding selection of material, peer comments and decisions.

Be specific

Try to use relevant **terminology** and refer to particular **performance skills**. Explain how you can use the skills to your advantage within your solo performance.

Sample response extract

I plan to utilise my performance skills to their maximum potential when performing my solo. For example, I excel at facial expression, so during my portrayal of different sports using different dance styles I will apply the relevant facial expression to draw the audience in, particularly using eye contact and projection.

Another performance skill I will be able to employ is dynamics; the different dance styles I incorporate all require contrasting dynamics. My ballet section will require smooth sustained movements, whereas the street dance section requires sharp, punctuated actions. This juxtaposition of different styles combined into one will highlight the theme of 'Unity' in bringing together all sports into the one event of the Olympics.

Good use of specific examples here to highlight how the planned performance techniques are going to be conveying the creative intentions.

Now try this

Look at the commission brief on page 79 and the aural stimulus on page 80. Explain how you would respond to the commission brief, focusing on creative skills, performance skills and production values.

Working from a thematic stimulus

The following pages look at different types of stimulus and how they might be used to prompt ideas for your performance proposal. You may be given a theme as a stimulus for your performance, which you will need to research. Themes are divided into four main categories.

Social

Social themes relate to society, for example:

- gender inequality
- poverty
- crime.

Homelessness is a sensitive and emotive topic for a performance.

Cultural

Cultural themes relate to customs, traditions and values such as:

- celebrations
- spirituality/religion
- tradition.

A performance based on a religious festival such as Diwali could make links between different world faiths.

> **Types of thematic stimulus**

Ethical

Ethical themes relate to morality/ what is right and wrong, for example:

- euthanasia
- abortion
- the death penalty.

You would need to consider your target audience carefully if you base your performance on an ethical issue.

Spiritual

Spiritual themes relate to the human spirit or religion, such as:

- faith
- forgiveness
- love.

Exploring spirituality can lead to a profound and resonant performance.

Now try this

1 Look at the theme of 'Unity' on page 80. Undertake some internet research and record **five** key words associated with this concept.

2 Create a mind map in which you analyse these words and list different ways in which your performance pathway could communicate them for the commission on page 79.

Working from a visual stimulus

You may be given a visual stimulus for your performance, which you will need to research. Visual stimuli are divided into five main categories.

Photograph

A photograph could be taken of a:
- landscape
- object
- person
- animal.

Painting

A painting could be:
- historical
- still life
- everyday scene
- landscape.

This image combines many of these aspects of painting.

Sculpture

Sculptures are three-dimensional works of art, made by one of these processes:
- carving
- modelling
- casting
- constructing.

Types of visual stimulus

Image

An image is a representation of a person or object in art.

Artefact

An artefact is an object of cultural or historical interest, made by a person.

An ancient object could generate ideas about universal issues and timeless concepts.

It could be a painting, a photograph or a digital image.

Using artefacts

Objects are often used in performances as they can provide an extra dimension, add interest or create a scene. They are referred to as 'props'.

Now try this

1 Focus on the three examples of visual stimulus presented on this page. Make notes on how you could convey each image in your performance pathway for the commission on page 79.
2 Describe **one** challenge presented by each stimulus.

Working from a textual stimulus

You may be given a textual stimulus for your performance, which you will need to research. There are five main categories of text.

Literary text

There are several types of literature, including:

- fiction
- non-fiction
- drama.

A literary stimulus could be a short extract from a book.

> Shall I compare thee to a summer's day?   (A)
> Thou art more lovely and more temperate.   (B)
> Rough winds do shake the darling buds of May,   (A)
> And summer's lease hath all too short a date …   (B)

Sonnets follow different rhyming patterns, which you could reflect by using performance motifs.

Short story

A short story is significantly shorter than a novel. It has five main components:

- character
- setting
- plot
- theme
- conflict.

Poem

Poetry is a form of literary expression and is often rhythmical, which makes it distinct from other texts. A poem could be:

- a Shakespearean sonnet
- a limerick
- blank verse.

 Blank verse does not rhyme, but includes a regular metrical rhythm. You could explore the rhythm in movement terms, to create a motif.

Historical

This text focuses on historical events that are:

- political
- social
- cultural
- religious.

Types of textual stimulus

Biography

This type of written text involves detailed description of someone's life. It provides the reader with insight into the subject's experience of life events such as education, relationships, work, family. There are three types of biography:

- biography (written by someone other than the subject)
- autobiography (written by the subject, usually covering their whole life story)
- memoir (written by the subject about aspects of their life).

The stimulus could relate to a significant historical figure such as Emmeline Pankhurst.

Read and reread

Make sure that you read and re-read the text stimulus. Think about the main message (or messages) and how this could be interpreted for performance. Remember to think about how the message relates to the commission brief.

Now try this

1. Focus on the text stimulus on page 80. Make some notes on how you could transform the text into monologue, vocals and/or movement.

2. What ideas does the text generate, and how could these be explored?

Working from a media stimulus

You may be given a media stimulus for your performance, which you will need to research. Media stimuli fall into three categories.

Magazines

A magazine headline, image or article could be provided as a stimulus.

Thinking about newspapers and magazines

Consider the main message that is being put across. How could this be translated into acting, dance or musical theatre? Think about the different considerations that would need to take place. For example, to portray an earthquake a script could be created, motifs may be developed or lyrics used to communicate the message, depending on the genre of performance.

Newspapers

A newspaper headline, image or article could be provided as inspiration for performance.

Types of media stimulus

Videos and film

A video or film could be the stimulus for your performance.

Thinking about videos and films

What is the main message or subject matter being communicated in the video or film? Remember that you may need to condense your ideas, as a video or film may be lengthy and your performance may be substantially shorter. It is essential to capture the main idea(s).

Now try this

Using the media stimulus on page 80, make a spider diagram of words that connect with the stimulus.

Working from an aural stimulus

You may be given an aural stimulus for your performance, which you will need to research. Aural stimuli fall into two main categories.

Music

There are many types of music that may be provided as inspiration for your performance. For example there is:

- classical
- electronic (UK garage, house and ambient)
- rock
- jazz
- popular
- country
- Latin (salsa, tango and merengue)
- metal
- punk
- rap
- reggae
- R&B.

Enhancing your performance with music

Even if music is not the stimulus for your performance, you may decide to incorporate music to enhance your piece. Think about why you are choosing a particular type of music and what it does to improve the piece. It may create an atmosphere, provide a regular beat, set a scene or add an extra dimension. Or it may do a combination of these things at different points within the performance.

Maracas feature in Latin music.

Types of aural stimulus

Sound

Sound can be used in a variety of ways in performance. For example, abstract sounds can form a backdrop for dance and movement.

In a play or musical theatre performance sound effects may be employed in order to help set a scene or convey a mood. For example, farmyard animal noises would conjure up a farmyard setting, and the sound of a doorbell ringing could signify the arrival of someone.

Found sound

Have you ever heard of found sound? Found sound is when everyday noises or sounds are incorporated into music. It is often created using whatever is available at the time, for example books, pencils, a table, and/or body parts (body percussion) such as creating rhythms by clapping, slapping thighs or tapping fingers on a table.

Now try this

Think about a recent performance you have watched. Give **two** examples of how music or sound were used to create an effect.

Primary and secondary research

You will need to research and explore materials and ideas in relation to your commission brief and stimulus. You will do some research in advance of writing your proposal and you may do some more when developing your performance later on. This research might focus on both the stimulus and the type of commissioning body you have been given.

Primary research involves carrying out research yourself and is discussed in the context of this task on pages 5–7. **Secondary research** involves gathering existing research, for example by using the internet and other digital resources, libraries and archives.

Internet and other digital resources

Considerable research is undertaken on the internet, as it is so fast and accessible. You can use search engines to help you gain access to information, ensuring that you type in key words in order to get the best results. Remember that not all websites are reliable in terms of providing accurate information.

Libraries

Books, journals, plays, notated dances and musical theatre scores are all examples of printed publications that you may find useful in your research. Showing that you have performed extensive research via different methods will demonstrate a thorough approach.

You may wish to visit your local library to access printed publications, or be able to access them at your school or college library.

Archives

You can access texts and performance material by visiting archives or digital archives. This may be helpful in terms of gaining familiarity with a certain style of dance, theatrical form or genre of musical theatre. Having watched performances you can then note the key components of the style and aim to transfer these elements to your own performance piece.

Plagiarism

It is essential that you acknowledge all of your sources when you are taking information from the internet, printed publications or digital archives. Make sure you write down websites and publishing/recording details as you conduct your research, otherwise you will forget where you found your information.

Remember to put quotations inside quotation marks.

Now try this

1 Taking the visual stimulus on page 80 as your inspiration, perform some internet research, making notes as you go along.

2 Trim the information so that you are left with the key points only.

 Remember to make a list of all websites visited.

Justifying ideas

You will need to outline your performance ideas and justify these ideas in a proposal, which means clearly linking them to the commission brief, its purpose, the target audience and the stimulus you have chosen.

Sample response extract

I have decided to convey the purpose of promoting sport to a wider audience by creating a one-man sports day. This relates to my chosen stimulus of Banksy's *There's always hope*, as sport can provide hope and motivation for people who may be disadvantaged in other ways.

I intend to deliver monologues that will focus on different sporting events as well as different people around the globe. My use of language and physical theatre techniques will emotionally draw in the audience, regardless of their age, because I will use such a variety of sound and movement as I perform short solos connected by musical transitions to suggest different parts of the world.

In each extract I will communicate how sport has motivated/helped each person to have hope. The type, age and gender of each character will be different and will reflect a wide variety of people, to tie in with the wide target audience. My use of sporting actions will engage the audience and be immediately accessible.

 There has been careful focus on the stimulus to make a link between art and sport.

 Clear intention followed by a justification. Effective description of performance skills used to achieve the intention.

 There is clear consideration of the target audience here.

Try to explain **how** you would use improvisation. What key words or starting points would you use (for example, ideas generated from the stimulus)?

Make sure that you explain the activities you will participate in, leading up to your performance. This does not mean providing lists or a plan, but **explaining** the process such as what resources you will be using, what creative tasks you will participate in and how research has shaped your decisions so far.

Sample response extract

I intend to use improvisation to help me generate material for my performance. I find this a useful tool and am able to create material spontaneously, which I record and then watch back. I will be drawing on research that I have undertaken, such as secondary research on the internet, which helped me to gain knowledge about different countries and how sport helps people in different ways.

I intend to wear a plain black costume so that I will be able to move easily. Lighting and set are not priorities as I want to take the audience on a journey via movement and dialogue. I will be using a flag as a prop, which I will make. This will be a collage of flags from different countries suggesting that sport creates links and, thus, hope.

Now try this

Based on some recent work that you have performed, write a paragraph explaining your intentions and ideas and justify them by linking them to the purpose of the performance and the stimulus.

Planning your written proposal

Before you write your proposal, it's a good idea to plan your response to make sure you include everything you need to say.

Read through the requirements for a written proposal below. How will you structure your response to ensure you cover all these areas?

Assume that the reader does not hold any information about the commission brief or stimulus. Explain clearly **why** you have selected specific ideas about the theme and stimulus.

You will need to provide solid reasoning about your intentions and how you came to these decisions. **How** do you propose to work within the requirements and constraints of the commission brief?

 1 Your rationale for ideas in relation to the chosen stimulus – why you have selected your ideas in relation to your chosen stimulus (for example, the media stimulus about track running).

2 Your ability to justify your creative intentions in relation to requirements of the commission brief – how you made decisions relating to the commission brief, including examples to back up your justifications.

Show interest and enthusiasm for the stimulus; what skills can you bring, and how does the stimulus inspire you?

See it from the commissioning body's perspective too. What do they want you to do? How can you best achieve this?

Requirements for a written proposal

3 Your ability to carry out activities and use resources that are justified and presented effectively – describe and explain the activities you undertook in preparation for the proposal, and provide detail on the resources you used.

You are trying to convince the commissioner that you are well informed, so make sure that the language you use is professional and direct with good grammar, spelling and punctuation.

Other pages in this Unit have given guidance on the research and preparatory activities you will need to undertake to fully understand your commission brief and stimulus. This will help to inform your decisions and boost your chances of success.

Writing your proposal

Keep reminding yourself of the assessment objectives throughout. Visit the Pearson website so you can download them. You could use these as a checklist for your writing as you go along. Keep calm and write clearly and accurately, and leave time to check over your work at the end.

Now try this

Taking the commission brief on page 79 and one of the stimuli on page 80, write a paragraph including points which would help to meet each of the above requirements.

Practical exploration of stimulus

In preparation for your solo performance you will need to explore your stimulus. You can do this practically. Try to challenge yourself and try out tasks or ways of working that may be new to you.

Practical exercises

You could participate in practical exercises that will help to develop your skills working on your own. For example, you could try starting off in character, initiating a scene with an opening line. Then switch immediately to a contrasting character to deliver your second line, which may mean changing your physicality. Then move back into the original physicality and character to deliver the third line of the scene. It will help to warm up your brain as well as explore characters!

Improvisation

Improvisation is an excellent way to explore your stimulus practically and, if you record your improvisations using your smartphone, this can help you to generate material for your performance. It involves spontaneity; in other words it requires no preparation. But keep your improvisations focused on your stimulus.

The more you can take risks in an improvisation the more exciting your results will be! Try to think outside the box and use your imagination as much as possible.

Try-outs

It is essential to experiment with your stimulus and commission brief, trying out new ideas and exploring their physical or aural potential. You can explore the:

- physicality of a character
- boundaries of a dance technique
- physical dimensions of a prop.

Aural experimentation might involve exploration of dialogue in acting, songs or musical theatre. You can experiment with rhythm, accent, tone or projection, for example.

Responding to feedback from peers

During the exploratory stages, it is useful to share your work with your peers. This will provide you with constructive feedback, which could help to shape and develop your ideas.

If you record your explorations using your smartphone, tablet or laptop, you can show the clips to your peers as well as watching them yourself to remind yourself of valuable material.

Now try this

1. Taking the media stimulus on page 80, make a list of words that the item evokes.
2. Using the words, experiment physically or aurally.

You could also try combining physical and aural experimentation, which may be particularly useful in developing characters. Remember to record your experiments!

Establishing links

You need to establish links between your chosen material and creative ideas, and the commission brief.

Establishing links

It is important to establish links between your commission and the stimulus right from the outset. If, for example, your commission is to create a solo performance to educate a teenage audience commissioned by a charity, this will bring with it certain requirements and constraints. Any ideas arising from the stimulus you choose will need to be suitably linked to the commission brief.

Consider the following questions:

- How can the stimulus help you to educate a teenage audience?

- How can it enhance the requirements of the commission?

You will need to strike a good balance between the commission brief dictating what ideas can be explored, and feeling free to experiment and explore your stimulus within these constraints.

You need to keep both the commission and stimulus in mind during the whole creative process, otherwise you may lose sight of the intention.

How can you use the stimulus to grab the attention of a teenage audience?

Selecting and rejecting ideas

During the creative process you will generate a large amount of material as a result of your exploration such as improvisation. Select the material that is more original and communicates your intention more clearly; reject material that is less innovative or does not fit the brief.

One way of helping with the selection and rejection process is to ask for feedback from peers.

Recording material and watching it is also a useful method of sifting out the stronger material.

You can adapt material or develop it, rather than simply discarding it.

Now try this

Look at the commission brief on page 79 and choose one of the stimuli on page 80. Explore the links between the commission brief and the stimulus.

Developing materials and ideas

You will need to develop and shape these ideas into performance material. Consider the guidance below in the early stages of creating your individual performance.

Exploring meaning within your chosen material

Once you have experimented with your stimulus and generated ideas, the next stage is to develop and mould your material. You will need to explore meaning within the material you have selected, so that it fits the commission brief effectively and communicates your chosen intention. You could ask your peers to provide you with their interpretations of the meaning of the material to help you.

Try not to get bogged down in trying to relate every small detail directly to the meaning, but make sure that the piece as a whole clearly conveys the meaning.

> There may be sections within your solo that have different meanings; you could use transitions to help communicate this.

Applying the chosen material in different ways

Depending on your chosen performance discipline, there are numerous ways in which you could apply your chosen material, and you should explore it from different angles to see what works best.

Your material may have more than one meaning. For example, using a visual stimulus such as an artwork, you may have explored pattern and emotion. You will then have choices to make. You may choose one meaning over another. You may decide to perform material that combines the two meanings in a performance that conveys patterns in space as well as emotional highs and lows.

Applying different forms, structures, elements and/or techniques to the work

Once you have generated material, you will need to apply different features in order to communicate your intention and meet the demands of the commission brief.

It is vital that you consider the following:

* What does the form/structure/element/technique add to the performance?
* How does it do this?
* Does it help to communicate meaning?
* Does it meet the requirements of the commission brief?

Your performance needs to have a clear structure, so make sure you invest time in planning this. You could create a spider diagram, timeline or mind map that focuses on the structure and the forms, elements and/or techniques you decide to use. This may make it easier for you to visualise the solo in its entirety, and work out whether it flows effectively from start to finish.

For example you may wish to apply a structure such as narrative, to convey a storyline through musical theatre. Alternatively, naturalistic techniques could be applied to material to produce a realistic and emotional performance.

Now try this

Consider a recent solo you have performed. Create a timeline that outlines the structure and the forms, elements and/or techniques it included.

Structure and present action

You will need to think about how to structure and present your performance. Bear in mind the following considerations.

Ordering of performance pieces and use of transitions

You are allowed to perform several short solos within your proposed time slot rather than one lengthier solo. If you decide to perform several solos, you will need to consider the length of each one, and your reasoning for performing in this manner. You will also need to consider how you transition between one solo and the next, so that the individual pieces hang together.

You could use different costumes to represent different characters.

You can introduce variety

It may be appropriate to perform a variety of short solos in different dance styles, characters or songs.

You may wish to use transitions as a means of connecting solo material to build a storyline. You could use musical extracts, dialogue, movement, mime, dance, acting or song to provide transitions.

Use of performance space

Using the space imaginatively can greatly enhance your performance. Use diagrams and sketches to plan how you will use levels, pathways and dimensions, and think about the position of your body and the shapes it is making in the space. Decide whether to use different parts of the stage space to help communicate your intention(s), for example in relation to character or plot. Also consider your use of personal and general space.

Think about your character in relation to the space. How would your character use different levels, dimensions, pathways and directions?

Imagine that the entire space above, beyond, under and around you is a blank canvas waiting to be explored. Ensure that you fully examine the space around you by moving around it all.

The performance space might have limitations, such as the floor being uneven or the dimensions being quite small. Try to work professionally within these constraints rather than letting this impact negatively on your performance.

High, low, medium levels and exploration of pathways and directions will enhance your performance.

Now try this

1 Taking the commission brief on page 79 and the thematic stimulus on page 80, make notes on how you could use transitions and the performance space to your best advantage.

2 Practise justifying your decisions by giving reasons for each choice you make.

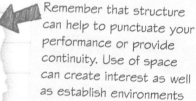

Remember that structure can help to punctuate your performance or provide continuity. Use of space can create interest as well as establish environments or characters.

Technical elements

You will need to consider props, set and costume as well as other technical elements when presenting your individual performance.

Props

You might want to use prop(s) in your performance, if you can justify their inclusion. Prop(s) may serve to:

- establish a character
- provide additional dimensions to explore
- enhance the mood/atmosphere
- create an environment/setting.

A prop should blend effectively into the performance and become an integral part of the piece. Remember to practise regularly with your prop so that your performance is seamless.

Props can help to add interest or spectacle

Set

It might be appropriate to use set as part of your performance piece, but it will probably be basic. Set may serve to:

- create an environment/scene
- establish a particular era
- suggest the style and tone of the performance.

A set is effective when it does not detract from the main performance but serves to support it, by providing a suitable backdrop or creating a mood, environment or era.

Set can also help to create a mood or atmosphere

Costume

Using basic costume as part of your performance piece might be appropriate. Costume can serve to:

- establish a character
- enhance the mood/atmosphere
- provide additional interest or visual effects, such as a mask or cape which moves in a certain manner.

An effective costume will not hamper your movement or distract the audience from your performance. It will add to your character or to the mood of the piece.

Lighting and sound

There are other technical requirements that you may need to consider, such as lighting and sound. Although these requirements are likely to be basic, you will still need to think about whether the whole performance space will be lit. Try to rehearse with lighting so that you are familiar with it. If you have a costume, it might look different under the lights.

Regarding sound, you need to consider whether you are using sound effects or music, as well as ensuring that the music is appropriate and you have rehearsed to it regularly before performance. If songs or monologue are part of the performance, consider whether vocals can be heard and whether you need to use microphones.

Now try this

1   Taking the commission brief on page 79 and the text stimulus on page 80, write notes on how props, set, costume, lighting and sound could help to enhance a solo performance.

2   Practise justifying your decisions by giving reasons for each choice you make.

Performance skills

You will need to communicate style and meaning in your individual performance, which you can achieve partly through the use of performance skills.

Communication skills

In your performance you will be required to exercise a range of communication skills.

mood   emotion   stimulus

You need to communicate ...

with the audience   style/form   intention

Developing confidence

Performance skills relate very closely to confidence. Try to develop your confidence by using breathing/relaxation techniques.

Practice is also vital in preparing your performance skills. You will need to have memorised your solo effectively so that it is second nature to you, otherwise you will be too busy concentrating on remembering your material to perform to your fullest potential. You can practise in front of a mirror or by performing to friends and family.

Performance skills that you can use to communicate

You can use some or all of the following performance skills to communicate style and meaning:

Schedule some time to embrace your character (if you have one), studying it and trying to get to know him/her. Communicate your character not just through your lines but also through body language and physicality.

- Awareness of other performance elements (lighting, costume, set)
- Focus
- Control
- Projection
- Expression
- Characterisation
- Phrasing
- Musicality
- Vocalisation
- Characterisation
- Conceptualisation
- Physical/vocal embodiment of a role
- Use of stillness
- Use of gesture
- Dynamics
- Breathing
- Timing
- Emphasis
- Facial expression

The quality of your movement can be enhanced by use of contrasting dynamics such as sharp, slow, smooth, heavy, fast and sustained. Thinking about details such as breathing and timing can help to build tension or add dramatic effect.

Use of gesture is important to support dialogue or song, as well as communicating meaning in dance.

Now try this

1   Which performance skills will you use to communicate style and meaning in your performance?
2   Think about the commission and your target audience, and make notes on the most appropriate skills for conveying your message.

Individual performance skills

You will need to apply your individual performance skills to the commission brief and think about how you can communicate your creative intentions effectively without other performers present.

Use of individual performance skills to meet the requirements of the brief

What can you bring to the performance? It could be that you are adept at performing particular dance style(s), musical theatre genre(s) or that you have an excellent ability to embody a character or deliver lines confidently.

Although you are following a selected performance pathway, it might be appropriate to borrow from other disciplines. For example, a performer on the acting pathway may also be a proficient dancer; these additional skills could be incorporated into the solo performance if they complement the commission brief.

Make a list of performance skills that you excel at. Focus on each skill and consider how you could put it to good use in the performance of your solo.

Similarly, list your areas for improvement and think about how you could work on these prior to your performance.

Be honest with yourself about your performance skills and also ask for feedback from your peers.

Communication of creative intentions to audience through performance

As well as identifying your individual performance skills, you also need to think about how you can best communicate your creative intention(s), linked to the purpose of the commission. There may be more than one intention. For example, you may have been asked to provide an entertaining performance which will inform *and* educate the audience. This requires a balancing act, as you have to bear in mind more than one requirement and ensure that both are considered equally.

Make a list of the creative intention(s) in relation to the commission brief and stimulus, and then map this to your individual performance skills. Think about how you could use different methods of communication, whether physical or aural (or both), as well as technical elements.

Share extracts of your solo performance with peers. Can they understand what it is about? Are you communicating clearly, or is the message(s) confusing? Take on board feedback and advice.

Now try this

Think about the purpose of the commission (see page 79). Make notes on how your solo performance would be affected by different creative intentions. Would you choose different performance skills if the purpose was to inform, entertain, celebrate or raise awareness of a topic?

Rehearse, practise and review

You will need to invest time into rehearsing, practising and reviewing your performance in order to achieve your maximum potential. Use the guidance below to help you prepare for performance effectively.

Following a practice regime

Working as an individual can have its bonuses; however, it means that you need to be proactive, creating as well as following your own practice regime. To some extent this may be dictated by scheduled sessions within your school or college, although you may also wish to invest additional time preparing your material. It will help if you plan how much time you are going to allow for practising your performance once it is completed, for example by setting weekly practice targets. Try to stick to your regime and reward yourself accordingly!

Selection and use of performance skills

It is vital that you select and use appropriate performance skills in order to achieve the highest possible standards. Decide which performance skills are the most significant in relation to your performance, and focus on practising them regularly in the run-up to your performance. For example, you may choose to focus on projection, musicality and facial expression.

It may feel daunting if you have not performed many individual performances previously, but rehearsing in front of family members can help to build your confidence.

Analysing progress, identifying problems and solutions to inform progression

You will need to analyse your progress, looking at strengths and weaknesses within your performance as well as ways to improve. When you identify problems, think rationally about how you can resolve them effectively. It could be that repetition of a specific exercise or task is required in order to improve a particular skill, such as coordination. Alternatively it could be that you are finding it difficult to piece together your material, in which case it will help to draw a plan showing how the sections link together. Some problems may be logistical, such as not having the desired resources at hand. But, whatever the problems are, try to think of positive solutions and be proactive.

Be realistic and honest about where your strengths and weaknesses lie. Regularly update your skills audit, so that you can see how and when your performance skills are improving.

Sharing performance work with peers and responding to feedback

It will be beneficial if you can share your material with peers leading up to your performance. Not only will this enable you to build your confidence and practise your performance skills, but you will also receive valuable feedback.

Strength: performance skills
Weakness: structure
Improvement: Look at transitions between sections

You could ask your peers to provide you with one strength and one weakness about your work, as well as specific ways that you could make improvements.

Ultimately it is your decision how to develop your work, but feedback can be very useful in helping you to consider alternative ideas that you may not have been aware of previously.

Now try this

1   Think about some recent performance work you have done and jot down some notes about how you analysed your progress.

2   Describe **one** problem you encountered and explain how you resolved it.

Managing your preparation time

Being organised and disciplined in the run-up to your performance will ensure you are fully prepared.

Memorising, learning and perfecting material

Having generated material, as well as shaping, developing and structuring it, the next stage is to ensure you are performance-ready. This means learning and memorising the material effectively – perfecting it. Performers use various methods in order to memorise material effectively:

Practising in front of a mirror.

- Writing notes
- Repetition
- Performing in front of others
- Being filmed and watching it back
- Blocking
- Breaking down the material to practise it in segments
- Formally reviewing, by analysing it yourself or gathering feedback from peers.

Making an audio-recording of songs and words and listening to it.

Managing available time to meet deadlines

You will need to consider the following when managing your time leading up to the performance:

- Prioritising tasks
- Making lists and schedules
- Avoiding procrastination
- Being proactive
- Being organised
- Using your rehearsal time wisely
- Spreading out your tasks
- Staying level-headed
- Setting yourself goals
- Trying to be self-motivated – you are your own boss!

Choosing and making best use of physical resources

You will have thought about your production elements and resources – such as lighting, costume or set – when writing your proposal. Remember, you will not be expected to use anything complex, so try to think of basic requirements. You should continue to check back to ensure these are still relevant now you have developed your performance. Don't be afraid to make changes if required. There may be resources available from previous productions, such as backdrops, that could be adapted to suit your requirements.

Now try this

1 Look at the strategies for memorising material listed above. Rank these strategies from 1 to 7, based on how effective they are for you, with 1 being the most effective.

2 Look at the time management strategies listed above. Choose the three strategies you would find most effective.

Preparing for your solo

Use the tips and information below to help you hone your skills and effectively prepare your individual performance.

During your performance you will need to show that you have:

- communicated creative intentions imaginatively and with assurance throughout the performance
- selected performance skills and techniques appropriately and used them imaginatively to realise intentions
- applied skills and techniques fluently and in an assured manner, showing outstanding control and consistency.

Performance tips

Try to consider the following in relation to your performance:

> If you make a mistake, try to carry on and don't be put off by it. If you react to it, then it will stand out more.

- Stay in character/performance mode throughout; be professional.
- Relax! Take a few deep breaths before you go onstage. A few nerves will not matter.
- Try to connect with your audience.

Performance checklist

Here are some things to think about when you are preparing for your performance:

1. Make sure you have rehearsed in full costume and with other production elements in place.
2. Memorise your material effectively so that you know it off by heart.
3. Think about all the possible things that could go wrong, and find solutions.
4. Make sure that you have packed everything that you will need on the day.
5. Consider potential health and safety issues such as wearing socks, jewellery or chewing gum.
6. Put any distractions to one side and enjoy your time on stage.
7. Remember that you can't rely on others as this is an individual performance, so be proactive in your preparation!

Now try this

Think about an upcoming performance.

1. Make a checklist of any equipment or clothing you will need for your performance.
2. Make a list of the performance skills you plan to focus on in this performance.

> Remember that at the start of your performance, which is filmed, you will need to state your:
> - full name
> - registration number
> - centre name
> - centre number.

Evaluation: artistic effectiveness

Following your performance you need to write an evaluation. Part of this involves evaluating the artistic effectiveness of your performance.

Execution of solo performance skills

Consider how well you have employed performance skills in performance. Think about the following questions:

- Which performance skills did you use?
- Were they successful?
- Did you find that you were better at some performance skills than others?
- Why was this?
- Did you feel that the commission brief and stimulus enabled you to use your performance skills to their full potential? If not, why not?

Evaluating performance skills

Think about **why** some of your performance skills were stronger than others. How did you achieve this? Was it through:

- ✓ experience
- ✓ practice and rehearsal
- ✓ specific exercises
- ✓ research
- ✓ tasks
- ✓ a combination of the above?

What could you have improved on, and how? Would this have enhanced your performance?

Clarity of interpretation

Consider how well you have interpreted your stimulus and ideas in performance. Watch a recording of the performance, and consult any feedback or notes you have taken since the performance. Think about the following:

- Is your message(s) clear?
- Are there parts that could have been clearer?
- How could you have achieved this?
- How did research help to inform your interpretation?

Did production/technical elements support the interpretation of your message?

Creativity and imagination

How well did you exercise your imagination and think 'outside of the box' in terms of development of material? Consider the following aspects of the exploratory process:

- Which exploratory techniques did you use?
- Were they successful?
- Did you find some techniques more effective than others?
- What were the benefits of improvisation?
- How did you use selection and rejection to develop material?

How did you record/ document your exploratory tasks?

Now try this

Write a paragraph about each category above, noting why each aspect is important to the performance process.

Be specific. Describe what you did and why it was successful.

Evaluating artistic effectiveness

You need to be able to prepare a written evaluation of your performance. In your evaluation you will need to consider your artistic effectiveness.

Evaluation checklist

The key things to remember for your evaluation are as follows:

✓ You can only get credit for what you put in your response.

✓ Remember to describe how you have **improved** your skills through performance.

✓ Remember to evaluate **both the good and the bad** elements of your piece.

✓ Remember to identify **possible improvements**.

Provide clear examples from your performance to support your conclusions along with appropriate specialist terminology.

This is your chance to demonstrate how much hard work you have put into your solo!

Sample response extract

My intention was clear, as I managed to communicate the commission brief relating to sport and the community through the form of musical theatre. I communicated this through dialogue, dance and song. I worked closely with the commission brief and stimulus to ensure that I was meeting objectives effectively.

I feel that my interpretation was expressive and clear, as I used key words in the dialogue and songs, and my structure followed the structure of an Olympic event, starting with the 'On your marks, get set, go!' motif.

I adopted a creative approach and was determined to be original; for example, I closely studied the movement of a discus thrower which I re-enacted while singing a song. I made this a comic sequence based on peer feedback. This was a good contrast to the more serious sections.

Sample response extract

Having watched the recording of the performance, I thought my performance skills had really improved overall. For example, I was more confident in my delivery as well as in articulating my lines at the correct volume and pace. I made eye contact with the audience and maintained a strong focus throughout. During the creative process I tried to go beyond the obvious by developing new ideas rather than just settling for the first one that comes along. I experimented extensively with the stimulus in order to achieve original and exciting performance material, sometimes recording myself and then watching it back. This helped me to refine and shape the material more effectively.

 Refer to the recording of your performance, and describe your individual strengths and weaknesses. Your response will be better if you provide **specific examples**.

 Try to mention **relevant skills** such as performance skills, interpretation, creativity and imagination.

 You could include specific examples of the ideas that were less original and were dismissed, or those that were more original and what the experimentation involved.

Now try this

Think about some recent solo performance work you have produced. Write a paragraph about your effectiveness in terms of your solo performance skills, your clarity of interpretation, and your creativity and imagination.

 Remember to provide specific examples. Say **why** something was effective, and also **how** you managed to achieve it.

Evaluation: professional effectiveness

Your evaluation should cover your professional effectiveness. This includes production values and the way in which you managed time, tasks and resources.

Production values

You will need to think about how production values enhanced your performance. Consider how the following aspects helped to communicate your intention(s):

- lighting
- sound
- costume
- set.

Evaluating production values

Although production values are not a significant part of your performance, they can still serve to enhance your performance material however basic they may be.

Don't use the evaluation to complain about how the space was too small or that your costume disappeared. Instead, you should explain how you turned these elements to your advantage. Of course, there may be hiccups along the way and the performance might not have run as smoothly as you had hoped. However, try to focus on the positives, demonstrating how you worked within limitations to the best of your ability.

Management of time, tasks and available resources

You will need to consider the following elements:

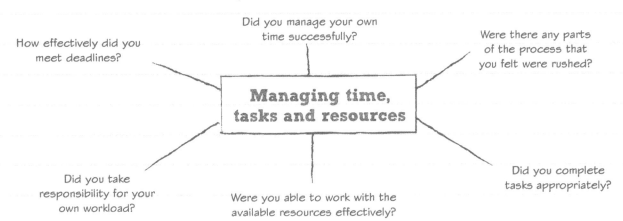

How effectively did you meet deadlines?

Did you manage your own time successfully?

Were there any parts of the process that you felt were rushed?

Managing time, tasks and resources

Did you take responsibility for your own workload?

Were you able to work with the available resources effectively?

Did you complete tasks appropriately?

Try to be honest about your strengths and weaknesses in this area. For example, perhaps at the beginning of the process you were not very punctual, or were poor at meeting deadlines. However, this might have improved as the process went on. You might have felt more motivated when you could see the piece taking shape. Working as an individual poses challenges as you bear the main responsibility for your own work, whereas with group work the responsibility is shared. This might be your first experience of working on a solo piece, so think carefully about how you managed the process.

Managing these elements is not easy but you will also learn valuable transferable life skills.

Now try this

Thinking about a recent performance, write a paragraph about how:

(a) production values enhanced your performance

(b) you managed your time, tasks and resources.

Evaluating professional effectiveness

In your evaluation you will need to consider your professional effectiveness.

Evaluation checklist

You will need to cover the elements below in your evaluation.

✓ Comment on production values.

✓ Comment on management of time, tasks and available resources.

Sample response extract

I spent time planning how I could use production values and I researched their uses. As I am already using music I didn't need to consider sound. I felt I could portray my role of the 'sporting hero' better with an appropriate costume so made a costume which, although basic, helped me to communicate the theme of community and sport. It was made out of a Union Jack flag. Also I used props – pieces of sporting equipment such as a football – within my dance sequences, which enhanced the visual qualities of the performance and was new and original and captured the audience's attention.

This is a positive point about how the learner overcame production constraints to produce an effective performance despite limited resources.

An example of how the production values specifically enhanced the solo performance and how the learner adapted their skills to produce an effective performance despite limited resources.

Sample response extract

I feel that I managed my time effectively to carry out exploratory techniques such as improvising with my prop using key words. This later led to several of my monologue ideas focusing on 'hope' in sport.

I feel that I worked in a professional manner throughout. I asked for peer feedback whenever possible and took on board comments to improve my material. For example, some feedback I received was regarding my performance being too long. I went away and thought further about how to focus my performance on just the key purpose of entertainment and ideas of 'Unity', to address this. As a result, I cut the section of my performance which had looked at different clothing in sport, because it was less relevant to the purpose of the commission.

Strengths and weaknesses

Remember that you can comment on weaknesses as well as strengths. For example, you could state your areas for improvement, as well as how they were addressed. It will not have an adverse effect if you admit that you had some areas for development. This shows a more realistic understanding of your skills.

Good example of how peer feedback can be used when developing material.

The learner effectively provides a specific example to support their decision.

Now try this

1 Which of the following areas are the most challenging for you: managing time, tasks or resources, or using production values?

2 Make a list of aspects you could improve, with suggestions of how you might achieve this.

You could also comment briefly on how working independently impacted on the process.

Evaluation: meeting requirements

Part of your evaluation should cover the extent to which the performance work addresses the requirements of the commission brief and uses the stimulus material.

Fulfilment of the objectives of the commission brief

Watch the recorded performance and look at any notes you made initially about your objectives.

Try to be as objective as possible when watching your performance. Make notes and also consult any notes you made during the creative process. Read through your proposal. Have you achieved what you set out to do?

When writing your evaluation, consider peer feedback you received during the process or following the performance.

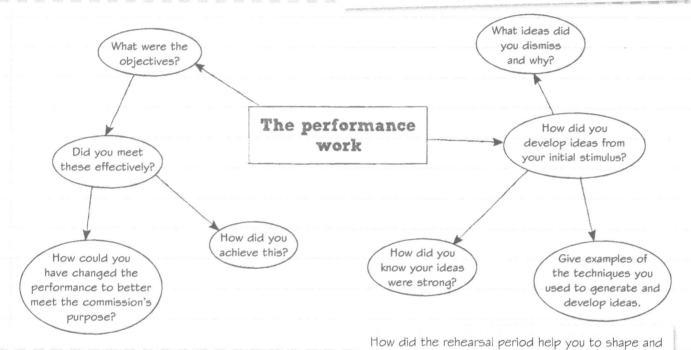

What were the objectives?

Did you meet these effectively?

How could you have changed the performance to better meet the commission's purpose?

How did you achieve this?

The performance work

What ideas did you dismiss and why?

How did you develop ideas from your initial stimulus?

How did you know your ideas were strong?

Give examples of the techniques you used to generate and develop ideas.

How did the rehearsal period help you to shape and refine your material in response to the stimulus?

Interpretation and use of the stimulus material

You will also need to consider your interpretation of the stimulus material and how effective this was. You may have met the requirements of the commission brief but feel that there were shortcomings in your interpretation of the stimulus or development of stimulus material. Consider the following questions:

* Was your interpretation effective?
* Why was this?
* How did you use the stimulus material to its full advantage?
* Are there any areas you could have improved?
* How could you have achieved this?

Think about what drew you to the stimulus you selected. Did it provide you with a lot of creative ideas, or did you struggle to generate material?

How did initial research, tasks and exploration help you with your interpretation of the stimulus?

Now try this

Focus on a recent performance that was based on a brief. Develop the mind map above, writing notes under each heading to evaluate how effectively you met the requirements of the brief.

Evaluating fulfilment of purpose

In your evaluation you should reflect on the extent to which the performance work fulfilled the purpose of the commission brief.

Sample response extract

As the commission brief required performances to target teenage audiences, I decided to incorporate up-to-date language in my solo. For example, I used 'buzz' words and mentioned current trends within my dialogue, such as the use of social media. Also the background music I used was current and popular, and would appeal to a young audience. The focus of the commission being celebration of sport also meant that it would be appealing to a young audience.

The songs I created were mainly upbeat and helped to engage people. For example, I performed a rap as part of my solo performance, which was about the Olympic Games and I used this as a recurring motif throughout my performance, repeating shorter sections of the rap at different points in the performance.

Is the appropriate audience being targeted here? Make sure you are consistent in addressing elements such as target audience.

Don't assume that the reader will know anything about your solo. Try to explain every point fully.

Good use of a specific example here.

Skills audits

Remember you can always input information from any skills audits that you have completed and include it in your evaluation. A skills audit is a good way of focusing your thoughts and producing concise answers. You can then expand on the key points you have made in your answers.

 Links See page 76 for an example of a skills audit.

Sample response extract

My goal was to produce an entertaining and stimulating experience for the audience so I decided to perform several short pieces and included transitions in between.
This would help people to engage, as they may have short attention spans. This seemed to work really well.

I feel that I combined sports and the performing arts effectively by blending the two in performance. I did this throughout the solo. I demonstrated a variety of sports in my solo, for example football, hockey, tennis, darts, swimming, rowing, volleyball, gymnastics, athletics and basketball.

How did you demonstrate some of the sports mentioned? Why did this help to meet the purpose of the commission?

Now try this

Write a paragraph about how you interpreted the stimulus material in a recent performance. Remember to include your strengths and weaknesses in your evaluation.

Try to work within the guidelines, making clear and informed decisions about what you did well and where you could have progressed, always relating back to your objectives.

Evaluating the use of stimulus

In your evaluation you should reflect on how effectively the performance work has interpreted and used the selected stimulus material.

I chose to use the actual aural stimulus in my performance as I really felt inspired by this piece of music. I liked it because:

- it is called 'Heroes' and links to sporting heroes
- it will help to inspire others and get them interested in sport
- it will provide a solid structure for my performance.

I enjoyed using this music and it helped to communicate my intention, which was to celebrate sporting heroes. I feel that I used the music to its full potential, particularly in how I interpreted it for performance. I responded to the dynamics of the music effectively, adapting the timing of actions to show slow motion and fast actions relating to sport.

I also mirrored the verse and chorus structure in my dance performance, varying movement whenever the chorus played, and developed motifs related to sport by adapting sporting actions and applying choreographic structures such as instrumentation and retrograde.

 For an evaluation, writing in full sentences and paragraphs is preferable to writing lists.

 Remember that your stimulus is the starting point for generating ideas. You don't need to necessarily 'use' the stimulus within your performance.

 Good use of specific examples and technical language.

Consideration of how the commission brief and stimulus interrelate is evident, as well as providing justifications for decisions.

I used research initially to explore the theme of unity. This provided me with additional insight regarding the key factors surrounding the theme. From the outset I made a list of the commission requirements and constraints, and considered how they could link with my selected stimulus. I kept this in mind throughout the process. For example, I thought that sport and unity connect really well, as they share a lot of common goals. Also I felt that creating a 5–8-minute performance would be an ideal way of showing a variety of different sporting events through a series of short pieces.

I felt that contrasting monologues would be appropriate to convey my intention, basing each one on a different sport. With the target audience being all ages, I felt that I would need to vary the types of sports to be all-inclusive.

Quality of written communication

Remember to use full sentences, correct punctuation and explain things as clearly as possible. Use specialist terminology wherever it is appropriate.

Try to explain fully. How can a variety of sports appeal to a wider audience?

Now try this

Write a paragraph about how you managed requirements and constraints in recent performance work. How will this experience help you in future projects?

Your Unit 7 set task

Unit 7 will be assessed through a task, which will be set by Pearson. In this assessed task you will need to justify your suitability for an employment opportunity, gathering and presenting evidence to support your application.

Set task skills

Your assessed task could cover any of the essential content in the unit. You can revise the unit content in this Revision Guide.

This skills pages are designed to **revise skills** that might be needed in your assessed task. They use selected content and outcomes to provide an example of ways of applying your skills.

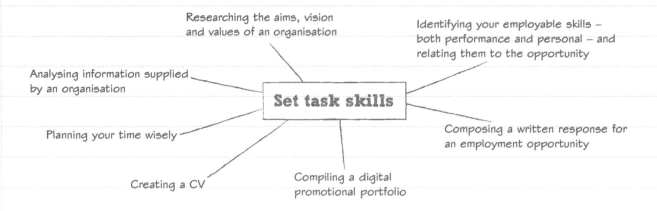

Researching the aims, vision and values of an organisation

Identifying your employable skills – both performance and personal – and relating them to the opportunity

Analysing information supplied by an organisation

Set task skills

Planning your time wisely

Composing a written response for an employment opportunity

Creating a CV

Compiling a digital promotional portfolio

Workflow

The process of applying for a performing arts employment opportunity might follow these steps:

✓ Review the information the organisation has supplied.

✓ Research the organisation's status and aims further.

✓ Assess your own suitability for the role.

✓ Compile a digital portfolio, promoting your experience and talents.

✓ Write an application, with supporting evidence.

Check the Pearson website

These skills pages are designed to demonstrate the skills that might be needed in your assessed task. The details of your actual assessed task may change from year to year so always make sure you are up to date. Check the Pearson website for the most up-to-date **Sample Assessment Material** to get an idea of the structure of your assessed task and what this requires of you.

Now try this

Visit the Pearson website and find the page containing the course materials for BTEC National Performing Arts. Look at the latest Unit 7 Sample Assessment Material for an indication of:

- the structure of your set task, and whether it is divided into separate parts
- the length of any initial preparation period
- how much time you are allowed for each section of the task and what marks are available
- what briefing or stimulus material might be provided to you
- the activities you are required to complete and how to format your responses.

Task information

Below is some sample task information, provided for revision purposes. This is different from the task information you will get in your real assessment, but it follows a similar model. The sample learner responses found on the following pages are based on the sample task information below and you can use this content to build an understanding of the assessment and to practise the skills required to complete the activities you will find in the real assessment.

Task information

Breakin' Barriers: Employment Opportunity

Breakin' Barriers is currently seeking applications from like-minded individuals to join us as workshop leaders for our latest project.

You are required to demonstrate your understanding of our organisation and how you can contribute to the work we do and what you plan to deliver in the workshop outlined below, using relevant examples to justify your ideas and skills. It is essential that you consider the age and profile of the group your workshop will target.

Organisational Profile

Breakin' Barriers is a performance company that produces alternative versions of classical works in any genre. By challenging historical approaches to casting, Breakin' Barriers breaks down the audience's preconceptions and sheds new light on well-known works. At Breakin' Barriers we believe that good performers shouldn't be restricted by their disability, race and gender.

Every year we deliver national outreach and education programmes in schools and a range of local community venues. Our emphasis is on equality of opportunity, so that everyone has a chance to access the performing arts. We have links with many Special Educational Needs (SEN) schools and schemes, and provide ongoing skills-building workshops to give everyone an opportunity to access this industry and enhance participation within the wider community.

We are a not-for-profit organisation and receive funding from a number of sources in the public and third sector. At times, our members will liaise with other organisations to help develop new revenue streams that will help us to continue our work.

Project Outline

We are planning a new production of Shakespeare's *A Midsummer Night's Dream*. The project's key focus is that of inclusion and creativity, as we take on the challenges of casting, staging and production. We aim to be innovative in changing the audience's perception of this well known play and we need full collaboration and input from all our members in order to do this.

The work is engaging and thought provoking, suitable for a range of age groups, locations and situations. The work aims to develop enquiring minds and creative thinkers and encourage positive ideas, messages and concepts.

Workshop Requirements

We aim to offer a workshop in addition to the performance outlined above. The aim will be to extend the understanding of the themes, ideas and concepts within the project. The workshop needs to be inclusive, fun and have clear objectives. We would like you to propose ideas for a workshop as part of your submission. We are looking for a talented individual to lead and develop this workshop.

Planning your preparation time

Before you can start on your preparatory work for your set task, it is important that you plan this time effectively. Check the latest Sample Assessment Materials on the Pearson website to find out exactly how much time you have to prepare in advance of your supervised assessment time.

The purpose of planning

Planning is your first step to completing this project. Knowing what you need to produce can help you in creating a schedule of activities, setting deadlines for yourself and ensuring that you are ready for the supervised assessment time.

Main tasks during planning

1. Reading the set task information and building an understanding of the organisation, the project and the workshop requirements

2. Linking your own skills to the demands of the employment opportunity.

3. Create extensive notes for your written response.

4. Create/collate the necessary documents/footage as evidence of your relevant skills, for your professional portfolio.

Example of a time plan

Step 1	Step 2	Step 3	Before your supervised assessment time
• Analyse and research the task information • Analyse my own skills and link to organisation and opportunity • Write preparatory notes for your written response • Identify or plan the content for the digital promotional portfolio	• Plan the structure of your written response • Record the digital content for your promotional portfolio and find any additional evidence	• Edit all the footage • Save digital content on USB stick • Review and print notes	• Check everything in advance of your supervised assessment time

Smaller tasks to plan

You could break down the tasks further, and use this as a checklist at the end of week. Include even the smallest job so that you can keep on top of your work.

Day 3
Plan the professional portfolio
• Contact photographer and arrange a date for next week.
• Make a list of the video footage needed and where to get it.
• Contact people about getting all the footage for next week.

Making a detailed list is a good way to guarantee that you remember to complete all tasks.

Review your schedule

At regular points you should review your schedule. By doing this, you can re-prioritise and work out what the most urgent tasks are in the time you have left.

Monday – Week 2
• Phone Dayle about the head shot. Confirm next Wednesday (anytime) to do the shoot. Images needed by Friday at the latest.

If you are depending on other people, you might need to remind them of your schedule.

Now try this

Look back at the sample task information on page 119. Write up a plan of the work you would do in preparation.

 Be as specific as you can.

Organisational requirements

There are many employment opportunities within the performing arts industry. Understanding the organisational requirements of a potential employer will give you a greater chance of being employed. You'll look more closely at all the areas below on the following pages.

Aims, vision and values

These can help you to consider whether or not the organisation would be a good fit for you as an employee. Ask yourself these questions:

- Do you have the same values?
- Would your skills help the organisation to achieve its aims?

> 🔗 **Links**   Revise pages 122–123 for more information on an organisation's aims, vision, mission and purpose.

Funders

How an organisation is funded can indicate what additional skills you will need to work there. For example, an organisation funded by the public sector might need to provide evidence of the work to satisfy the funder. You may need to develop:

- report-writing skills
- ability to use a camera
- ability to use editing equipment.

> 🔗 **Links**   See pages 129 and 130–132 for information on different funding sources.

Creative intentions

Knowing the creative intentions of the performing arts company will allow you to provide the necessary information about your skills and experience.

For example, if a performing arts company creates original physical theatre works, you will need movement skills, acting skills and vocal skills (and circus skills would be a bonus). You would also need devising and teamwork skills, and experience of the theatrical style.

> Seeing an organisation's performances will give you a good idea of the performance skills required in order to work for them.

Structure

The legal constitution and structure of an organisation helps you to understand its focus and how decisions are made.

- Is it not-for-profit?
- Is it for-profit?
- Is it for-profit but with a community focus?

Needs of the audience

The audience pays money to watch the performance and therefore it is necessary for their needs to be taken into account.

This could be in terms of the structure of the building (disabled access, baby-changing facilities) or the nature and content of the work being produced.

Now try this

Vocalworks is a not-for-profit organisation that runs an outreach programme in homes for elderly people. It receives funding from the Big Lottery Fund and is looking for outreach workers.

(a) Identify the skills that Vocalworks might be looking for in its workers.

(b) Make a list of your own skills which would support your job application.

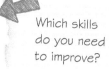

Which skills do you need to improve?

The purpose of an organisation

All successful performing arts organisations will have decided what their purpose is. To establish who they are and what they do, a performing arts organisation will identify their **aims**, **objectives**, **vision** and **mission**. You can learn about vision and mission on the next page.

Aims

An organisation will have one or more overarching broad **aims**. For example, they may aim to provide a service whilst achieving growth and fulfilling a social responsibility.

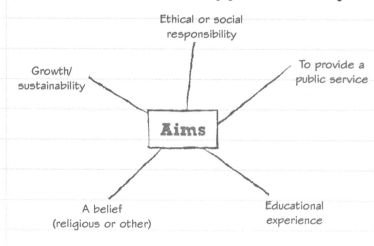

Ethical or social responsibility

Growth/ sustainability

To provide a public service

Aims

A belief (religious or other)

Educational experience

1 To provide a high-quality performing arts experience for young people aged 6–16 years in the local area.

2 To raise awareness of current issues that are relevant to our target audience.

An example of the aims of one performing arts organisation.

Objectives

Objectives are **specific targets** that an organisation sets out to achieve. Objectives are made to help the organisation reach its aims. Objectives can change over time as an organisation progresses, and a good organisation would review their objectives regularly.

SMART objectives

A successful performing arts organisation will set objectives that are SMART.

S pecific
M easurable
A chievable
R ealistic
T ime-bound

1 For each season of events to include at least two performances and workshops aimed at every age group between 6 and 16.

2 Each year to commission the development of at least two new drama works that have themes based around current issues.

An example of the objectives of one performing arts organisation.

Organisations often include information about target audience in their aims and objectives.

Now try this

Your World is a Theatre in Education (TIE) company that produces performances about current events for 14–16-year-olds. Write a set of aims and objectives for Your World.

You can make up any additional details you like about the company. Don't forget to make your objectives SMART.

Vision, mission and values

The vision, mission and values of an organisation shape the way in which the aims and objectives are achieved.

Vision

An organisation will have a vision of what it intends to become in the future. The vision is based on the aims, objectives and mission of the performing arts business. It is important for the organisation's vision to be clear and easily understood. It would include information on the work to be produced or the services provided. For example:

> Our vision is to be a financially secure theatre company that produces groundbreaking physical theatre productions with excellent links with local schools and communities.

Mission

The organisation's mission is to make its vision a reality. The mission statement is mainly for members of the organisation and its employees, giving them purpose and focus. It would describe the way an organisation will behave in order to be successful. For example:

> Our mission is to create groundbreaking physical theatre productions by being brave, experimental and innovative in the rehearsal room. We will strive to connect with the local schools by being accessible and open to opportunities.

Values

Values are the organisation's beliefs and ideals – its ethos – clearly stated and shared across the company. They give the members of the organisation an idea of how to approach the world and their work.

Characteristics of values
- they define an organisation
- they form the foundation of the organisation
- they never change
- they encourage behaviour that supports success.

> Values do not describe the practical things an organisation will achieve, but the spirit in which they will achieve them.

Examples of general values

'The customer is always right.'

> An organisation dealing with a complaint might use this value to ensure that the customer is listened to and believed.

'Be innovative.'

> This could encourage employees to be creative and find new ways of doing things.

'Be efficient.'

> This could support a company's approach to administration, to the environment, or how quickly they work.

'Be accessible to all.'

> This could affect pricing policies, funding applications or the building's physical structure.

Now try this

Using the vision and mission statements above, write down some values you think the organisation might have.

Think about how the theatre company's employees would need to behave in order to be successful.

Intended audience and stakeholders

A performing arts organisation needs to make decisions about what it will offer. It can do this by determining the needs of its intended audience and stakeholders.

Intended audience

The product or service will be targeted at a specific audience. Factors to consider include the following:

- gender
- age
- location/geography
- occupation
- socio-economic status
- earnings
- lifestyle
- technology
- psychological factors
- life stages
- physical conditions.

> **Links** You have explored creating work for a target audience in Units 3 and 5. See pages 49, 87 and 88 to revise these points.

Appealing to the audience

Identifying the audience can help the organisation to make better business decisions. For example:

- **Theatre A** puts on performances aimed at children up to 14 years old. It is a family theatre.
- **Theatre B** produces cabaret performances aimed at adults.

The theatres would need to market their performances totally differently from each other in order to reach their intended audience.

Stakeholders

A stakeholder is a person who has an interest in the organisation, either as a business partner, someone who benefits from the service, or a person who takes part in the organisation. Each stakeholder will have an objective or idea about how the organisation should be run.

To be successful, organisations have to listen to their stakeholders while maintaining their vision and objectives.

All stakeholders can influence the direction of an organisation.

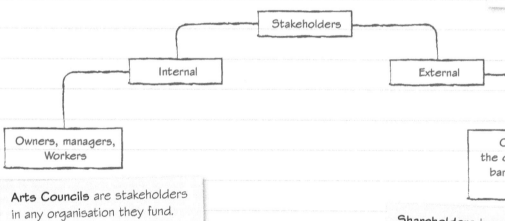

Arts Councils are stakeholders in any organisation they fund.

Shareholders have a financial share of incorporated organisations but may also be able to make decisions as stakeholders.

> ### Now try this
>
> Take the list of potential stakeholders and write down what you think the objective of each group would be.

 For example, a worker might want to be paid well, and a supplier might want higher prices for the goods.

Scope

Scope means the reach of an organisation. The scope of a performing arts organisation has a big influence on how they decide to approach aspects of their work.

Geographical scope

Scope can be geographical, referring to the size of the audience that the organisation is aiming to reach.

Local

Warwickshire

Regional

National

International

Local performing arts organisations

This can be a small theatre, a dance school or theatre group that caters to the needs of the local area.

National performing arts organisations

Arts Council England is a national organisation that funds and promotes the arts across England.

Regional performing arts organisations

The Northcott Theatre in Exeter caters to the Devon region in the UK. It is a professional theatre that provides 'a varied programme of the highest quality drama, opera, music, dance, comedy and family theatre.'

International performing arts organisations

Frantic Assembly has 'performed, created and collaborated in 30 different countries around the world'.

Scope of business activities

Scope can also refer to what an organisation does to sell a product, sell a service, or both. For example, Theatres A and B offer the following services.

Theatre A	Theatre B
Can be hired for shows, has a bar, serves general theatre snacks, commissions new work by upcoming artists and runs an education programme.	Can be hired for shows, has a bar and serves general theatre snacks.

Theatre A has a **broader scope** than Theatre B.

Now try this

Looking at Theatre A and Theatre B in the table above, write a list of advantages and disadvantages to having a broad or narrow scope.

Think about how this could affect the mission and the income.

125

Types of legal constitutions

When applying for an employment opportunity in a performing arts organisation, you should be aware of the type of legal constitution it falls under, and how this may affect how it operates.

How does type of legal constitution affect an organisation?

- How the organisation operates.
- The function of the board of directors and their personal liability.

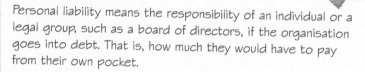

Personal liability means the responsibility of an individual or a legal group, such as a board of directors, if the organisation goes into debt. That is, how much they would have to pay from their own pocket.

What is a board of directors?

A board of directors is a group of people who are responsible for overseeing the running of the company. This can also be referred to as a management committee or board of trustees and members. The board does not deal with the day-to-day running of the business.

Incorporated organisation

An **incorporated** structure means that the organisation has its own legal identity.

Legal identity means:
- the organisation can own property
- it can take out loans
- the board of directors has limited liability for any debts (this can be as little as £1)
- the organisation must be registered with Companies House and there are legal requirements that must be met each year.

Legal identity

Unincorporated organisation

An **unincorporated** structure means that the organisation does **not** have its own legal identity.

No legal identity means:
- the organisation cannot own property
- it cannot take out loans
- the individual members of the organisation become liable for all debts
- there is no need to register with Companies House.

No legal identity

Examples of types of legal constitutions

Choosing the correct legal constitution has important implications for an organisation and whether it can achieve its aims and objectives.

Unincorporated
- Associations (e.g. amateur drama groups)
- Trusts
- Charities (e.g. The National Youth Arts Trust)

Incorporated
- Company limited by guarantee
- Company limited by shares
- Industrial and provident society
- Charities

Charities can be both incorporated and unincorporated. However, they must all adhere to rules set out by the Charity Commission as well as the rules of their specific organisational structure.

🔗 **Links** See page 132 for more on trusts.

🔗 **Links** See pages 127-128 for information on different organisational structures related to type of legal constitution.

Now try this

You and your friends have decided to get together to put on new plays in a small local theatre. You each make a weekly payment that goes towards the room hire and the final production. This could be described as a membership fee. You and your friends run your group together and have written down some rules to make things run smoothly. Decide which legal constitution would suit your organisation.

There are advantages and disadvantages to both types. Think about which model offers the best opportunities for your organisation.

Types of organisational structures

Performing arts organisations can be structured in a variety of different ways.

Sole trader

You work on your own and are classified as self-employed. You are responsible for everything to do with the business.

Many actors, dancers and singers operate as sole traders.

You can team up with another person and create a **partnership**. This has similar rules to a sole trader.

Community interest company (CIC)

A sole trader or unincorporated association can also register as a CIC, but must then comply with additional demands such as:

- producing a report to accompany their annual accounts
- demonstrating that they are serving the community.

This type of organisation is ideal for social enterprises.

Unincorporated association

This structure is mainly used by voluntary or community groups such as amateur drama groups or clubs. The members of the group determine the rules.

Company limited by guarantee (CLG)

A CLG has a board of directors who are limited by guarantee. If that company goes into debt, the individuals are only liable for a set amount (as little as £1). CLGs must be registered with Companies House for business and tax purposes.

Charity

A registered charity is regulated by the Charity Commission, and it must have a solid social or environmental purpose. There are two types of charity:

1 **Charity incorporated organisation (CIO)**. This organisation will have a board of directors (trustees) but also a wider membership who may be able to vote and influence the running of the charity.

2 **Charitable company**. This organisation:
   (a) is limited by guarantee (see above)
   (b) has no shareholders
   (c) cannot pay the board of directors.

Company limited by shares (CLS)

A CLS has shareholders, who contribute a set fee (which could be as little as £1) to the company in return for a share of the profits if the organisation is successful. If the organisation goes into debt, shareholders are only liable for the amount contributed.

Shakespeare's Globe Theatre on the South Bank in London is an educational charity and a company limited by guarantee which receives no government subsidy.

Now try this

Star Maker Academy is a performance school that provides after-school and weekend activities. The principal employs around 10 part-time staff. Select the most appropriate structure for the organisation.

Remember that the structures have different legal requirements to suit different organisations.

Advantages and disadvantages of different organisational structures

Organisational structures	Opportunities	Restrictions
Sole trader	👍 Can have a business name. 👍 The individual keeps profits after income tax. 👍 The individual has sole control over the business.	👎 The individual is responsible for losses, purchasing equipment and keeping records of income. 👎 Each year a self-assessment tax form must be completed.
Unincorporated association	👍 Its members make its own rules. 👍 Its members are responsible for the money. 👍 It is easy to set up.	👎 The group does not exist as a company in the eyes of the law. 👎 Individual members are responsible for the money, including debts. 👎 If it makes a profit it must pay corporation tax and file a company tax return.
Many community arts organisations are Community interest companies, such as Bee Arts Community Interest Company. Lipa is an example of a company limited by guarantee.	👍 Ideal for social enterprise. 👍 Can be not-for-profit, for-profit or democratic ownership. 👍 Directors can be paid. 👍 It has its own legal identity. 👍 Profits can be asset-locked.	👎 Not relevant for non-social enterprise. 👎 Profits can be asset-locked. 🔗 **Links** Asset-locked profits are discussed on page 129.
Charity	👍 There are tax exemptions and reliefs. 👍 Raising funds can be easier – more access to grants and public donations.	👎 Directors cannot be paid. 👎 Closer regulation because of the benefits they receive. 👎 Restrictions on sales.
Company limited by guarantee	👍 Directors can be paid. 👍 It has its own legal identity. 👍 It can own property. 👍 Profits can be shared between the board of directors.	👎 Profits are not asset-locked. 👎 Annual accounts must be sent to Companies House. 👎 It has to notify Companies House if there are any changes to the board of directors.
Company limited by shares	👍 Can attract private investors. 👍 Shareholders benefit from the success of the organisation. 👍 Directors can be paid. 👍 It has its own legal identity.	👎 Profits are not restricted. 👎 It needs to be independently financed as it cannot access grants.

Social enterprise

Social Enterprise is a company that has a social conscience and aims to better the world we live in, for example *The Big Issue*. It is not a legal organisational structure in its own right. It could be a CIC, charity or a company limited by shares or guarantee and would have their same advantages and disadvantages.

Now try this

Think of an example for each type of organisational structure listed above.

 Some internet research on different organisational structures will be helpful.

Funding restrictions and opportunities

Many performing arts organisations rely on money from a combination of three areas: public, private and third sector (not for profit). The legal constitution of a performing arts organisation will determine where it can get its money from.

Types of funding

Public sector	Private sector	Third sector
This is money that comes from any organisation that is supported by taxpayers (the general public).	This is money that comes from any organisation, e.g. businesses that are not under direct government control.	This is money from trusts or charities in the form of grants, bursaries and donations.
Arts Council England is an example of a public sector body that gives money to performing arts organisations.	The Wolfson Foundation is an example of a private body that gives money to performing arts organisations.	A donation from a charity may be appropriate for individual performers or a small performing arts organisation

Accessing money

A registered **charity** will be able to access grants from the third sector

Industrial and provident society relies on private investment, and would rarely access third sector funding.

Unincorporated associations will find it difficult to access public and third sector money due to its lack of legal identity

A **company limited by guarantee** relies on loans, private investment and the profits of the sale of goods or services

A **community interest company** (whether limited by guarantee or shares) may be able to access public and third sector money due to its community slant, but for-profit companies will be limited unless their assets are locked

Funding opportunities

A **company limited by shares** relies on money from profits, loans, private investment and shareholders

 Links See page 127 for definitions and explanations of these different structures.

Asset-locked: where an organisation sets out exactly how much money (a maximum amount) can go to shareholders or the Board of Directors.

Other restrictions

Using public money means you are answerable to the government and to the people. Therefore, certain rules are put in place to protect the money. Private and third sector bodies can draw up their own funding stipulations and restrictions.

Public sector restrictions

HM Treasury sets out the following values which recipients of public money must embody:
- ☑ transparency
- ☑ accountability
- ☑ achieving value for money
- ☑ being in the public interest.

Now try this

1 Visit the website for Arts Council England and familiarise yourself with its content: www.artscouncil.org.uk.

2 The Advice and Guidance section contains useful guides to funding in the performing arts. Download a few that you think will help further your understanding of funding. Read through the pages and make notes.

 This information will be useful when you are creating your written response and portfolio.

Public sector funding

The public sector funds a variety of services across the UK through different government bodies. Public sector funds can be accessed by individuals and organisations within the performing arts.

Accessing public sector funds

Public funding can be accessed from several areas:

- government departments
- local authorities
- non-departmental public bodies.

> ### Remember!
> As public sector funds are mostly raised through taxes, this money is subject to scrutiny. Organisations that handle public money must be transparent and accountable which is why unincorporated companies can find it hard to gain public funding.

Criteria for using public sector funding

Public funders publish criteria for receiving funding, how the process works and how decisions are to be made.

Grant money is carefully monitored – organisations need to provide proof that they are using the money as they said they would. This includes submitting budgets, accounts, written reports, video or photographic evidence, and feedback from the public.

Grants have to be spent within a short time frame. This is not a wholly secure method of funding for the day-to-day running of an organisation.

Application forms for grants tend to be extensive, requiring a lot of information from the applicant and clear plans as to how the money will be spent and how it will benefit the community.

The National Lottery

Money from the National Lottery is also considered public funds.

The National Lottery donates money to good causes – around 30% of its ticket price. This is defined as public money as people have given money through purchasing lottery tickets.

The National Lottery has many different grant schemes. All have their own focus, criteria and requirements, ranging from granting £300 to many millions of pounds.

Local government funding

Local authorities will also award grants to performing arts organisations, although there is now a shift from grants towards contracts and service level agreements.

> ### What is a service level agreement?
> This is a contract between organisations that determines the type and standard of service being supplied.

Non-governmental organisations

The UK government gives money to the Arts Councils in England, Scotland, Wales and Northern Ireland, non-governmental public bodies that each run a grant programme to support the arts.

> ### Now try this
>
> 1 Write down a community project idea: anything that you think will benefit your local community.
> 2 Visit an Arts Council website and find out what sort of projects they fund. Does your project fit into their funding categories?

Make a note of the different criteria for funding, the processes and the obligations.

Private sector funding

The private sector is not run by the government. Private sector funding for the performing arts comes from organisations that aim to make a profit.

Pros and cons of private sector funding

Private grants can sometimes be offered by for-profit organisations.

Advantages of private funds	Disadvantages of private funds
👍 Can be less paperwork to complete than public grants.	👎 They do not have to be transparent in their selection of successful applicants.
👍 Fewer organisations apply for these grants so there is more chance of being successful.	👎 Smaller grants are likely to be available compared to those from public funds.
👍 The money can sometimes be transferred more quickly than public funds as there is less bureaucracy.	👎 They might grant the money but offer no project support.

Loans

A loan is a sum of money that is borrowed and must be paid back in full, along with interest (additional money).

A loan can sometimes be placed against an organisation's assets. An asset could be the building it is based in, or anything that has a monetary value. If the company cannot pay back the loan, then the bank may take the assets as payment instead. If a company does not have any assets, the organisation's financial track record would be taken into account and a loan may still be granted.

A producer would avoid raising money through loans to fund a show.

Investment

Private investors can give an organisation money in return for a stake in the business. If the business is successful, the private investors would receive a share of the profits. These private investors become shareholders and own a share of the company.

Only certain types of organisations can raise money through shares:

- companies limited by shares
- community interest companies (limited by shares).

🔗 **Links** See page 127 for definitions of these organisational structures.

Sponsorship

Private companies often give organisations money in return for commercial marketing. This can be through product placement, company logos being included on the organisation's website, brochures, and so on.

Being associated with a successful cultural event can raise the profile of a business, and ultimately attract more customers.

Benefactor

This is a person who makes a large gift (mainly money) to an organisation.

Benefactors often receive special benefits as a result of their donations, acknowledging their contribution. These could be:

- opportunities to go to special events and meet the organisation's directors
- private tours
- preferential treatment by way of services or goods.

Now try this

Changing Faces Acting Company is looking to raise funds and wants to attract benefactors. Brainstorm some ideas of special benefits that the company could offer people who give them large donations.

 Think about what sort of access they can have to the company that is normally not permitted.

Third sector funding

Third sector organisations, such as funds and charities, fund the performing arts by providing performing arts organisations with grants. You can find out more about grants on page 131.

Nature of the funding

Features of third sector funding organisations include:

- being value driven
- not driven by profits (i.e. not-for-profit organisations, outside of the private sector)
- independent from the government
- aiming to improve public welfare and the environment.

The third sector in society

The third sector is also referred to as the:

- ✓ voluntary sector
- ✓ community sector
- ✓ non-profit sector
- ✓ civic sector
- ✓ social sector.

Trusts

Funding from the third sector is mainly generated from charitable **trusts**. These trusts are built on equity – the money they own earns more money in the bank through interest. This money is then available to distribute to successful applicants through grants.

In general, trusts have the following features:

- They can be very specific about what kind of projects they want to fund.
- Funding for profit-making organisations might be restricted.
- As a trust is separate from the government, it may not closely monitor expenditure to the same extent as public sector funding.

Charities

Charities can also fund the performing arts through grants.

- Charities cannot be political.
- They must work in the public's interest.
- Trustees (the people who run the charity) cannot be paid.
- A charity has no shareholders.

Organisations that are funded by the third sector

- Organisations that can most often access third sector funding are registered charities, social enterprises and community interest companies due to their community slant. For-profit organisations will find it harder to gain this type of funding unless their assets are locked.

Many voluntary clubs or societies are unincorporated associations.

Now try this

Visit your favourite theatre company's website and find out how it is funded.

You might find that its funding comes from a combination of public, private and third sectors.

Access to funding: grants and contracts

Applying for funding can be a long and complicated process. There are several routes and you should be aware of them when working with an organisation that may be working through them.

Definitions

What is a grant?

A grant is money given to an organisation to help it meet its objectives.

What is a contract?

A contract is a legally binding document that records two parties' agreement to services or goods. It is specific, and identifies what service is being paid for, by when and for how much money. Contracts can last for longer periods of time than grants.

What does tendering mean?

Tendering is a process in which different organisations bid and negotiate for the same contract.

Grant cycle

To apply for a grant, an organisation must **prepare** and **apply**. If successful it will **receive** funding and must then **deliver** the service which is a condition of the grant.

Preparing to bid for a grant

To prepare your bid for money, an organisation must first do some **research**.

To do list – research

1 Use funding databases to search for grants that suit the needs of the organisation.
2 Find out as much as possible about the grant and the funder.
3 Identify deadline dates so that a realistic schedule for completion can be made.

Applying for a grant

In order to write a successful application, an organisation must identify what the funder wants it to do. For example, the funder may want you to complete an application form or submit a written proposal. The funder may also ask for evidence of:

- charitable or not-for-profit status
- organisation structure
- clear plans for the use of the money to be granted, and evidence that this plan can realistically be implemented.

Tendering for a contract

A lot of preparation and research is required if to tender for a contract. An organisation will need to know the following information:

- who the people are that deal with the contract (procurement officers)
- what the exact required service is, and whether it includes administration or is just the service/product
- whether there are there any hidden costs.

Successful tendering

To gain a contract, an organisation will need to:

- advertise itself so that there is more awareness of its activities
- network with people in the public sector to raise the organisation's profile.

Tendering for contracts requires negotiation and includes the process of bidding. An organisation might be directly competing with several other organisations.

Consider different methods of putting across a message.

Now try this

The local authority is putting out to tender a contract for an organisation to run a project in schools that addresses the increase in obesity.

1 Write down a list of possible performing arts-related projects.
2 Considering the information above, which project is most likely to win the tender? Develop your best idea.

Fundraising and direct selling

Many performing arts organisations use fund-raising or direct selling to support themselves.

Fundraising methods

Social media is the main vehicle for promotion, and this encourages donations.

This method guarantees a lump sum of money.

Crowdfunding
This is an online fundraising campaign. Many organisations or individuals use different crowdfunding websites to post a specific campaign.

Membership schemes
Some community-based organisations run a membership scheme, in which members pay an annual fee and in return receive some benefits.

Methods of fundraising

Events
Organising events, such as fetes, car boot sales, sponsored events.

Donations
Fundraisers on the street can raise one-off donations by using a donation box, or raise regular donations by asking people to sign up to monthly subscriptions.

You can turn almost any activity into a sponsored event, ranging from running a marathon to being silent.

Securing regular donations is a growing priority for many charities.

Donations

A donation is a gift given by a person, normally for a good cause. It can be cash, services, or new/used goods.

If the charity is registered with the government and the donor pays tax, the charity can get more money through a government scheme called Gift Aid (by reclaiming the tax, the charity can receive an additional 25p for every £1 donated).

One-off vs regular donation

The one-off donation in a tin is a good way of raising money. However, organisations prefer regular donations as this enables them to plan more effectively in the future. For example:

- donating £3 a month by direct debit = financial stability for the charity
- making a £5 one-off donation = no financial stability and a need to encourage more donations.

Direct selling

This is a sales method where the sale of goods happens away from a shop. An individual salesperson sells a product to the customer at their home, their place of work or any other location. The salesperson would normally receive additional money for a sale (commission).

Direct selling from organisation to person

A representative of the organisation would speak to an individual and try to sell them their product/service. They could use practical demonstrations.

Direct selling from an organisation to other organisations or businesses

This would take place through a pitch. Representatives from an organisation may conduct a presentation, pitching their ideas to management of another company.

Now try this

The local amateur theatre company is putting on the musical *Hairspray* for their summer production. It needs to raise funds. Write a list of different fundraising methods it can use. Which are the most suitable for a local group?

Remember, fundraising can range from a cake sale to an evening event.

Marketing, HR and finance

There are many different types of roles and functions in an organisation. The key features are outlined below and on pages 136 and 137.

Finance • Human Resources • Training

Marketing •
Technical

Director

Creative •
Policies and Procedures

Outreach • Education

Even the smallest organisation has to cover these roles and functions.

Marketing

The marketing department is responsible for raising and maintaining the profile of the performing arts organisation. Without successful marketing, the organisation will not be able to reach its target audience.

Examples of marketing roles are:

- director of marketing
- marketing officers
- graphic designers.

Marketing responsibilities

- ✓ To write press releases promoting the activities of the organisation.
- ✓ To develop marketing strategies that will raise and maintain their profile.
- ✓ To design and produce leaflets, brochures, posters as required.
- ✓ To liaise with newspapers, media outlets and organisations.
- ✓ To use social media effectively as a promotion tool.

Human resources responsibilities

- ✓ To uphold the policies and procedures set out by the organisation and abide by government law and employment law.
- ✓ To organise the contracts for staff, contractors and volunteers.
- ✓ To help the staff's professional development.
- ✓ To support and lead in staff recruitment.
- ✓ To support in disciplinary or redundancy action.

Human resources

This department looks after the interests of the company by keeping up to date with the current employment laws and guiding staff and the organisation as appropriate.

Examples of roles are:

- director of human resources
- human resources officers.

Finance

The finance department works to ensure that the organisation is financially secure. A background in finance or accountancy is required.

Examples of roles are:

- director of finances
- finance officers
- fundraising officer.

Finance responsibilities

- ✓ To develop a budget.
- ✓ To balance the books (monitor income and expenditure).
- ✓ To find new sources of income through fundraising and grant applications.
- ✓ To allocate funds within the organisation.
- ✓ To send annual accounts to Companies House (if incorporated) and abide by financial regulations and employment law.
- ✓ To organise payment of its employees.

Now try this

Think about a recent or upcoming show at your school or college. Plan a marketing strategy for the show.

 Make a list of different ways you can raise awareness of the show.

Organisational operations

Without effective training and solid policies and procedures, an organisation's outreach work might be difficult to achieve.

Training

Learning is lifelong. The more skilled a workforce, the more effective it can be. Good organisations support their staff in continuous professional development.

Those involved in developing training might be directors, managers or human resources employees. A small company might invite outside organisations to help them.

Skilled workforce Effective workforce Successful organisation

Without training, an organisation's success might not be sustained.

Examples of training needs
- ✓ Staff may need first-aid training.
- ✓ An outreach worker may need safeguarding training and risk assessment training.

Policies and procedures

All organisations must create a set of policies and procedures. These will state what the organisation does and how it achieves this.

Policies are designed to guide employees and employers on how certain situations should be handled.

Examples of policies
- ✓ Maternity/paternity policy (how the organisation pays and supports new parents)
- ✓ Equal opportunities policy
- ✓ Staff development policy
- ✓ Health and safety policy
- ✓ Safeguarding policy

Example of a procedure
- ✓ Grievance procedure (how the organisation deals with issues between any of its employees)

Outreach

The purpose of outreach work is to reach people who would not normally have access to the organisation. This often means travelling out to them. It can help with integration, widening participation and opening access to the arts. It can also be to raise the profile of an organisation for gain, (for example, workshops related to the performance of a play). Outreach can include practical theatre activities in schools, out-of-hours clubs and other organisations that will liaise with the community around them.

An example of an outreach worker conducting a workshop with the older generation.

Now try this

The Royal Shakespeare Company (RSC) is looking to develop its outreach programme. Find out what the company currently offers, and brainstorm some ideas for new activities.

Education, creative and technical areas

The creative and technical departments are essential to the success of a performing arts organisation's performances, which can be created for educational purposes.

Education

Many theatre companies have an educational aspect to their business. Making contact with children is not only a good way of communicating a message, it can also inspire them to be performers in the future.

Roles in the education department include the workshop leaders and the officers who liaise with the schools. In smaller organisations, this can be the same person.

Education and outreach are closely related.

 Links See page 136 for more information on outreach.

Education responsibilities
✓ To develop educational programmes to offer to schools, colleges and universities.
✓ To liaise with organisations to arrange workshops and organise payments.
✓ To deliver the workshops.

Teacher packs and programmes

Organisations may develop workshops specific to a play, dance, musical or physical theatre piece. They may also create teacher packs that schools can purchase to help deliver their qualifications.

Creative department

The operational function of the creative department is to produce the high-quality performances or develop community theatre. Employees essentially help to produce the product, and are often part of a theatre company that produces its own performances.

Performers are usually auditioned and employed based on the production's requirements.

General
• Develop a theatrical product

Performers
• Rehearse and refine the theatrical product to a professional standard
• Take direction and act on corrections

Responsibilities of creative department

Artistic director
• Create a vision of the final product
• Liaise with the technical team and work collaboratively
• Work with performers

The creative department is at the heart of a performing arts organisation.

Examples of creative roles
✓ Artistic directors
✓ Choreographers
✓ Designers (set, props, lighting, sound, costume, media)

Examples of performer roles
✓ Musicians
✓ Dancers
✓ Actors

Technical department

This team supports the production. Technicians are responsible for the smooth running of the performance.

Examples of technical roles
✓ Lighting   ✓ Crew
✓ Sound   ✓ Stage management

Now try this

Consider the last performance you took part in. Write a list of the different jobs carried out by people on the production side of the show, and describe their responsibilities.

Analysing information

You need to be able to extract and analyse the essential information you need about an organisation, and any employment opportunity it is offering, from any information they supply. The examples about how do this below are taken from the sample task information on page 119.

First impressions

Noting down your first impressions of the revision task information is a valuable exercise. You can return to it throughout your preparation time. Here is an example.

> Strong values. All about equal opportunity.
> Looking for performer and workshop leader.

Annotating the information

Once you have noted down your first impressions, you can start to underline or highlight important words within the information. Select the words or phrases that tell you something about Breakin' Barriers as an organisation.

Use your first impressions to work out the overall vision of the organisation.

Sample notes extract

> Breakin' Barriers is a <u>performance company</u> which produces alternative versions of classical works in any genre.'

Produces performances of classics with a twist. Part of organisation mission may be to be innovative and original.

Who else does this? Matthew Bourne in dance. Any other companies?

Annotation can help you brainstorm ideas.

Sample notes extract

Objectives – to produce new versions of well-known works regularly.

> Breakin' Barriers is a performance company that produces alternative versions of classical works in any genre. By challenging historical approaches to casting, Breakin' Barriers breaks down the audience's preconceptions and sheds new light on well-known works. At Breakin' Barriers we believe that good performers shouldn't be restricted by their disability, race and gender.

You can use the information to identify the qualities of the organisation.

You could research similar companies on the internet and find out what their missions are, to help you identify what Breakin' Barriers' mission might be.

Values – equal opportunity, inclusion, open minded.

Aims – change how audiences see old works and provide opportunity to people who wouldn't normally be given certain roles.

Vision – have an excellent performance company based on talent and not looks.

Now try this

Look at paragraph 4 of the set task brief on page 119. Can you add to the aims, objectives, vision, mission and values above?

Researching the organisation

You will need to undertake some research to further your understanding of the organisation and fill in any gaps in your knowledge.

Answering your questions

Your analysis of the revision task information might have produced several questions that you could not answer by yourself. The best way to answer these questions is by researching organisations that are similar in some way. You might already know of one through your experience on the course.

Researching similar companies can help you to imagine the profile of Breakin' Barriers.

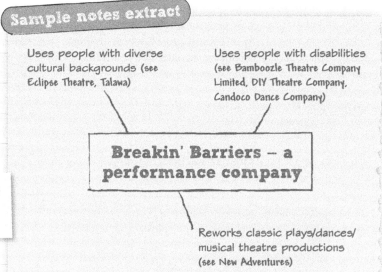

Sample notes extract

Uses people with diverse cultural backgrounds (see Eclipse Theatre, Talawa)

Uses people with disabilities (see Bamboozle Theatre Company Limited, DIY Theatre Company, Candoco Dance Company)

Breakin' Barriers – a performance company

Reworks classic plays/dances/ musical theatre productions (see New Adventures)

Using search engines

Choose your words carefully and be specific.

Example 1

| Equal opportunity companies | Search |

The word 'companies' will be used in virtually every business with a website. All businesses should have an equal opportunity policy. Your search will be too wide.

Example 2

| Performing Arts and disabilities | Search |

This search uses more specific words and therefore will produce more relevant pages.

Avoid plagiarism

If you use exact words from the website in your notes, use quotation marks. Otherwise, when you return to it later you may think you wrote it yourself. And always reference your sources fully.

Referencing

When referencing websites, you need to include:

- website address (copy and paste this from the browser)
- title of the web page
- paragraph number
- date you last accessed the source.

For example:

www.theatrestudies.com, Epic Theatre, para 4, last accessed on 1 September 2016.

Be efficient in your note-taking

Avoid printing off lots of web pages as this could lead to you spending precious assessment time reading instead of writing your written response. You need to collect all the information you need together clearly in your notes, during your preparation time.

Now try this

Visit www.candoco.co.uk and scroll down to the bottom of the page. Identify what sorts of funding it receives. Could Breakin' Barriers receive similar funding? If so, how will you show that you can work with Breakin' Barriers as an organisation?

Skills for professional practice

Your employability will improve if you evaluate and develop your communication and performance skills.

Performance skills

Developing your technical and performance skills will enhance your overall performance. This means engaging in technique classes, using every opportunity to improve, and approaching rehearsals with discipline and commitment.

 Links See page 147 for a comprehensive list of skills specific to your specialism.

You also need to consider personal lifestyle choices and how this could affect you at work.

A healthy diet will give you the energy needed to perform.

Communication skills

The most employable people are excellent communicators. You will need to develop strong skills for communicating on paper and in person.

Writing skills	Non-writing skills
Be clear and succinct	Maintain eye contact
Vary your vocabulary	Listen carefully
Use appropriate vocabulary (no slang)	Put across ideas coherently
Use correct grammar	Be confident
No spelling mistakes or typing errors	Make good use of vocabulary

Employability skills

There are two types of employability skills: transferable skills and competencies.

Transferable skills
- Team work
- Personal motivation
- Personal organisation
- Time management
- Listening skills

Competencies
- Learning
- Interpersonal skills
- Critical thinking skills
- Presentation skills
- Numeracy skills
- IT skills
- Literacy skills
- Leadership skills

Areas to develop

When working as a professional, you need to use the professional work environment to further your own abilities.

By evaluating your work carefully, you will identify areas to improve for next time.

Evaluate

Carry out the plan

Identify areas to develop

Create a plan of action

Circle of evaluation

Now try this

1 Use the circle of evaluation to evaluate your written skills.
2 Identify areas for improvement and explain how you could do this.

Experience for professional practice

During your lifetime, as well as the duration of this course, you will have gained useful experience that will support your career progression.

Performance

All of the performances you have taken part in will have furthered your experience in the performing arts industry. Every performance gives you the opportunity to showcase and develop your skills.

Experience in lots of different styles and disciplines gives you the opportunity and confidence to say 'I **can** do this!'

Devising work shows an ability to work as a team and collaborate.

Choreography demonstrates an ability to develop ideas, lead people, and create a final product.

Work

All employment, whether it is inside or outside the performing arts sector, provides evidence of your skills. You need to identify exactly what you achieved, and relate your experience to an employability skill.

 See page 140 for more on employability.

Make sure that you include professional performance experience for which you have been paid. This is excellent evidence of your employability.

What is my work experience?

1 I taught dance at a local dance school – this shows good planning and leadership skills.
2 Answering the phones at a small business improved my communication skills.
3 Serving tables in a restaurant showed that I can multi-task, communicate well, work as part of a team and use IT.

Examples of work experience

Volunteering

You should also consider volunteering work when assessing your own skills. This can be serving food in a homeless shelter, helping at a charity shop or answering phones at a not-for-profit organisation.

Voluntary work can demonstrate commitment and passion for a good cause. This could be linked to the values of a performing arts organisation.

Areas to develop

It is important to review your experience often and make sure that it is up to date. By doing this, you can spot any gaps in your skill set and think about how to fill them.

The value of voluntary work and work experience

Reflecting on these experiences and working hard gives you a chance to develop your professional approach.

Now try this

Think about any work experience you have had, either paid or voluntary.

Can you transfer your experience into employability skills?

(a) Write down exactly what you did.

(b) Identify what skills you needed to do this work.

Effective communication skills

Communicating in a work environment is different from interactions with friends, and it requires some formality. This page gives information on non-written communication. See the next page for revision of writing skills.

Communicating at work

If you work in the performing arts industry you are likely to meet lots of people. Knowing how to establish a good rapport with someone new requires confidence, and you need to communicate clearly.

Non-verbal communication is very important. It can help to reinforce what you say in words, or suggest that you are not being truthful. When you speak to someone, think about the importance of the following aspects:

- your posture
- eye contact
- your facial expression
- physiological changes, for example sweating and shaking
- body movements, for example hand gestures and nodding.

Non-verbal communication can be more powerful than speaking.

Clarity

Taking a long time to make a point means that your audience will probably lose interest. Being concise and clear with your use of language helps to move the conversation along.

Think about what you are going to say before saying it.

- Can it be said with fewer words?
- Does it need to be said?

Example

What was said:

'On the way here I stopped off for a coffee which I wouldn't normally do, but today I thought I would, and now it seems I need to go to the toilet.'

Translation:

'Where is the toilet?'

Effective speaking

This means being confident and clear while maintaining your individual personality. You can apply skills learnt in your voice classes for professional communication.

Links   See page 147 for more information on vocal skills.

Accents and dialects add to individual personality, and can be important skills for employability.

Effective speaking tips

- ✓ Open your mouth.
- ✓ Project.
- ✓ Don't forget to say the end of the word.

Being friendly, listening well and using humour also show that you have good communication skills.

Now try this

1 Record yourself speaking, and listen to the recording.
2 Could you be understood easily? Make a list of areas where you could improve.

You could read a short poem. You could use a voice-recorder app on your phone to record yourself.

Effective written communication skills

Good writing skills are vital as a job application is often the first communication with an organisation, and first impressions count.

Writing

A promotional portfolio includes written work such as a personal statement or letter of application in response to the employment opportunity. Excellent writing skills will support a successful application.

The main things to look out for are:

- spelling
- grammar
- punctuation.

Some organisations reject any Curriculum Vitae (CV) that contains a spelling or grammatical error.

Checking for mistakes

Spelling – Beware of typing errors too. Our minds tend to work faster than our typing skills.

Grammar – Write in full sentences. Reread your writing to make sure that the sentences make sense.

Punctuation – Incorrect punctuation can change the meaning of what you're trying to say. Check your use of capital letters and full stops.

Format, structure and tone

How you communicate depends on who you are communicating with and why. As you are applying for a job, you need to apply a professional approach that reflects your ability to meet the demands of the employer. Different formats you could use include a letter, a report, a CV, a presentation and/or a webfolio. The structure and tone should meet professional expectations, for example:

Hi George	should be …	Dear George Jarvis
Bye for now	should be …	Yours sincerely,
Harley Quinn (Aka. The Guvnor)	should be …	Harley Quinn

Clarity of written communication

When you write a personal statement, make sure that your intentions are clear. Writing a long statement which has no clear direction is a waste of time and energy, and will not impress the reader.

Always think about whether you could be more precise in your use of language, and whether the content is necessary.

Referencing

When writing a job application, the employer wants to hear from **you**. Avoid copying other people's writing, even if you change it to reflect your position.

If you include a quotation in a personal statement, make sure that you reference it appropriately.

- Use quotation marks.
- After the quotation, state in brackets who said it and where.

Vocational language and terminology

Using the correct vocational language and terminology can show an employer that you understand your subject area.

For example, instead of saying:

'I am able to be loud when acting'

you could say:

'I am able to *project*'.

Take plenty of time over a job application, and make sure that you check it for errors.

Now try this

Describe a rehearsal or training process you have recently undertaken. Review your writing and check for spelling and grammatical errors.

When you review your writing, have you made the same spelling mistake or grammatical error more than once? If so, you might need to look up the spelling or check the grammatical rules!

Pitching ideas

To succeed in pitching ideas to an organisation, you need to have confidence in your own planning and delivery.

Engage the audience

- Think about your posture – don't slouch.
- Use your performance training to sound positive and hide your nerves.
- Use different methods to visually engage the audience (diagrams or handouts of plans, schedules, funding breakdowns and your assessment of the risks involved).

Apply communication skills

- ✓ Speak clearly.
- ✓ Project appropriately.
- ✓ Use eye contact.
- ✓ Use open body language.

A successful pitch communicates good ideas clearly and with enthusiasm.

Communicate clear ideas and intentions

1. **Plan and structure your pitch.** Include an introduction, main body and a summary (like writing an essay).

2. **Practice it beforehand.** This will help you to evaluate whether it runs smoothly or if there is missing information.

3. **Make a clear link** between your project and the organisation's plans for the future.

Plan your pitch

Before your pitch, make sure you know the answer to these questions:

- ✓ What is the project?
- ✓ How will it run?
- ✓ How much will it cost?
- ✓ How much money could it generate?
- ✓ Is there any additional funding available?
- ✓ How many people (hours of work) would be needed?

Facts and figures

Make sure you have thought about all of your project's requirements in the planning stage.

Include the most important information in your pitch prominently, with the detail placed later or less prominently. Be open about any risks – this shows that you understand your project, and will encourage the organisation to trust you.

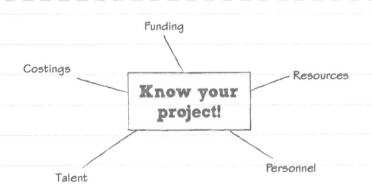

Now try this

A local college is looking for new ideas for widening participation in performing arts. You have the idea of a series of drama workshops in schools, leading to a large performance in the local theatre. Create a short pitch to present to the college management.

You can make brief notes or create a few PowerPoint™ slides.

What is a promotional portfolio?

You need to be able to produce a promotional portfolio containing examples of your practical work and experience. This will prepare you for future job applications in your chosen performance pathway.

Contents of a promotional portfolio

A promotional portfolio is a collection of work that showcases your knowledge, skills and techniques in a performance style.

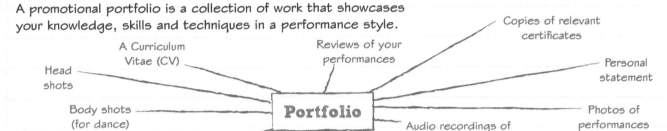

Head shots — A Curriculum Vitae (CV) — Reviews of your performances — Copies of relevant certificates — Personal statement

Body shots (for dance) — **Portfolio** — Audio recordings of performances — Photos of performances

Show reel(s)

There are some portfolio components that you must include, such as you CV, headshots and at least one show reel. Others with depend on your specialism but you always need to emphasise your skills and success.

Format

It is wise to produce physical (hard copy) and digital copies of your promotional portfolio.

It is possible to include all of your items (such as video footage, CV, personal statement) in the same document, such as a pdf.

Remember to back up on another device anything you have saved digitally. You could use a USB stick, or even create a backup on several devices.

Promotional website

Some performers present their promotional portfolio on their own website. Links to video footage and further information on experience and skills can be easily included.

Links See page 146 for more details on web portfolios.

Curriculum Vitae (CV)

A CV is one to two sides of A4 that gives information about you and your history. For a performing arts CV, you need to include:

- your contact details
- basic description of your appearance (height, eye and hair colour)
- a small version of your head shot
- relevant training
- relevant experience.

Head shots

Employers will want head shots to be formatted in a specific way:

- showing head and shoulders
- 8" × 10" (approx. 25 cm × 20 cm) portrait photo
- black and white (although some employers may want colour).

Example of an actor's head shot

Now try this

Using one sheet of A4, write down all the information needed for your CV.

 Use the bullet points above as a starting point.

Alternative portfolio formats

You could consider different formats for your portfolio. Many digital platforms are now used to present portfolios.

Web portfolio

A growing trend is the web portfolio. You can pay for a web address and build a website to showcase your skills and experience.

Include the conventional content of a portfolio shown on page 140, along with links to videos, a blog and links to social media accounts.

Managing your online presence well is increasingly important when looking for work opportunities.

Links to social media accounts

Including links from your website to your social media can be beneficial, as an employer can see how you network and connect with the general public. However, be aware of these issues:

- Links to pages where your personal and social life is exposed can be off-putting to an employer and undermine your credibility for the job.
- Links to inappropriate video footage or posts will make you look unprofessional.

- About
- Training and Experience
- Gallery
- Videos
- Contact

An example of a professional performer's website

 Case study

A children's entertainer, Micky Chuckles, has a company website and email address for customers to contact him. The website is professional and encourages custom with excellent photos of Micky at work. One of his services involves working at children's birthday parties and therefore he is contacted by a lot of parents.

A parent has watched Micky Chuckles in a performance at the local theatre and wants to hire him for their child's upcoming birthday party. Having lost his business card, the parent types his name into a search engine, which produces many pages. One link is to his personal Facebook page which is not set to private and can be accessed by anyone. The parent clicks the link and sees photos of Micky drinking with friends on a night out and posts related to his relationships with women. In particular, in one post he describes his ex-girlfriend in a derogatory way.

Outcome

The parent decides that this entertainer is unsuitable for running a party for their child, and decides to find someone else.

Many employers will also run an internet search to find out more about candidates for a job.

Now try this

1 Check your online profile, using a search engine look yourself up.
2 What information can you find? Evaluate how this may be perceived by potential employers, and review your privacy settings.

Many performers use their head shot as their profile photo – this ensures that a good image of themselves is the first thing people see.

Highlighting discipline and skills

Your portfolio should clearly show how you have developed your skills and can apply them within your chosen performance pathway (discipline). Below are the areas you should consider covering when describing your skills in your portfolio.

Skills

Some skills apply across all disciplines within performing arts:

- planning
- responding to direction and corrections
- collaboration and team work
- time management.

This page lists just a few of the skills related to different disciplines. You can refer to other units to revise skills not listed here.

Lifestyle and approach

These points relate to performers in all disciplines:

1 **Nutrition** – Eating healthy food provides more sustainable energy and will support you through a day of practical activities.

2 **Rest and burnout** – Many injuries are caused through tiredness. Practical work in performing arts is energetic and taxing, but you can reduce the risk of physical and emotional complications by getting proper rest.

3 **Safe practice** – you will be able to participate and perform better if you wear suitable clothing, focus during rehearsal, warm up properly and manage injuries.

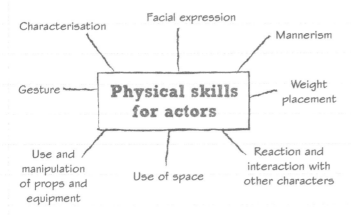

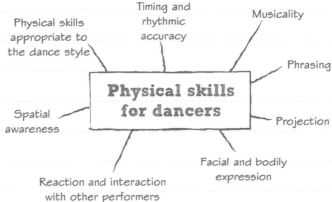

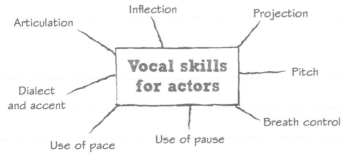

Variety

Variety develops existing skills, such as acting, dancing or musical skills, whilst mastering additional skills such as magic, impressionism, comedy or using specialist equipment.

Now try this

Using the skills listed on this page, conduct a skills audit for your performance pathway. Rate yourself between 1 and 5 for each skill.
1 = excellent, 3 = requires improvement, 5 = no skill evident.

In the future, you may want to revisit any skills audits you may have completed as part of your other units.

Highlighting relevant skills

Your promotional portfolio should express your commitment to performance and developing skills.

What shall I select?

In order to select the appropriate material for your promotional portfolio you need to understand how it relates to the employment opportunity, your own skills and what evidence you have to back you up.

Make sure your portfolio is varied. Don't just include lots of videos and nothing else. You will need to evaluate each piece of evidence you have.

- Is the quality of the evidence professional enough?
- Is there a better way to show a skill, such as a written response, certificate, CV, or video?

'I am an excellent dancer/actor/performer'

'I have the skills and techniques for the job'

> **The material in my promotional portfolio should express ...**

'My experience means I know what I am doing'

These statements should help you to select the appropriate material for the portfolio.

'I am an excellent dancer/actor/performer'

You will want to showcase the styles appropriate to the discipline, for example:

- **dance** – contemporary, ballet, jazz, street dance
- **acting** – naturalism, epic (Brechtian), comedy, Shakespeare/verse speaking.

Your portfolio should communicate your passion for performance.

Links See page 150 for advice on plugging gaps in your portfolio if you need to demonstrate more skills.

'I have the skills and techniques for the job'

Consider the skills and techniques of your discipline (dance, acting, musical theatre) and employability skills, for example:

- transferable skills
- competencies
- skills particular to the discipline.

Links See pages 140 and 147 for more on these skills.

You need to link each skill to something you have achieved, such as work in class or performance experience. If, for example, you have lots of evidence in communication, you can pick the best two or three pieces of evidence to use.

'My experience means I know what I am doing'

Your experience will be written in your CV, and you don't need to produce video footage of every performance you have taken part in.

Be selective, and consider the relevance of your experience.

How many skills can I show?

One piece of video footage can showcase several skills at once. This will reduce the amount of evidence you have to find.

Rejecting material as evidence

Bear in mind the employment opportunity when listing past achievements. Swimming certificates may not support an application for an actor, unless the piece was about swimmers.

Now try this

Choose a skill from page 147.

(a) List **three** of your performances in which you have demonstrated this skill.

(b) Write a short description of each performance, and link them to other skills.

These can be transferable skills, competencies or communication skills.

Understanding practical work

Your professional portfolio can be boosted by carefully selecting the relevant content as evidence of your experience and abilities.

Video footage

Video footage of performances can give employers a good idea of your capabilities. However, there may have been workshops, rehearsals, work-in-progress performances in class, and technique classes that did not finish with a final performance. Video footage of your participation in these could not only fill gaps in your experience but also demonstrate your professional approach to work.

Rehearsal extracts

Selecting appropriate rehearsal clips can show an employer you have the following skills:

- positive response to direction/corrections
- self-discipline, for example listening, focus and concentration
- safe practice, for example suitable clothing, behaviour
- effort and commitment
- interpersonal skills.

Individual projects

Projects where you have worked independently or were in charge are also good forms of evidence. This could be choreographing a group dance, directing extracts from a play, or leading a workshop. Good video footage might show rehearsals, with you leading physical or vocal warm-ups.

Compare with the final product

Footage of the final product will demonstrate your creative output and development.

Technique classes

Vocal and physical technique classes can develop your skills. If you cannot demonstrate these skills in a final performance, footage or written evidence of your participation in technique classes provides good evidence of your skills.

For example, you may be outstanding at speaking in regional accents, but always use your own in performance. Evidence could be:

- participation in voice classes where you focused on accents and excelled
- the tutor filmed you performing a short poem in a regional accent.

In-class performance extracts

Sometimes, a project does not always come to fruition. Perhaps there wasn't enough time, or maybe that was the original intention. These in-class performances can also be valuable forms of evidence as they can show you:

- performing a style different from your main performances
- using performance skills outside a live audience performance context.

Workshops

Participation in professional workshops is invaluable experience. This is like attending a master class, when you work with a professional from the industry. Footage could be strong evidence of how you respond to professional direction.

Attending technique classes and workshops shows dedication to your discipline.

Now try this

1 Think about a different unit you have studied on this course. Briefly identify what you did in the classes.

2 Could you use anything from your experience of that unit to showcase your skills and techniques? Make notes on how you can apply your skills.

 Identifying transferable skills will enhance your portfolio.

Selecting relevant video footage

Selecting the most appropriate footage for your promotional portfolio is key to gaining an interview.

The ticks and crosses in the table below illustrate footage that is appropriate in the given contexts.

The job	Video footage			
A contemporary dancer is required to work in a children's theatre	X A performance in **Cabaret**	X A performance in a street crew	✓ Footage of leading a workshop for young people	✓ A performance of children's theatre
A high-profile theatre company is looking for actors to cast in their production of **Twelfth Night**	X A stand-up comedy routine	X A jazz dance	✓ Footage of a strong vocal technique class	✓ A Shakespearean monologue or play
A leading producer for the West End is casting for the musical **Sweet Charity**	X Singing a rock song	X Performance of a monologue in a Jacobean play	✓ A performance in **Cabaret**	✓ Attending a musical theatre workshop

Other points to consider

Quality of the video footage

- Has the camera picked up the sound effectively, or is there interference?
- Is the camera still or shaking?
- Are you clearly visible at a time where you should be the focus of the camera?

Gaps in your experience

- If compiling your portfolio has shown obvious gaps in your experience, trawl through other projects and try to make a film montage of previous performances such as monologues, solo songs or dances.
- You could also prepare solo performances and film them in a studio setting to fill the gaps.

Now try this

A new, upcoming producer is looking to cast the musical *Rent*, a rock opera about the lives of struggling artists in downtown New York.

(a) Write down what you think would be good audition pieces.

(b) Which skills would you need to emphasise?

Promotional intent

You need to organise your portfolio so that it addresses the needs of the organisation, demonstrates your skills, communicates your artistic intent and focuses on the requirements of the job opportunity.

Using your discipline to communicate your intent

A potential employer should understand your artistic intent before watching a video. Include a short description underneath each video link in your pdf to cover this information.

The five Ws
- ☑ What is this performance?
- ☑ When was it performed?
- ☑ Where was it performed?
- ☑ Why was it performed?
- ☑ Who is performing?

Solo performance of The Windy City from Calamity Jane. Performed at the Abbey Theatre in Northampton as part of a Musical Theatre showcase. September 30th 2015.

Performing arts skills and techniques

You should select video footage that not only reflects the requirements of the job, but that showcases your skills to the highest level.

Example

The job: Actor in Shakespeare play

Video footage:

1 The production of **The Comedy of Errors**.
2 A short monologue from **Macbeth**.

In **The Comedy of Errors** you bumped into a chair and forgot a few lines. You performed the short monologue from **Macbeth** with no hitches. Which one do you pick for your portfolio?

Cataloguing your video footage in this way makes selection of evidence easier for future job applications.

Designing the portfolio for the employer

Choose an appropriate order for your videos to keep the potential employer engaged by identifying the primary focus of the employment opportunity. This table has two examples.

Employment opportunity	Order of clips
Performer	Place clips of you performing first, and then any other footage.
Workshop leader	Place the clips of you leading workshops first, and then move on to performance and other clips.

Direct the portfolio towards the organisation

You will need to consider the following aspects of the organisation. You should mention these in your portfolio for the employment opportunity and then link your experiences directly to them.

 Links Revisit pages 121–137 to remind yourself of the purpose, function and requirements of performing arts organisations.

Now try this

Write a short description of a clip you may use in your own promotional portfolio. Use the 'five Ws' above to help you.

Are you right for the job?

Your application should demonstrate that you are a good match for the organisation's values, ethics and purpose. The written aspect of your portfolio should be clear, accurate and informative.

Matching your values and work ethic to the requirements

In order to match your skills to the requirements of the organisation, you have to undertake some research into the organisation. Find out the following:

- What is their organisational purpose?
- What is their legal and operational structure?
- How are they funded?
- How do they operate?

Answering these two questions will influence your selection of material as evidence:

- Is the job performance orientated?
- Do you need to evidence a passion for community work?

> Ensure that you clearly explain how your skills are well matched to the structure, funding model and scope of the organisation. For example, you may have experience working in a rural area with a broad range of people, and you can describe what you liked and what you gained from this experience in your written statement.

Drama Club Organiser

We are looking for an innovative and dynamic theatre practitioner to lead our hugely successful business. The successful candidate will be an outstanding classroom practitioner with extensive experience of drama leadership.

> Through the Big Lottery Fund we are now able to expand our successful community project 'ACCESS'. We are looking for a community worker to help bring the performing arts to the small villages in our county. The successful candidate will be inspiring and able to work with a diverse group of people.

Supporting written information

As we saw on page 143, written information can include:

- a written response (or personal statement)
- a tailored CV
- any references
- any copies of certificates.

Achieving a professional presentation

To make the best impression, make sure that all written evidence is:

- ✓ word processed
- ✓ formatted well
- ✓ correct – check spelling, grammar and punctuation.

Further refinement

Work, training and performance history can be laid out in the CV. Therefore practical work can be refined further to enhance qualities relevant to the job.

Be careful of selecting evidence because you like it. You need to think of a reason for including every piece of evidence that is linked to the organisation and employment opportunity.

> For example, evidence of your ability to do a regional accent through footage of a voice class should be rejected if the employment opportunity is for a workshop leader.

> For example, the employment opportunity is for a street dancer. Video footage of you performing contemporary dance or ballet can be rejected.

Now try this

Choose a competency or transferable skill. How can it be evidenced by a written document from the list above?

You can pick more than one way to evidence the skill.

Ensuring professionalism

Your promotional portfolio must be of a professional standard to be taken seriously by an employer.

Structuring your portfolio contents

Once you have selected the appropriate content, you will need to bring it all together. Your promotional portfolio will be in a pdf format where you will be able to embed sound clips and video footage as well as import word documents such as your CV.

You could use this order:

1. A short introductory statement followed by a list of contents

2. Your head shot

3. Your CV

4. Your written response/personal statement

5. Your audio or video clips

6. Any additional evidence

Editing your videos

- **Identify timings for each video** – where does the crucial clip start and finish?

- **Use video editing software** to cut the footage at the right places.

  Edit video footage to support the skills and techniques you want to showcase.

- **Add effects** such as 'Fades in and out' to add smoothness to the clip.

  It would not be appropriate to include the video for the entire musical you performed in. Select a good part and edit it.

Workshop ideas

If you are asked to provide workshop ideas include a few options. This will reflect your creative abilities.

- Outline the theme.
- Explain the idea that came from the theme.
- Include a brief workshop plan so they can see how it would work.
- Explain how the workshop would fit into their requirements (organisational, funding, operational, etc.).

Written response

Your written response to the employment opportunity will allow you to demonstrate your knowledge of the performing arts organisation.

- Introduce yourself.
- State why you want the job.
- State why you would be perfect for the job.

A written response could have an essay or report structure. It could also be formatted like a letter.

The final product

Once you have completed your written response and promotional portfolio, take a step away from it for a short while.

When you return, go through the final product carefully and assess the content.

- Do you tick all of the performing arts organisation's boxes?
- Does the portfolio have a professional appearance?

 It is hard to evaluate something that you have worked closely on. Show your portfolio to a tutor or friend and ask for feedback unless you are working under assessment conditions.

 Always proofread your writing.

 Check that the audio and video clips all work.

Now try this

Use a search engine to find a professional performer's web portfolio. Write down **three** observations about the portfolio that give it a professional appearance.

Relating the employment opportunity to your skills

You need to understand the organisation's purpose, structure and work in order to relate the task to you and your abilities. If you understand the organisation, you will be able to present yourself in a way that suits its requirements.

Checklist of what to identify

- Aims, objectives, vision, mission and values.
- Legal constitution and organisational structure of Breakin' Barriers and how this affects the company.
- Intended audience (performance work and outreach/educational work).
- Scope of the organisation.
- Possible viewpoints of the stakeholders in Breakin' Barriers.
- What kind of funding does it receive?
- How might this affect how the company works?
- How big is the company? Does it have few staff covering lots of different areas, or lots of staff in separate departments?

> Every year we deliver national outreach and education programmes in schools and a range of local community venues.

> At times, our members will liaise with other organisations to help develop new revenue streams that will help us to continue our work.

Sample notes extract

Workshops in schools and other venues across the UK.

1 My ability to travel, e.g. driving licence
2 Experience of touring?

The learner is using the task information to identify the organisation's mission. They are then thinking about how it relates to their own skills.

Sample notes extract

Help the organisation find funding

1 Might have to pitch to other organisations for contracts.
2 Need to know how to find funding.
3 Will need to apply for and secure funding.

This learner has read the text carefully to draw out the requirements of this employment opportunity.

Note-taking

Your notes can be phrases, bullet points or sentences. Try to avoid full sentences in your preparation as you need to be able to access the information quickly.

Finding gaps in your knowledge

Don't be afraid to use a question mark to indicate where you don't know an answer. You can come back to this later. If you don't know the answer, or cannot see it in the task brief, you will have to research it. Write this in your notes for when you start your research.

Now try this

Read the task information on page 119 and identify **three** possible funding sources for not-for-profit organisations.

Thinking of workshop ideas

In your written response, you will need to present ideas about how you will help to achieve the organisation's requirements. The task information states that all performers in Breakin' Barriers are also workshop leaders.

These workshops are going to be linked to the performance of 'A Midsummer Night's Dream'.

The aim of the workshop will be to extend the understanding of the themes, ideas and concepts within the project. The workshop needs to be inclusive, fun and have clear objectives. We are looking for people with excellent leadership, organisational and performance skills.

Breakin' Barriers has identified two features required of the workshops – to be both inclusive and fun. You will need to describe how you will achieve these two things, as well as identifying other clear objectives of your workshop, based on the organisation's overall project aims.

I will need to demonstrate my strong performance, planning and leadership skills in my written response.

You could do initial research into the job description of a workshop leader to help inform the ideas your propose in your written response.

Sample notes extract

Reading the script and watching other performances are good ways to research a play.

Magical world controlling everything

Falling in love with the wrong people

Being lost in the woods

A Midsummer Night's Dream

For each idea, you can identify how you could explore the theme in the workshops. For example, the concept of falling in love with the 'wrong' people could lead to a movement workshop based on falling, or perhaps an improvisation on people's perception of differences.

Falling out with people and impact on other people's lives

Running away from home when your parents order you to do something

Sample notes extract

As Breakin' Barriers explores lots of different disciplines in the performing arts, pick one where you are most confident and experienced.

Tongue-twisters for articulation and speaking out loud

Zip Zap Boing, for coordination, rapid response and focus

Drama workshops

To help with planning, think of the skills the learners are building and from this create some fun dynamic ideas to support them.

Throwing and catching a ball (like hot potato), for hand-eye coordination, rapid response and focus

Now try this

Come up with your own idea for a workshop based on **A Midsummer Night's Dream**. Which skills could you be building, and which exercises would help you achieve this?

Your performance skills

Reviewing your own skills and relating them to the requirements of the employment opportunity will help you to decide what to write about in your written response and include in your digital promotional portfolio.

Matching your skills to the organisation

Breakin' Barriers is looking for dancers, singers or actors for their new production of **A Midsummer Night's Dream**. The first stage would be to assess your own qualities as a performer focusing on your own specialism.

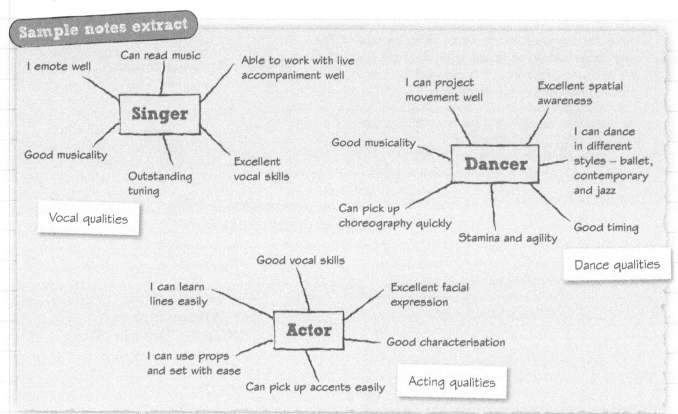

Sample notes extract

I emote well

Can read music

Able to work with live accompaniment well

Singer

Good musicality

Outstanding tuning

Excellent vocal skills

Vocal qualities

I can project movement well

Excellent spatial awareness

Good musicality

Dancer

I can dance in different styles – ballet, contemporary and jazz

Can pick up choreography quickly

Stamina and agility

Good timing

Dance qualities

Good vocal skills

I can learn lines easily

Excellent facial expression

Actor

Good characterisation

I can use props and set with ease

Can pick up accents easily

Acting qualities

Evaluate your skills

You are likely to have completed a skills audit before, for example in Units 3 and 5. Either refer to your answers there, or complete an analysis of yourself as a dancer/actor/singer. For example:

Strengths	Weaknesses
Embodying a style of dance	Accuracy of timing

Thinking of additional skills

Additional skills

Breakin' Barriers is also looking for additional performance skills. You can draw on different activities and experiences from your childhood/adolescence.

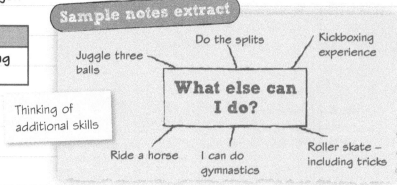

Sample notes extract

Juggle three balls

Do the splits

Kickboxing experience

What else can I do?

Ride a horse

I can do gymnastics

Roller skate – including tricks

Now try this

Brainstorm what additional skills you may have.

 Think back to after-school activities. Could you transfer skills learnt at that time?

Writing about your performance skills

Now you have identified your own skills, you can link these skills to the employment opportunity in your written response.

Read through these sample extracts from learner responses and the annotations, to understand how you might do this.

Sample response extract

Breakin' Barriers is clearly an innovative, creative organisation aiming to engage a youthful and varied audience nationally, with ethical values. I am a like-minded individual as I have previously used Theatre in Education to deliver workshops for young people aged 11–16. There was a diverse range of acting abilities in the group, and I have included video evidence in my portfolio of how I modelled strong listening, communication and vocal skills using an activity based on the traditional 'Chinese whispers' game and showed them the importance of clear projection to an audience.

This helped them to play to each person's strengths to improvise short pieces for an end-of-workshop performance. I will employ these same skills in the workshop I am proposing for Breakin' Barriers, but in order to shed new light on *A Midsummer Night's Dream*, as per Breakin' Barriers' objectives, I will introduce a number of modern props into scenes and engage all students in thinking about how everyone, including students with limited physical mobility, can use them for comic effect. In my portfolio I've included photos of my creative use of props in a scene from the musical *Cabaret* last year to show the arrival of Cliff on the train at the start.

 The learner has clearly interpreted the aims and values of the organisation.

 Clear linkage of the experience to the organisation's aims and activities.

 Description of skills and how and why they were employed, with reference to evidence in the digital promotional portfolio.

 Clear link to how skills will be relevant in achieving the organisation's objectives.

Understanding of organisation's target audience.

Now try this

Using your brainstorm of additional skills from page 156, link **three** of these skills to the workshop ideas you are going to propose, explaining why they are relevant.

Your employment skills

The whole focus of this unit is on employment opportunities so, alongside your performance skills, it is important to identify the skills that make you employable.

Identifying your employability skills

Analysing the task information will help you to ensure that you tick all of the employer's boxes.

> Our emphasis is on equality of opportunity and we build links with many Special Educational Needs (SEN) schools and councils in order to enhance participation in the performing arts.

This extract tells us that Breakin' Barriers is looking for performing arts specialists who can communicate effectively with others to develop and refine workshop plans and ideas.

From this analysis we could conclude that the organisation needs someone with the following skills:

- teamwork
- listening skills
- learning
- interpersonal skills
- leadership skills.

You will need to prove that you have these skills when you complete your written response and portfolio.

Proving you have the skills

First of all, brainstorm occasions within your experience where you have demonstrated those skills.

Sample notes extract

Devising work – e.g. 'Not on my Doorstep' was a devising piece based on gun crime

All movement work when rehearsing for a performance

Teamwork

I work part-time in a restaurant, and have to work with two chefs and bar staff to serve the customers on time

> Using the information from the brainstorm you can plan the most appropriate physical evidence to showcase these skills.

Devising – include comment in written response and/or photos of devised piece or video footage of a clip.

Movement work – include comment in written response and video footage of me in rehearsal.

Restaurant job – include comment in written response and list this in my CV.

Sample notes extract

Personal organisation

Interpersonal skills

Personal motivation

Teamwork

> We are looking for people with excellent leadership, organisational and performance skills, who value inclusion and relish a challenge. They must be able to contribute to evaluative reports of our workshop delivery and be able to evidence our organisation's activities within the community.

Leadership skills   Literacy skills   IT skills   Presentation skills

Now try this

1. Brainstorm the skill of literacy. List the many occasions in your past experience when you have demonstrated this skill.

2. How could you apply your literacy skills to this employment opportunity?

Your communication skills

Communication skills are vital to securing any job, and you will need to provide evidence of your communication skills in your written response and your digital promotional portfolio.

Sample notes extract

This can either be verbal contributions in a meeting or written contributions to a report. I will need to prove that I can communicate effectively in both ways.

They must be able to contribute to evaluative reports of our workshop delivery and be able to evidence our organisation's activities within the community ... At times, our performers will liaise with other organisations to help develop new revenue streams that will help us to continue our work.

This will probably mean pitching ideas or a product to companies such as schools or funding bodies. Delivering a pitch requires verbal and written communication skills:

* verbal – presenting information
* written – handouts, creating a PowerPoint presentation.

This part of the task brief tells us what kind of communication skills Breakin' Barriers is looking for. Read it carefully to identify different skills required.

* **Clear tone/speak clearly** – I can record a short introduction to the digital portfolio so they can see how I speak.
* **I can listen** – demonstrate collaborative work, such as my experience as director of extracts from 'Blood Brothers'.
* **My vocabulary is mostly good** – make sure I use subject-specific terminology and appropriate words.

Verbal communication skills evidence

You will need to identify your verbal communication skills: what are you good at, and where do you need to improve?

Sample notes extract

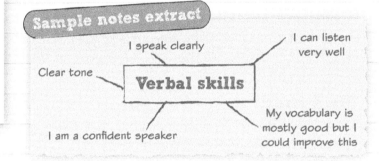

* **Write essays and reports** – show this with a high-quality written response; include GCSE English Language and Literature certificates.
* **Complex words** – use sophisticated vocabulary in the written response.
* **I can spell** – all written work within the assessment must be spelt correctly.
* **Good grammar** – this must be evident in all written work within the assessment; GCSE English Language and Literature certificates.

Written communication skills evidence

You will need to identify your written communication skills: what are you good at, and where do you need to improve?

Sample notes extract

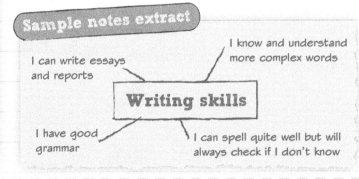

Now try this

You can draw on past experience as evidence of your communication skills.

1. Make a list of skills you have learnt and used in previous activities and work situations.
2. How can you apply them to this employment opportunity?

Planning your written response

When you have completed your preparatory work, organise your material into a good structure in preparation for the written response. A standard structure will be an introduction, the main body and the conclusion.

Introduction

On the left below is a sample plan for the introduction of one learner's written response. On the right is the full introduction for their written response.

Sample notes extract

Introduction
Introduce myself and my key experience
What is my own experience (related to employment opportunity)?
Spent two years developing my skills as a performer – BTEC, extensive performance experience. Have been teaching dance to children with Down's syndrome for past three years which has developed my communication, listening and collaboration skills.
Why do I want the job?
Breakin' Barriers = leading company, strong ethos of integration and equal opps and feel my values and workshop proposal will be a good fit.

Allow plenty of time to organise your material. Write out a list of headings and place your notes under these headings.

Sample response extract

My name is Erin Smith and I am an 18-year-old dancer who has experience of teaching children with disabilities. I note you are looking for performers and workshop leaders who can uphold the ethos of Breakin' Barriers. I have trained as a dancer, completing a BTEC qualification in Performing Arts, and I have extensive performance experience working closely with others developing original and innovative work. I also have experience of teaching dance to children with Down's syndrome and I have developed listening, communication and collaboration skills this way, as well as the ability to relate to others. I therefore understand how important your company's work of integration and equal opportunities is in the current industry and I believe my workshop proposal below would be a strong fit with your company whose values I share.

Main body

The following extract from the main body of one learner's written response will help you understand what kind of format your written response might take.

Clear statement of objective for proposed workshop that links to Breakin' Barriers' aims and values.

Clear identification of a specific skill they have that will support the workshop.

The learner links the workshop outcomes to the larger Breakin' Barriers project aim.

Detail of how skills have been developed the past, with evidence and subject-specific terminology.

The learner could go on to explore how funding might be obtained to support the workshop plan.

Sample response extract

The first objective of my proposed workshop will be to develop and enhance key dance skills for all students, in a fun, positive and inclusive environment. This is to support Breakin' Barriers' overarching aim of building links with communities and instilling a love of performance in young people regardless of background. I am well placed to do this as I have a strong sense of musicality and will use uplifting, positive music with a strong beat to inspire students to improvise with movement. We will aim to portray key characters, such as Bottom, from *A Midsummer Night's Dream* in a new way in order to support Breakin' Barriers' larger project of developing a new production of the play. There is lots of potential for fun comic input here, as well as enhancement of modern dance techniques. An example of where I have done this before is in the development of the characterisation of a cat in my solo performance for my BTEC National course, using rhythm and articulation in the style of Merce Cunningham and I have included body shots of this in my portfolio. I was also inspired by DV8 Physical Theatre, which shares many of the same values as Breakin' Barriers, and would show clips of their performances to the students as a starting point for their ideas for inclusive and innovative movement.

Planning your digital promotional portfolio

It is a good idea to plan your promotional portfolio so that all of your best pieces of evidence can be included to boost your application.

Evidence of your skills and experience

Once you have decided on the skills Breakin' Barriers requires, and how you can prove your own skills, make a list of the types of evidence you have. For example:

- GCSE certificates
- performing arts exam certificates
- photos of performances
- videos of workshops
- teacher testimony
- reviews
- CV
- head shot
- body shots.

Select images that will have the most impact on the employer.

Page order

Structure your evidence into a coherent order. Think about how you would like to guide the employer and keep their interest. If they get bored after the first page, they may not want to scroll any further.

Suggested order:

- introductory page
- CV
- head shot
- body shots
- video footage (include reviews if related directly to the video)
- photos of performances and workshops
- review (if not related to the video footage)
- certificates
- testimonies/references.

Compiling digital recording list and order

Planning the length of each digital recording clip will help to ensure you have everything covered in the allotted time. If, for example, you have 8 clips of video or audio, aim to make them no longer than roughly a minute long after you have edited. This is plenty to demonstrate key points, and there is some contingency possible. It will help to write out how you plan to divide this time across clips, for example:

Video 1............... 1 minute 30 seconds

Audio 1 .... 2 minutes

Video 2 .... 2 minutes

Video 3 .... 30 seconds

Video 4 .... 1 minute

Video 5 .... 2 minutes

    Total: 9 minutes

← Check the Pearson website for the most up-to-date **Sample Assessment Material** to find out how long your digital recordings can be.

Introducing clips

Remember that if you decide to introduce each clip, you will have to cut off approximately 15 seconds from each one to allow for the introduction.

Create a montage

You could group some clips together to create a montage that demonstrate similar skills. For example, you could merge into one clip footage of you leading different workshops.

Review

Review all of your notes and annotations you have made on the task information. Make sure that you have mentioned each of the key skills required in your written response AND provided evidence of these skills in your digital promotional portfolio where most relevant.

Know how you will structure your digital promotional portfolio before you go into the assessment. You can amend your plan as you progress through your preparation time to keep checking it is structured as clearly as possible to match all the required skills you have referenced in your written response.

Now try this

Write a promotional portfolio plan based on the evidence that you think Breakin' Barriers would like to see for this employment opportunity.

Content of your digital promotional portfolio

Compiling the content of your portfolio can take time, which you need to plan for.

Gathering and reviewing your evidence

You need to be organised when collating your evidence as you might have to wait for other people to source some items, for example:

- teachers for video footage of previous shows
- parents or other family members to help locate certificates.

Once you have the evidence, check every item before you decide to include it. There is an emphasis on professional presentation, so discard any video footage that is blurred or poorly filmed. It might be better to produce a new recording rather than present poor footage.

To help you complete your CV, collect the lists you have made about your performance and part-time work experience.

Creating new evidence

You might decide to produce some new performance material to reflect the employment opportunity.

Example of new evidence

All of Amelia's previous performances were of contemporary plays. She wanted to perform a monologue from **A Midsummer Night's Dream** to showcase her ability to perform Shakespeare. As Breakin' Barriers creates new takes on classics, she decided to be unconventional with her choice of monologue in terms of character. She has selected a monologue from the character Oberon.

Make sure, when you select new material, that it is appropriate to the set task information.

Rehearsing

Choosing new material to perform is not a decision to take lightly. With only two weeks of preparation time, rehearsal and filming time is limited. If you do select new material, bear this in mind in your initial planning.

Use rehearsal time effectively and apply self-discipline and commitment to realise your full potential.

We are looking for people with excellent leadership, organisational and performance skills, who value inclusion and relish a challenge.

Sample notes extract

I value inclusion.

Past job – teaching performing arts to children with disabilities.

Evidence:

- Teacher's testimony of how well I taught the group.
- Photos of me teaching the children specific workshop, with a note about its objective and its outcomes.

Review your notes on Breakin' Barriers' employment opportunity. Match your skills to its requirements and link this to the evidence needed.

Now try this

Take the suggested video footage plan on page 161. Can you identify examples from your own experience that would make you perfect for Breakin' Barriers? Do video or audio files exist of these experiences and, if so, how difficult would it be to get them?

Creating your CV

Your CV is an important document which should summarise your capabilities and experience.

Centre your name

Owen Bradley

Your head shot on right side

Contact details on left side

Contact: 23 Mulberry Close
Stratford, CV23 1QU

Phone: (01165) 223224

Mobile: 07735 123123

Email: owen.bradley@asp.co.uk

Personal details:

Height: 1.70m

Build: medium

Place personal details of yourself underneath

Hair: black

Eye colour: brown

List your training

Training:

2014 – 2016 Riverside College: BTEC Level 3 Extended Diploma in Performing Arts
2012 – 2014 Humbervale Academy: GCSE Dance (A); GCSE Drama (B)

Additional skills

- Accents
- Role-playing age
- Driving licence holder
- Aerial skills, circus skills
- Scuba diving
- Microsoft office and web-design skills

 Links See pages 121, 147 and 156 for the importance of listing additional skills.

List your performance experience. Don't forget to include what is relevant to the employment opportunity.

Credits

Year	Type	Role	Production	Company	Director
2016	Play	Willie	Happy Days	College Theatre Co.	Steven Marshall
2015	Play	Macbeth	Macbeth	Midlands Theatre Co.	Jenni Stewart

Details could include: year of performance, type of theatre – play, dance piece – your role, name of the production, performance company and director. You should give details of the experience that is most relevant to the job opportunity in your written response.

Additional experience

2016	Workshop Leader	Hayworth Summer School
2015	Town Council	Play scheme leader

You can find many examples of performers' CVs on the internet. Look at a few to gather ideas on how best to structure **your** CV.

Now try this

Create a 'Credits' section for your own CV, listing your performance experience and giving detailed information about each performance.

Preparing video evidence

Including video footage in your promotional portfolio is an ideal opportunity for you to demonstrate your skills and experience.

Organising footage

The video footage you select may already exist. If this is the case there are several steps to organising this footage.

- Source the video footage.
- Select the appropriate clip to fit into your promotional portfolio.
- Edit the clip.

Boost your video skills

You could also ask media colleagues for some help on working with video footage as you prepare for the assessment.

Editing clips

You will need to cut the clips to the length of time you have determined previously.

There are many different software packages available for editing media clips.

Make sure that the file formats and editing software are compatible. Amending formats can reduce the quality of the video, depending on how you work. Find out what file formats the software accepts and ensure that you record any footage in the same file format.

Introductions

You may want to include a short introduction to the video footage or to each clip. This would involve you speaking directly to the camera, using good communication skills.

It may help to write a short script, which you can memorise and rehearse before recording.

Special effects

Sometimes using special effects can enhance the professional quality of your video footage. For example, use of fade in and out can smooth the clip at the start and end.

You could also include a title credit at the start of the clip to introduce the content.

Recording new evidence

If you need to create new evidence of your skills, remember these points:

- Ensure that you have time to rehearse, record and edit the footage.
- Use good lighting and a space without sound interference.
- Ask somebody to run the camera for you and watch back the footage immediately, before packing everything away.

File naming

Remember to save your files with recognisable file names so you can easily identify them during the supervised assessment period. For example 'Grade 6 LAMDA Certificate'.

Presenting certificates

After sourcing relevant certificates you need to convert them to a digital format. You can scan documents from most printers.

Check the images you create on the computer: is there any discolouration that makes it look unprofessional? If so, find a different device to scan it on.

Now try this

Practise introducing yourself to camera.

Use the camera on your own phone or ask a friend to help.

Selecting relevant video footage

Select the items that will go in your digital promotional portfolio carefully.

Sample response extract

This is an informal video recording of a singing performance in a school. It is embedded into the digital promotional portfolio of one learner. It takes place in a music room and is from a recital conducted as part of the course. A more formal performance, with lights and a costume, is not required. However, if the recording had been blurry, or other people had moved in a way that distracted from the performance, this learner could have converted the file to an audio recording.

This information will be clear from the clip. You need to give the examiner more detail.

Sample response extract

This is me singing 'Close every door to me' at my school.

Remember to:
• use full sentences
• use correct grammar
• list the titles of songs, monologues and dance pieces appropriately, identifying where they are from and, if necessary, the writer.

Improved response extract

My solo singing performance of 'Close Every Door' from 'Joseph and the Amazing Technicolour Dreamcoat' in 2014. It demonstrates, particularly at 0:45, my strong vocal range, which would be helpful in delivering the vocal experimentation workshop I have proposed for SEN children aged 10–16.

It is important that you give details about the clip to the examiner so that they know what they are about to watch. Explain what the video is and why it is relevant to the job opportunity.

Now try this

Think about a recent performance and write a short introduction to an extract of a video of the performance as if you are using it as evidence in your digital portfolio.

Remember to give details. If you do not know all of the details, can you ask someone to help you complete the missing information?

Planning your supervised assessment time

Creating a plan for your assessment time is crucial to success. Visit the Pearson website for the most up-to-date Sample Assessment Material to see how long each activity will take in your actual assessment. Once you know the time frames, you can identify how much time you should be spending on specific activities.

Sample notes extract

Written response – suggested time plan

Step 1: Read through my notes and plans. (10 minutes)

Step 2: Start the introduction. (15 minutes)

Step 3: Start the main body. (50 minutes)

Step 4: Start the conclusion. (15 minutes)

Step 5: Read through my response, alongside my notes to make sure everything I planned has been covered. (15 minutes)

You should link your points to the evidence in your digital promotional portfolio as much as possible.

Step 6: Proofread and make any amendments, repeating until satisfied. (15 minutes).

Before Step 6, you could print off the written response and have a moment away from it so you can look at it with fresh eyes.

Sample notes extract

Digital promotional portfolio – suggested time plan

Step 1: Read through my notes and plans. (15 minutes)

Step 2: Write all the descriptions I need for each video. (1 hour)

You should link your different types of evidence to the skills you have highlighted in your written response as much as possible.

Step 3: Write the introduction and contents page. (30 minutes)

Step 4: Start importing my files into the pdf file and formatting the portfolio in a logical clear order. (4 hours)

Step 5: Read through the portfolio alongside notes to make sure everything I planned has been covered. (15 minutes)

Step 6: Proofread and may any amendments until satisfied. (1 hour).

Step 7: Check that all video footage works including saving, closing and re-opening the portfolio to ensure everything works as it should. Make any corrections. (1 hour)

Checklist for items to take into the assessment
- ☑ Notes for written response, including plans
- ☑ Notes for the promotional portfolio, including plans
- ☑ A USB stick with your digital files
- ☑ A back-up USB stick just in case
- ☑ Pens
- ☑ Paper

Checklist for items on your USB stick
- ☑ Your CV
- ☑ Your head shots
- ☑ Your body shots (if applicable)
- ☑ Any references/testimony you have
- ☑ Scanned certificates
- ☑ Photos of performances/workshops
- ☑ Images of posters or reviews etc
- ☑ Show reel(s) and any videos

Now try this

Evaluate the time plans above in terms of your own skills, and create your own. Make adjustments if you need to.

Answers

Unit 1 Investigating Practitioners' Work

These answers are in no way prescriptive and should be used for guidance only.

4. Assessment outcomes

The plan could be in the form of a spider diagram, a table, a list of bullet points or notes. It should include reference to the four assessment outcomes and clearly articulate your aims and objectives. An aim is what you hope to achieve and an objective is how you are going to achieve it.

5. Selecting primary sources

Learners' questions could include the following:
- Do you like Oscar Hammerstein II's work? Why/why not?
- What themes appear in his work? Are there any that link to identity?
- Have you seen any other Oscar Hammerstein II performances? If so, is this performance typical of his work?
- What do you think Oscar Hammerstein II is influenced by?
Questions should be specific and clear.

6. Selecting secondary sources

Answers should detail what types of sources were located and include effective acknowledgement of sources. For example, the learner could present some Kneehigh Theatre Company quotes found on websites, links to YouTube clips, DVDs found on Amazon and media reviews of Kneehigh's work. The research should focus on the theme of identity.

7. Research

Answers should include specific examples from some or all of the following sources:
- primary research – performing a survey, watching a live performance or conducting an interview
- secondary research – information relating to contextual factors, creative intentions and performance styles. This can be achieved by carrying out an internet search, looking in books, journals and theatre scores, visiting archives, looking at recorded/digital sources, reviewing case studies or reading key theories.

8. Different formats

1 Founded in 1926 by Martha Graham · Initially only women in the company · **Martha Graham Dance Company** · Still performing Graham's work today · Performed in more than 50 countries · Nurtured many of the leading choreographers of the 20th century

3 Learner's own response, for example:
From the research that I undertook, I discovered that Graham's company is still successful and performs not only Graham's work but also performs newly commissioned work by choreographers who were inspired by Graham's legacy. The repertory of original work includes `Lamentation' and `Appalachian Spring.' At first she just had women in her company but then men joined at a later point. Some of the dancers/choreographers the company nurtured were Merce Cunningham, Paul Taylor and Erick Hawkins.

9. Collating information

Arms 1, 5 and 6 on the spider diagram are of the least relevance, as they do not directly relate to Graham as a practitioner. Arms 2, 3, 4 and 7 are useful.

10. Sources, formats and collating details

Learner's own response. Answers could include reference to how the performance related to the theme of identity, whether it was typical/atypical of their work, whether it linked to other factors (historical, cultural, economic, political, technical social, geographical, physical), whether it was relevant in terms of influences, themes, collaborations, responses, creative intentions, target audience or genre.

11. Documenting research sources

Answers should display comprehensive and accurate referencing.

12. Footnotes and your bibliography

Answers should display effective referencing using the guidance provided.

13. Historical and cultural factors

Answers should relate to cultural and historical factors, providing specific information including examples of works and/or quotations. For example, Oscar Hammerstein II's *Carmen Jones* deals with racial identity and war, both cultural and historical factors. The work is set in the Second World War at a time when segregation and civil rights were major political issues. The leading role of Carmen Jones was played by Dorothy Dandridge, who was the first ever African American actress to receive an Oscar nomination.

14. Economic and political factors

Answers should include reference to economic and political factors, providing specific information including examples of works and/or quotations. For example, some of Martha Graham's works have been viewed as political. Deep Song is a response to the Spanish Civil War; a solo piece where she expressed man's inhumanity to man. Immediate Tragedy was also choreographed in response to the Spanish Civil War and fascism, in recognition of Spanish women fighting along with the men.

15. Technical and social factors

Answers should include reference to technical and social factors, providing specific information including examples of works and/ or quotations. For example, Martha Graham collaborated with set and costume designers such as sculptor Isamu Noguchi and fashion designer Calvin Klein. These are both technical and social factors. Graham's works were consistently well costumed. Particularly innovative was the shroud worn in Lamentation. In terms of set, Noguchi and Graham collaborated for years, with Noguchi creating sets with a purpose; however sparse, they always enhanced the intention of the piece.
In relation to technical advancements, answers could include suggestions about technical elements distracting from the main intention(s) of a work, or monopolising a performance.

16. Geographical and physical factors

Answers should include reference to geographical and physical factors, providing specific information including examples of works and/or quotations. For example, Kneehigh Theatre Company are very much influenced by their Cornish locality; they draw inspiration from the culture, people, landscape and history of Cornwall, inspiring people to visit Cornwall and see it for themselves. 'Tristan and Yseult,' which is one of their most popular productions, is based on a Cornish legend. Kneehigh also recognise that Cornwall has a history of international trade and cultural exchange, which is reflected in their innovative approach to theatre which has global appeal and recognition.

17. Other influences

Answers should include reference to the influence of other practitioners and performers and the influences from education, teachers and mentors. For example, Martha Graham was influenced by the work of Denishawn. In 1911, Graham saw Ruth St. Denis perform in Los Angeles. This inspired her to enrol at an arts college and, subsequently, the Denishawn School. The Denishawn School was founded by Ruth St. Denis and her husband, Ted Shawn. It taught American and world dance techniques. Graham studied and instructed there for eight years. Previously, as a child, Graham was inspired by her father who was a doctor with a specialism in nervous disorders. Her father believed that the body could express its inner senses, which Graham found fascinating, going on to create a dance technique that clearly expressed human emotion.

18. Themes

Answers should include reference to war, morality or romance. For example, many of Oscar Hammerstein II's works include romance/love as a theme, including *Show Boat*, *Carmen Jones* and *South Pacific*. In *Show Boat* there is a theme of tragic, enduring love. In *Carmen Jones*, the theme of love again has a tragic ending, with the protagonist strangled by her former sweetheart. In *South Pacific* the theme of love centres around an American nurse who falls in love with an expatriate French plantation owner and struggles to accept his mixed-race children. Hammerstein II's themes of love are often interwoven with racial themes.

19. Intentions, genre and target audiences

Answers could include examples such as Martha Graham's creative ideas and intentions in relation to social factors (the fact that she was influenced by her father who was a physician for nervous disorders, and how this affected her focus on the realism of movement – 'movement never lies').

20. Influences on others, collaborations and responses

Martha Graham created a new language of movement (and more than 180 dance works) transforming dance and heavily influencing dance as an art form in a reaction to the limitations of ballet. Her influence has been compared to that of Picasso for his influence on art. She rejected structured techniques in favour of movements which conveyed the expression of inner feelings, which was pioneering at the time. It was so different to most styles of dance at the time, which were lyrical and fluid, and some struggled with this. Others thought that Graham was too obscure and took herself too seriously. Many, however, applauded her originality and form of expression, which was able to communicate themes such as female identity and human emotion with dramatic effect. She continued to use her angular technique and was not affected by the negative criticism she received.

21. Collaborations

Answers should include reference to factors on pages 13–20, and be in a condensed format. This will mean recording the key points only, by using bullet points for example. Each point can then be expanded on to create paragraphs.

22. Critical analysis: getting started

Answers should show analysis – explanation, examination, discussion and your personal opinion – rather than just description. Answers should also include reference to a work. Here is an example of an analysis to compare with an example of description.

Description: Factors relating to collaboration link to Martha Graham and *Appalachian Spring*, as Graham collaborates with Aaron Copland (music) and Isamu Noguchi (set). Geographical/ physical factors link to the theme of *Appalachian Spring* in relation to Martha Graham as an American citizen; it is about a celebration of the American pioneers of the 19th century. Analysis: Martha Graham's work has been influenced by many factors, for example collaborations with other practitioners and geographical/physical factors. This is exemplified in the work *Appalachian Spring* in which Graham collaborates with Aaron Copland to produce the music and Isamu Noguchi to create the set. Graham successfully collaborated with Copland and Noguchi, who helped her to express the theme of American identity through movement as well as production elements. However, the piece also holds universal meaning, conveying optimism and hope.

23. Critical analysis: the next stage

Answers will need to include reasons as to why the information selected has been prioritised. Consideration of its strengths and weaknesses, why it is significant and a personal viewpoint will need to be presented.

24. Making condensed notes

Answers will need to demonstrate the learner has condensed their research.

25. Critical analysis skills

Answers should include critical analysis of identity in connection with Martha Graham or Oscar Hammerstein II. For example, for Oscar Hammerstein II, answers could include a discussion of racial identity and human/social identity. Here is an example: Oscar Hammerstein II's work includes themes of racial identity, often interwoven with love themes, for example in *Carmen Jones* and *South Pacific*. He also considers human/social identity in his works, promoting human understanding by tackling issues such as racism and cultural differences. He believed in celebrating differences and even created a musical revue aimed at schools, addressing prejudice, tolerance and self-esteem. Certain songs can be directly linked to his handling of identity, such as 'You've Got To Be Carefully Taught' from *Show Boat*. His philosophy can be summed up in the words from 'Pipe Dream': 'It takes all kinds of people to make up a world.'

26. Further critical analysis skills

Answers should develop or challenge the arguments(s). All decisions should be backed up effectively and include effective acknowledgement of sources. Here is an example: Oscar Hammerstein II was clearly influenced by his family, as he 'was born into a great theatrical family on July 12, 1895, in New York City' (http://www.notablebiographies.com/Gi-He/ Hammerstein-Oscar.html, para 1, last accessed 21 June, 2016). He was named after both his famous grandfathers, one of whom was a famous anti-slavery newspaper publisher (which could have had an influence on his views on race). The other grandfather was an opera promoter, which again could have influenced his interest in music and the theatre. His father was the manager of Victoria, one of the most famous vaudeville theatres of its time. His uncle was a well-known producer. In the end, all family members would be overshadowed by Oscar Hammerstein II himself.

27. Performance styles: repertoire

For example:

Text: integrated text from historical American documents to help communicate meaning, although this is not typical of her work.

Choreography: uses choreography to communicate intentions. Main method of communication for Graham. Her technique is used in the choreography to express meaning.

Martha Graham

Score: this is integral to Graham's work. Music often used to support the mood and emotional content as well as to make her works more dramatic. She often commissioned music especially rather than use already existing music.

Style: focused on basic human movement, concentrating on contraction and release. She used sharp and jagged movements rather than long and fluid ones.

Genre: contemporary dance. It is significant because Martha Graham is one of the pioneers of the genre, having created her own technique.

Content: she wanted to reveal inner expression through the creation of her own technique. She also wanted to communicate themes relating to identity and heritage.

28. Performance styles: the performance

For example:

Dynamics: Graham's technique has been described as 'dynamic'; she often includes sharp and angular movements which were a reaction to the softness and fluidity of classical ballet technique.

Pace: more directly relates to acting, so not of great relevance to Graham.

Spatial awareness: important in all her works, whether awareness of the stage space or of other performers onstage, as well as her dancers utilising the space expressively.

Movement: Graham created her own technique. She believed that movement comes from three places; the action of contraction and release, the pelvis and the emotional inner self. She introduced cupped hands and flexed feet which gave an angular effect, as well as spirals and use of breath.

Martha Graham

Character: Graham focused on human emotion in relation to character; for example in 'Xochitl' she played the part of an Aztec maiden and 'Frontier' is a performance about the pioneer woman.

Gesture: significant as she used gesture and movement to convey emotion, often using blunt and powerful gestures.

Voice: not generally significant in Graham's work.

Timing: links to dynamics, so also significant. There is a rhythmic energy to her movements. She provides the composer with timings when commissioning a piece, so that the music fits to the movement rather than vice versa.

Musicality: significant. Graham worked with composers Louis Horst and Aaron Copland. Horst taught Graham about musical form and encouraged her to work with contemporary composers. She believed that the music was secondary to the dance, that it should support the emotional content.

29. Performance styles: relationships

For example:

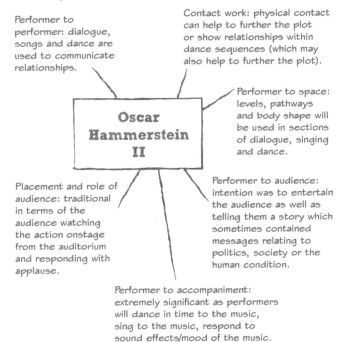

Performer to performer: dialogue, songs and dance are used to communicate relationships.

Contact work: physical contact can help to further the plot or show relationships within dance sequences (which may also help to further the plot).

Oscar Hammerstein II

Performer to space: levels, pathways and body shape will be used in sections of dialogue, singing and dance.

Placement and role of audience: traditional in terms of the audience watching the action onstage from the auditorium and responding with applause.

Performer to audience: intention was to entertain the audience as well as telling them a story which sometimes contained messages relating to politics, society or the human condition.

Performer to accompaniment: extremely significant as performers will dance in time to the music, sing to the music, respond to sound effects/mood of the music.

30. Performance styles: production

Martha Graham used set to help create meaning, such as in *Appalachian Spring* where she uses the rocking chair and bench designed by Isamu Noguchi to support the mood and suggest the environment. Probably her most famous use of costume is *Lamentation*, where Graham uses a long tube of material to show various feelings such as the ability to stretch inside your own skin. Graham did use make-up, although in later years she rejected ornateness and her dancers were devoid of make-up. Lighting and sound are significant to Graham's work in that they support the dance. For example, in *Lamentation* the repetitive nature of the music builds tension and echoes the repetition of movement motifs. The pale blue lighting detaches Graham from the rest of the stage, as well as revealing the dancing figure. Puppetry is not evident in Graham's work, although apparently she was inspired by a puppet show in her hotel drawing room, which gave her a deeper understanding of theatre.

31. Investigating performance styles

Answers should include concise notes that relate clearly to the four elements of repertoire, performance, relationships and production.

32. Summarising key information

Learner's own response. Answers could include suggestions for improvement such as notes being more concise, clear, relevant, neatly presented, logical, easier to navigate. Reasons for supplying additional material could relate to gaps in information, to have more equal coverage of assessment topics, or in order to provide more comprehensive answers.

33. Comparisons, conclusions and further research

Learners could acknowledge links between Graham and Kneehigh Theatre Company in terms of the visual imagery which is used in the repertoire of both practitioners. For example, in Graham's 'Lamentation' the use of the tube-like shroud has a strong visual impact on the audience, and in Kneehigh's 'Tristan and Yseult' the image of the couple suspended in mid-air is striking. In the work of both practitioners, production elements are significant such as costume, set and props which help to convey their intentions. Learners may comment on the fact that both practitioners aim to tell stories which relate to humanity.

Also they are both renowned for their collaborations with others. For example, Graham famously collaborated with the composer Aaron Copland and set designer Isamu Noguchi. Kneehigh have collaborated with many practitioners such as the conductor Charles Hazlewood in their production of 'Noye's Fludde' (Noah's Flood) which has been described as a community opera.

34. Communicating your key points

Answers should include evidence of conclusions, with information summarised effectively. Skills could include providing different viewpoints with specific examples, using quotations and referencing them effectively, using a range of sources when researching, analysing, drawing conclusions and use of discussion.

35. Presentation of findings

Answers should include consideration of format/structure, tone, language and use of subject-specific terminology. Learners could consider how these aspects could be improved.

36. Presenting judgements

'Oscar Clendenning Hammerstein II (1895–1960) was perhaps the most influential lyricist and librettist of the American theater.'
(http://www.pbs.org/wnet/broadway/stars/oscar-hammerstein-ii/, para 1, last accessed 21 June 2016)
Plan:
- clear introduction stating what the starting point for analysis is
- presentation of the argument that Oscar Hammerstein II was perhaps the most influential lyricist and librettist of the American theatre, using quotations and examples from different sources to back up this theory
- discussion of the meaning of the statement
- analysis of contrasting viewpoints
- presentation of own opinions with justifications
- discussion of the validity of the evidence
- drawing of conclusions to summarise the argument

37. Analysis and presentation

The introduction should be clear, concise and effective, detailing what the intentions of the investigation are and the theme to which it relates, the different elements of the investigation and an outline of the conclusion that will be reached.

Unit 3 Group Performance Workshop

These answers are in no way prescriptive and should be used for guidance only.

41. Types of stimulus

- Ethical themes such as euthanasia, abortion, the death penalty
- Historical themes such as the emancipation of women, war, the Industrial Revolution
- Social themes such as poverty, crime, health
- Cultural themes such as celebrations, spirituality/religions, traditions

42. Theme as stimulus

Here is an example:
The Industrial Revolution
A period in time – 18th and 19th centuries – when rural societies in Europe and America became industrial and urban.
(http://www.history.com/topics/industrial-revolution, para 1, 23 March 2016)
Scientific advances and technological innovations brought growth in agricultural and industrial production.
(http://www.britishmuseum.org/research/publications/online_research_catalogues/paper_money/paper_money_of_england__wales/the_industrial_revolution.aspx, para 1, 23 March 2016)
Key words: urban, agriculture, industrial, scientific, growth.

As the basis for an improvisation, you may wish to create an action, word or lyric for each word. You could then expand on the motif by adding transitions to create phrases, sections of dialogue or songs.

43. Visual stimulus

Ten example words: lines, fly, open, closed, wings, swoop, curves, wide, sky, stark.
Five starting points for devising material, any five of the following: lines, swoop, curves, open, closed, stark.

44. Text stimulus

Answers could include notes about mirroring and the use of facial expression and physicality to show emotion.

45. Aural stimulus

Learners need to consider elements such as the speed, dynamics and rhythmical pattern they are creating. To develop the motif into a soundscape, learners could think of ways to extend the motif through repetition and variation. The motif could be recorded using instruments or sound equipment.

46. Media as stimulus

For example:

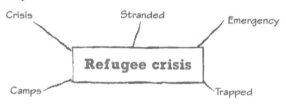

The above words could be translated into performance through improvisation for example, or by using the words as a basis for dialogue, narrative or lyrics.

47. Responding to stimulus

Learners should try to use a full range of movement and vocals, experimenting with different ways of using their bodies and voices.
Key-word notes could look like this:
- flight – swoop, pounce, weightless, soar
- open – free, stretch, lines, expand
- closed – protect, prepare, curves, introverted
- motion – fast, slow, direct, meander.

48. Analyse your stimulus

Learners should consider the texture, weight and colour of the piece of clothing. They should think about where they can put it and what unusual things they can do with it. For example, using it for another purpose such as for a shield, blanket, straitjacket or raft.

49. What, for whom and how?

For example:
Acting – trying to convey equality; this could be achieved through movement and dialogue; will be performing to a selected audience; the theme will be communicated through physical theatre.
Dance – trying to convey inequality; this could be achieved through movement and dance; will be performing to a selected audience; the theme will be communicated through contemporary dance (Graham technique).
Musical theatre – trying to convey change; this could be achieved through songs, dance and dialogue; will be performing to a selected audience; the theme will be communicated through Bollywood musical theatre style.

50. Where and who?

Learners should consider specific ways to improve. For example, alignment could be improved by correcting oneself in front of a mirror and repetition of movements. Diction could be improved by repetition of tongue twisters and lip trills to help relax your lips. Pitch could be improved by recording yourself and listening back to it, and practising intervals to develop muscle memory.

51. Primary research

Sample questions for dance, acting and musical theatre:
- Is this work typical of your repertoire? This could help with establishing what is typical of the practitioner's repertoire.
- What are the main features of your work? Provides valuable information about characteristics.
- Do you read reviews of your work? This relates to whether the practitioner applies feedback from audience/critics.
- How has your work progressed/changed? This relates to whether the practitioner's work evolves over a period of time, perhaps taking on technological advances, for example.
- Are you influenced by other practitioners? Provides insight regarding the creative process and how other practitioners could have informed their work.
- How do you create your material? Valuable in relation to the creative process and how material is generated; information could be applied to learner's work.
- How do you select performers? This may provide information about the particular skills required of performers which are specific to the company and practitioner.
- What genre do you consider your work to fit in? Perhaps the practitioner's work does not easily fit into a genre or overlaps into several genres. This could relate to how different people may perceive their work.

52. Secondary research

Learners should research the newspaper article, keeping a record of the websites they use, and trim the information to include key points.

For example, using the internet search 'humanitarian crisis in Greece, March 2016' the following information was found:

1 'In an excoriating indictment of official efforts to handle the emergency, Human Rights Watch said a humanitarian crisis was unfolding in the Athens port of Piraeus that needed to be addressed urgently. "Thousands of asylum seekers and migrants … face appalling conditions as the crisis for people trapped in Greece due to border closures intensifies", a report released by the group said on Thursday.' (https://www.theguardian.com/world/2016/mar/24/aid-agencies-greece-warn-growing-humanitarian-crisis)

2 'UNHCR is warning today that Europe is on the cusp of a humanitarian crisis. This is in light of a rapid build-up of people in an already struggling Greece, with governments not working together despite having already reached agreements in a number of areas, and country after country imposing new border restrictions. Inconsistent practices are causing unnecessary suffering and risk being at variance with EU and international law standards.' (http://www.unhcr.org/cgi-bin/texis/vtx/search?page=search&skip=45&docid=56d564ed6&query=Mediterranean)

3 'As of last night (Monday), the number of refugees and migrants in Greece and needing accommodation had soared to 24,000. Around 8,500 of these were at Eidomeni, near the border with the former Yugoslav Republic of Macedonia. At least 1,500 had spent the previous night in the open. The crowded conditions are leading to shortages of food, shelter, water and sanitation. Tensions have been building, fuelling violence and playing into the hands of people smugglers.' (http://www.unhcr.org/news/briefing/2016/3/56d564ed6/unhcr-warns-imminent-humanitarian-crisis-greece-amid-disarray-europe-asylum.html)

53. Research and analysis

For example:
Notes on 'Eastern Jam' by Chase and Status:
- Dubstep song on a Drum n Bass album
- contains sample of 'Silsila Ye Chaahat Ka', performed by Shreya Ghoshal and written by Nusrat Badr
- 'Silsila Ye Chaahat Ka' is a song from the Bollywood film *Devdas*.
- *Devdas* is a film about a man whose life spirals out of control after he is forbidden from marrying the woman he loves.

Sources:
https://www.discogs.com/Chase-Status-Pieces-Eastern-Jam/release/1460353
http://www.whosampled.com/Chase-%26-Status/
Find out more about *Devdas* on IMDb:
http://www.imdb.com/title/tt0238936/?ref_=fn_al_tt_1

54. Discussion skills

Here are some examples:
Brainstorm:

Organised brainstorm:

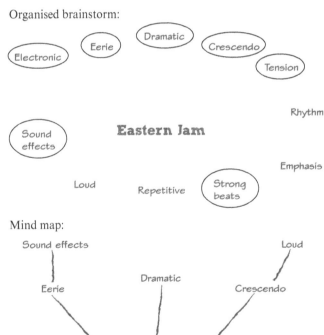

Mind map:

55. Improvisation

Learners will need to consider which movements and/or vocals relate to the stimulus most effectively.

56. Let's experiment!

1 Learners should consider how physical and vocal skills can communicate the stimulus of the Chaplin quote in a variety of ways, through experimentation. Key words: happy, sad, cry, laugh, mirror, look, reflection.
2 Digital Log Entry: 'I explored the stimulus of Chaplin's quote initially by focusing on the words 'happy' and 'sad' and the posture and facial expressions that correspond with those emotions. I then experimented with contrasting postures relating to happiness with facial expressions relating to sadness, and how messages were then confused as the body and face were not consistent. I then explored sound in relation to the words 'laugh' and 'cry', playing around with timing and rhythm, for example by slowing down or speeding up different types of laughing and crying sounds (sobbing, shrieking, giggling, whimpering).

57. Let's get technical!

Answers should include five production elements and/or performance techniques relating to their chosen pathway, that will have a positive impact on their performance piece. Answers should include reference to specific exercises and tasks that will need to be completed in order for them to have their full impact on the performance.

58. Thinking about structure

Definitions: Structures
- binary – two contrasting but related sections (AB).
- ternary – three sections (ABA). The second section contrasts with the first. The third section is a restatement of the first section in a related format.
- rondo – three or more themes, always returning to the main theme (ABACADA)
- narrative – follows a story line
- theme and variation – dance phrase/section is followed by phrases or sections that are variations of the original (A, A1, A2, A3).
- abstract – pure dance movement containing no plot
- chance – selected isolated movements are assigned sequence by random methods such as tossing a coin

Definitions: Devices
- motif development – a movement, gesture or short phrase which has the potential to be developed in the dance work.
- stillness – use of pause
- canon – the same movement/phrase is performed by individuals/groups beginning at different times
- unison – two or more people performing the same movement at the same time
- contrast – differences such as high/low, big/little
- climax – what something builds up to in a performance (could be a grand finale)
- highlights – parts of a performance that really stand out
- dynamic variation – differences in dynamics such as fast and slow, heavy and light
- symmetry – a balanced, even design (like a mirror's reflection)
- asymmetry – unbalanced proportion (unlike a mirror's reflection)
- retrograde – movement/phrase is performed backwards.
- inversion – inside out/upside down (for example a forward step would become a backwards step)
- instrumentation – when a movement/motif is performed with a different body part

Learners will need to provide research in response to the above terms, as well as examples of when they may have used them previously.

59. Developing physical performance skills

Answers should include the physical skills listed on page 59. Examples should be provided about why these skills were important to the role. For example, spatial awareness would be an important consideration for an ensemble piece because there would potentially be a large number of people on stage at the same time. Consideration of space would be essential so that performers do not bump into each other or have accidents. Answers should include specific ways to improve.

60. Developing vocal performance skills

For example, you could choose range, application of breathing techniques, modulation, inflection and resonation. And your brainstorm could include answers like this:
Modulation: Adjusting the voice, such as changing key or to a different quality such as whispering. Breathing through the diaphragm and warming up properly are key to this.
http://topsinginglessons.blogspot.co.uk/2011/03/5-tips-to-modulate-your-voice-and-sing.html

61. Developing musical performance skills

Answers will need to include consideration of music skills whichever pathway is selected. For example, for learners following the dance pathway, music skills such as rhythm and timing will be important in keeping in time with the beat and following cues, as well as being expressive through effective response to the music. Answers should also include specific ways to improve.

62. Developing communication skills

For example: 'I used expression in a previous acting performance, in order to portray my character which was intimidating and threatening. I used my face, posture and dynamics to demonstrate my characterisation effectively, which communicated my personality effectively to the audience.'

63. Develop, shape, create!

When thinking about whether or not learners did improve in response to feedback, they should consider if improvements have been made and how improvements were made.

64. Developing early stage ideas

Learner's own response. Entries should demonstrate how visual evidence can enhance the digital process log, such as providing variety; providing a broader perspective; capturing performance effectively and evidencing the creative process more effectively; providing insight into creative ideas and how the piece evolved.

65. Developing more early stage ideas

The answers should contain information on the performance skills involved and specific guidance on how to improve. For example, in order to develop vocal projection in performance the learner may write about how to control the volume and capacity of the voice, or physical projection in terms of communicating energy and expression through the face and body. Ways to improve may include breathing and vocal exercises (vocal) or practising facial expression and eye-line in front of mirrors/peers (physical).

66. Personal management skills

For the rehearsal checklist, learners could include any of the following: appropriate clothing, water/fluids, any relevant notes/notebook, recording equipment, bobble to tie up hair if necessary, script, score, notation, music.

67. Rehearsal skills

Answers should include some of the techniques listed on pages 59–62, and perhaps others not listed.

68. Teamwork and collaboration

Blindfold exercise:
- Get into pairs.
- One person from each wears a blindfold.
- The sighted partner guides the blindfolded partner across the room using vocal guidance.
- This can be made more difficult by putting obstacles in the space.

The main skills needed are trust and listening skills. The most difficult skill to master is trust, as the blindfolded person is completely reliant on the sighted person in order to keep them away from danger.

69. Developing mid-stage ideas

Answers should make reference to personal management, teamwork and collaborative skills, making the learner's personal contribution clear.

70. Continuing to progress

Learner's own response. Tasks could include specific exercises carried out such as regular stretching to improve flexibility which impacts positively on technical performance, tasks/activities such as refining material, a script/score for performance which helps to communicate meaning more clearly.

71. Performance preparation

Learner's own response. The checklist could include what needs to be packed for the performance, such as costumes, music and props. It may also include information about rehearsal times and specific performance skills that need to be honed or particular sections that need to be practised.

72. Process review

Learner's own response. Answers could include the following information:
- It is important to evaluate interpretation of stimulus and ideas during the process, so that effectiveness can be measured. Are you achieving what you set out to achieve? Learning from weaknesses during the process will help to improve working methods.
- It is valuable to evaluate use of exploratory techniques, as a lack of improvisation or thinking 'outside the box' could lead to less-imaginative ideas and less-exciting material for performance.
- Evaluating your personal development and your own contribution during the process is crucial in order to see where you exercised effective teamwork skills and contributed ideas, as well as seeing where you could improve your contribution.
- Your performance skills will have been employed throughout, as well as your creativity in developing and shaping work. It is useful to consider how well you employed particular performance skills leading up to the performance itself so you can improve them.

73. Process strengths and developments

Learner's own response. For example, when discussing contribution of ideas, the learner could point out that they contributed some effective ideas such as the transition sections but could have improved by making a more consistent contribution throughout the process.

74. Performance review

Learner's own response. Answers could include the following information:
- It is important to evaluate the effectiveness of the performance in realising creative intention so that you can work out whether you achieved what you set out to do. What you learn from this evaluation will help to inform future performance work.
- Evaluation of performance skills in realising the creative intention is vital, as the performance is the ultimate goal. Did nerves affect the success? Were you better in rehearsal? Why? What can you do about it in future?

- It is valuable to consider what changes you would make if the production were to be on a larger scale, to see beyond the task and think about the piece on a professional stage. It may be that not much content would change, but you would make more of the production elements.
- Consideration of your performance skills in terms of a larger-scale production is also important, as it will enable you to measure the success of your skills and see what adaptations or improvements would be required if performed in a professional context.

75. Performance strengths and developments

Learner's own response. For example:
Attitude and commitment during performance: I was committed to the piece except during the end section where I felt tired and lost momentum. I could have improved by being totally focused during the whole performance, as well as increasing my stamina leading up to performance.

76. Reviewing the process

Learner's own response. Ways to improve could include examples such as: improve flexibility in second position by doing regular stretching exercises, such as sitting on the floor with legs in second position, opposite a partner and using each other's weight to increase the stretch by gently pulling each other forwards by the wrists.

77. Reviewing the performance

Learner's own response. This could include points such as:
- improving on performance skills through specific tasks/exercises
- further consideration of production elements by, for example, linking them to the stimulus more effectively
- more effective use of time so there was more time to explore ideas and develop material
- use of different forms and structures/devices to communicate the intention(s) more clearly.

Unit 5 Individual Performance Commission

These answers are in no way prescriptive and should be used for guidance only.

81. Understanding commission briefs

Objectives of the commission – to celebrate, to entertain, to make performing arts more accessible to local residents, to promote performing arts, to combine sport and performing arts, to celebrate sport and the community, to mark the Olympic Games.
Type of commissioning body – local authority commission aimed at the general public, all ages, all genders, solo performances in a choice of performance styles, five to eight minutes long.
Links to previous or planned future projects – the local authority wants to put on a broader programme of events than previously; it wants to expand its performing arts provision.

82. Commissioning bodies (1)

Answers will need to refer to the 'Our Projects' page on Arts Council England's website and reference sources effectively. For example:
The 'Right Up Our Street' project in Doncaster meets the needs of the community by offering community projects that are relevant (consultation helps enable projects to match the needs of target groups). Also, putting on large-scale theatre productions will enable a wider audience to access performance opportunities.

83. Commissioning bodies (2)

Answers will need to identify the aims of a performance commissioned by a local authority or a commercial company and reference sources effectively. Answers should include details regarding successes and weaknesses of commissions, as well as consideration of performance disciplines. For example, are the commission objectives clear? Does the commission meet the needs of the target audience? Does it take into account the requirements and constraints of the local authority or commercial company that commissioned it?

84. Commissioning bodies (3)

For example, a tourist board could commission:

1 a dance performance on a local beach to advertise the beach area before the season starts and to promote performing arts and/or raise the profile of the performers
2 a musical theatre performance in a local shopping centre to attract more customers and to promote the area to tourists, as well as promoting the performing arts and/or raising the profile of the performers
3 a series of monologues based on areas of local interest, performed at a tourist spot, aimed at educating and creating interest, as well as promoting performing arts and/or raising the profile of the performers
4 multiple performances across all disciplines at a local festival to boost the event/area as well as promote performing arts and/or raise the profile of the performers
5 a 'parks performance tour' where performances across all disciplines are toured to promote local parks that may appeal to tourists, as well as promote performing arts and/or raise the profile of the performers.

85. The purpose of a commission

Answers could include:

Entertain: encourage audience participation, include songs/dialogue conveying a lack of unity which is then resolved within the performance (this will create tension and excitement). Using musical theatre you could invite the audience to join in with songs or use popular musical theatre songs with lyrics that relate to unity. Dance and acting are a popular and can provide variety and interest.

Educate: consideration of key points relating to unity that you are trying to educate the audience about; short bursts of information to keep the audience's attention; also needs to be entertaining. Using musical theatre, songs, text and dance can be used to help educate, as they can be altered to include snippets of information. Songs can also be written solely for this purpose. Using dance, information can be communicated non-verbally through a narrative structure. Using acting, information can be communicated through text or dialogue.

Inform: consideration of key points relating to unity that you are trying to inform the audience about; short bursts of information to impart the relevant facts; also needs to be entertaining. Using musical theatre, songs, text and dance can be combined to inform. Powerful messages can be communicated through the medium of dance. Text and dialogue can be used by actors to inform.

Celebrate: being sensitive to the type of celebration, for example if it is cultural or spiritual; being knowledgeable about the type of celebration. Using musical theatre, a variety of relevant songs, texts and dances can be included that communicate unity and relate to the celebration. Dance can include relevant movement that communicates unity and relates to the celebration. Through acting, relevant text and dialogue that communicates unity and relates to the celebration can be used.

Commemorate: sensitivity to the subject; having background knowledge about the focus of the commemoration (for example person, event or war); performing the necessary research to make informed decisions about performance material that is relevant. Musical theatre can combine songs, text and dance to provide a more varied commemoration. Dance can show sensitivity to the subject through movement and carefully crafted choreography. Acting can communicate detail relating to the person, event/war through text and/or dialogue.

Raise awareness of an issue/topic: consideration of how best to communicate the main objective(s); interesting and original methods of conveying intention(s); ensuring that the message is clear and current. Musical theatre can combine text, songs and dance to create a varied approach to a topic. Dance can offer an alternative way of communicating about a topics through the medium of movement, including gesture to put across meaning. Using acting, information relating to the topic can be communicated through text and/or dialogue.

Target audience will need to be a consideration for all commissions.

86. Considering commissioning bodies and their purpose

Answers could include notes relating to the different aspects of the aural stimulus that the learner may focus on when creating material, such as: lyrics; musical arrangement; the fact that the microphone is moved further and further away from David Bowie when he is singing (so at the end he is almost shouting); connotations of the song (heroes) even though that is not the original meaning (it tells the story of two lovers, one from East and one from West Berlin); the dynamics of the song. Notes could include reference to performing research, exploring the stimulus through creative tasks, links between the stimulus and commission brief, structure, styles, forms and techniques, in relation to the creation of material. In terms of linking material to the commission brief, learners should consider the fact that the performance should be accessible (and make performing arts more accessible) as well as being sensitive to the locality (the community) and target audience (all ages and genders). In terms of the purpose of the commission, notes should include reference to the fact that the objective is celebration, with material created to meet this requirement.

87. Target audiences

1 general public
2 all ages
3 mixed gender

Considerations would need to take place such as appealing to a wide target audience; embracing all ages; making material appealing to young/older people by the type of language, songs, dance styles, costumes and music; current and previous trends included to show relevancy. Past local events could be referred to, which would appeal to older people. Accessibility will be a key objective – creating material that is not too complex or highbrow.

88. Connecting the work to the audience

Age appropriateness – language will need to be appropriate as the target audience is so wide; performance styles will need to take into account all ages; music will also need to be diverse, and costumes must not offend!

Being aware of potential social and cultural issues – although the main focus is sport which tends to embrace all of society, there may need to be additional considerations such as appropriateness of costumes and language.

89. Considering the target audience and context

Material could be generated by the text stimulus in many ways. The actual words from the text could be used within a performance; to form lyrics; as the basis of improvisation to create movement/dance; as the starting point for creating material related to the quote such as a mime, piece of physical theatre, monologue (for example from the perspective of a sports personality or someone who finds it difficult to access sport). Key words could be selected, for example: power, inspire, unite, hope, despair, language, barriers that could form the basis of a performance.

Answers could include reference to the target audience in terms of different ways and various types of sport that appeal to a wide audience; and use of sport-related language/terminology. Discussion of context could relate to the Olympic Games and their significance in making sport more accessible, bringing communities together with a sole aim. In this instance, previous or future projects do not have much impact.

90. Requirements and constraints

Working to timescales and deadlines: when you are working on an individual performance you are your own boss, which can makes things more tricky. Don't leave everything until the last minute; set alarms, make schedules, set yourself realistic goals.

91. Assessing requirements and constraints

Requirements and constraints – Banksy's *There's always hope* links well to the theme of sport and the community, as it could be seen as suggesting that sport provides hope for people. It ties in with the themes of unity and celebration surrounding a sporting event. The figure of the girl provides a link to children/young people, and the balloon could be used as a prop/stimulus for material. Constraints may include available resources and/or language/music/performance style choices, due to the wide target audience.

92. Generating ideas for performance

Creativity and imagination – take the lyrics, musical arrangement, dynamics, meaning or connotations of the piece as the basis for improvisation and creation of material.
Performance skills – consider strongest individual performance skills to showcase.
Production values – consider the availability of resources and whether production elements will add anything to the performance.

93. Working from a thematic stimulus

All answers will need to include acknowledgement of sources.

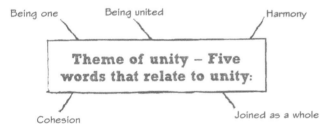

Learners should provide an analysis of each word/phrase, as well as how they can be communicated. For example, for 'Harmony': relates to music in terms of pleasant sounds but also means to be in perfect accord with someone or something. Would be communicated well through musical theatre using different harmonies in songs to echo the meaning.

94. Working from a visual stimulus

Answers should include examples of different ways of using visual stimuli as well as the challenges faced by visual stimuli. For example, bringing a two-dimensional piece of art to life (photo, painting, image); recreating an artefact as a prop (such as a mask to be used within the performance); exploring the dimensions of a sculpture; exploring abstract art in terms of lines, curves, shapes, patterns; basing material on the appearance/movement of people/animals which feature in the artwork. Challenges could include available resources and expertise in terms of recreating an artefact as a prop; the end product could be simplified or an alternative solution provided, such as using face paint instead of a mask. Exploration of the dimensions of a sculpture could be difficult practically if only an image of the sculpture is available. Accessible sculptures/structures could be explored in order to gain familiarity with moving across different dimensions and recording the results.

95. Working from a textual stimulus

Key words within the text could be used as the basis for creating material, for example incorporating some of the words into a monologue/lyrics or using them as a foundation for a monologue/lyrics for the acting pathway. In terms of movement/dance, key words could form the basis for motifs that are developed. For musical theatre, a combination of the above could be included, as well as using an established melody, but altering the lyrics to incorporate key words/phrases, or writing new songs to communicate the text.
The text generates powerful, inspirational connections with sport that could be communicated through a combination of creative thinking, performance skills and production elements.

96. Working from a media stimulus

For example:

97. Working from an aural stimulus

Answers should include examples of how music and sound were used. For example live music, recorded music, sound effects. They could be effective in terms of creating an atmosphere; helping to convey character/theme; suggesting a period in time or location; providing a rhythm to move/dance to; enhancing a mood.

98. Primary and secondary research

Websites should be referenced and information trimmed to retain key points only. Turn your notes into key points by sifting out information that is less relevant and keeping the most significant pieces of information only.

99. Justifying ideas

Answers should include justifications to back up ideas. For example:
I decided to use gestures to mirror the stance of the girl in the image, who is reaching up to the balloon. I incorporated reaching gestures throughout my performance, particularly directing them upwards. I also used an upwards focus at points to reflect the visual image and show a feeling of hope and aspiration.

100. Planning your written proposal

The paragraph should include reference to the items in the spider diagram and post-it notes. For example:
I have chosen to use the text stimulus in connection with the commission brief. Firstly I read and re-read the text, selecting key words which were the most meaningful to me as well as their potential to translate into performance material. I selected the words 'power,' 'change,' 'despair' and 'barriers.' My aim was to simultaneously encourage the target audience to celebrate sport and recognise its potential, in addition to highlighting the difficulties that sport can help people to overcome. I wanted to communicate the hope but also the struggle. In order to achieve this I conducted secondary research relating to the text as well as primary research, asking friends, peers and family what the quotation meant to them. I also showed them the four selected words and requested that they provide thoughts relating to each word. I collated my findings and used the research when developing material for my performance. For example, I discovered that many people found sport 'life-changing' and so I considered how to communicate that through my chosen discipline of acting. I decided to develop a series of monologues that relate to people of

different ages across the world, where sport had changed their lives. I added interest by using physicality as a means of expression, so that I was not solely reliant on the words. For example I used gesture and mime to enhance my performance.

101. Practical exploration of stimulus

The list of words could include: exercise; health; happiness; keep fit; nature; fresh air; positivity; environment; tired; gym; indoors; training; workout. Learners may incorporate the actual words into their improvisation or use their meaning as the basis for creating material.

102. Establishing links

Answers should include links between stimuli and the commission brief, referring to sport and the community. For example, 'Heroes' relates to the theme of sport (sporting heroes) and is often played at sporting events that involve the community. The text stimulus has direct links with sport and community. The theme of unity relates to how sport unites people within communities. The visual stimulus connects to how sport can provide hope for communities. The media stimulus is based on trail running which is a sport and accessible to the community.

103. Developing materials and ideas

Timeline of solo:

0:00–1:00: I start off by introducing the theme through stylised movement, to communicate the stimulus of 'Heroes'. I perform a lyrical jazz solo relating to sporting heroes and play an instrumental version of the song in the background.

1:00–1:15 : Transition 1 is to show a change in the structure; this is achieved through a change in the music, which stops. I remove some of my costume. Also I move in slow motion towards the audience (downstage).

1:15–3:00: I perform a street dance solo that links to heroes from athletics and gymnastics, in which I use props such as a hoop and a ribbon. I use hip-hop music that includes lyrics relating to heroes.

3:00–3:15: Transition 2 is to show another change in the structure; this is achieved by again moving in slow motion as previously, but this time upstage to suggest going back in time.

3:15–5:00: I perform a contemporary solo to music from the 1950s. I use a voice recording that I made, which talks about sporting heroes from the 1950s. My movement relates to the content of the dialogue, which I achieve through gesture, facial expression and dynamic changes.

5:00–5:30: I end my performance by travelling on a diagonal across the stage, from upstage right to downstage left in silence. I travel using different movements incorporated from a variety of sports. I end by reaching up (towards the heroes who have passed away) and the lights dim slowly.

104. Structure and present action

Answers should include ideas relating to the theme of unity in connection with transitions and exploration of space such as levels, dimensions, pathways and directions. For example:
I am going to be using the space by approaching the audience gradually for each section, so that I end up downstage. This is to increase the intensity as well as creating intimacy between the audience and myself. During the transition sections I am only going to be moving using my personal space (exploring levels and shape that relate to sporting prowess), in order to contrast with my journey downstage during the main sections.

105. Technical elements

Answers will need to include suggestions relating to how props, set, costume, lighting and sound could help enhance a solo performance. For example:
Props may be used to add an extra dimension; help to set a scene; add interest; help to establish a character.
Set may be used to create a mood; suggest an environment or location; add interest.
Costume can reinforce or suggest character; add spectacle; create visual effects.
Lighting can help to create mood; establish a setting; draw attention to performers (spotlights); create visual effects.
Sound can provide a beat/rhythm; provide sound effects to establish a setting or period in time; provide musical accompaniment to songs; create/enhance atmosphere; help to further the plot.
Each choice needs to be justified.

106. Performance skills

Answers will need to include examples of performance skills as featured in the list. Answers will also need to include how performance skills are employed to communicate style and meaning, for example: using diction to effectively convey the objective of sport and community through a series of monologues; using co-ordination in the execution of a dance with a balloon to convey hope; using facial expression to perform songs that relate to motivation and unity.

107. Individual performance skills

The purpose of the commission brief is celebration (and entertainment), so this would need to be considered in the selection of performance skills to be used. The messages relating to sport will need to be exuberant and celebratory, therefore this will need to be reflected in performances which should be mainly upbeat and positive, focusing on the advantages and successes within sport. However, if the intention was to inform/raise awareness of sport in relation to health problems the tone may be different. Performances would focus more on imparting information, and the messages communicated may be more hard-hitting.

108. Rehearse, practise and review

For example:
In a recent performance that I was in, I analysed my progress throughout, at weekly intervals. It was an individual performance and I used the analysis to help inform my progression. For example I examined weaknesses such as structure and creativity and addressed how they could be resolved. I decided to alter the structure slightly from an ABA to an AB structure; once I had done this I felt like it fitted to my 'Night and Day' theme a lot more clearly. I also addressed creativity issues by doing further improvisations and explorations, so that I was thinking more 'outside the box' and thus producing more original and innovative ideas. I also asked for peer feedback in order to improve the quality of my performance. I then analysed the feedback and looked at methods of addressing the points made. For example, I incorporated more use of gesture to connect with the contrasting states of night and day.

109. Managing your preparation time

Learner's own response.

110. Preparing for your solo

For example:
1 I will need: costume, make-up, props, set, music.
2 I will be focusing on the following performance skills:
   - projection: sending energy out to the audience to help communicate meaning
   - facial expression: because I am performing in different characters, use of facial expression is vital to my performance
   - use of dynamics: in order to show my contrasting characters' physicality, dynamics are an important element when considering how I move in performance (slow, fast, heavy etc.).

111. Evaluation: artistic effectiveness

Answers should include reasons why the three elements are important, for example:

- Execution of solo performance skills – to communicate meaning effectively. For example: Performance skills are vital and integral to the success of a performance. By using a combination of performance skills such as musicality, facial expression and projection, for example, it is possible to communicate intentions effectively. Fulfilling the objectives of a commission brief could not be achieved without the use of performance skills, as essentially they are employed to help communicate meaning. In order to hone performance skills it is necessary to practice them regularly, such as exaggeration of facial expression using a mirror and peer feedback.
- Clarity of interpretation – to convey objective(s). For example: Clarity of interpretation is essential to the effectiveness of a performance, and to delivering your message successfully. When an interpretation is unclear the performance loses impact and the intended meaning can be lost. In order to achieve clarity of interpretation, successful research in relation to the stimulus can help to inform material. Remaining on task throughout the process, as well as continually checking that each element (such as structure, repertoire and production elements) is aimed at communicating the intention is vital. You can use methods such as recording your work and watching it back/asking for peer feedback, to see how clear your interpretation is.
- Creativity and imagination – an original perspective on a common theme. For example: Employing creativity and imagination can really make a difference to your performance, making it stand out from others. Using improvisation techniques and exploration can help you to generate material that demonstrates thinking 'outside the box.' Often people can be afraid of being involved in improvisations, as it demands a certain level of confidence. However, with practice it is less daunting. Physical and verbal material can be generated through the use of improvisation techniques by, for example,

using key words as the basis for exploration. Recording yourself and watching it back can help you to select the most significant material, discarding that which is less relevant.

112. Evaluating artistic effectiveness

Answers should include reference to the three main areas of discussion and include specific examples.

113. Evaluation: professional effectiveness

Answers should include consideration of how production values improved the performance and how effectively time, tasks and resources were managed. Answers should contain specific examples.

114. Evaluating professional effectiveness

Answers could include examples such as facing challenges related to:

- resources available
- limited amount of space
- insufficient time to prepare
- difficulties in working independently (not being able to share ideas/collaborate in any way)

Ways in which to address these issues could include:

- trying to be resourceful in relation to production values. Can you adapt an item of clothing you already have or help to paint an old piece of set? Production elements should not be vital to your performance anyway.
- working as effectively as you possibly can within the confines of the rehearsal space, knowing that you will perhaps be able to utilise a bigger space more effectively in performance.
- If you have already lost valuable time you will really need to focus your energy on making a schedule that you will stick to, and working at a faster pace.
- You can always ask for peer feedback to help inform your decisions. Try to be proactive and work with initiative; give yourself goals to meet.

115. Evaluation: meeting requirements

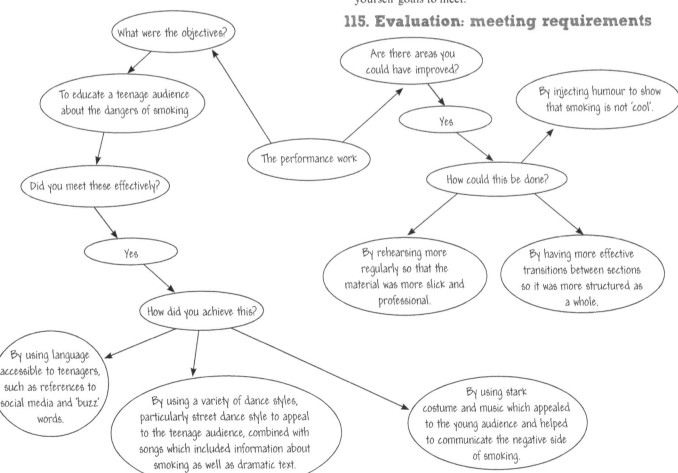

116. Evaluating fulfilment of purpose

Answers could include possible ways to improve, as well as what worked well and less well.

For example:

I interpreted the stimulus material fairly well, although I feel that I could have used the 'Heroes' track more successfully as a starting point. For example, I took the track and decided to write different lyrics which related to the theme of sport more clearly, with the intention of then performing the adapted song. I think I did this fairly well, although my lyrics could have been more original and creative, as well as fitting more effectively to the rhythms within the song. This was evident during rehearsal when I asked for peer feedback; however, it was then too late to change it. If I were to perform this task again I would allocate more time to it and play around more creatively with words and rhythms.

117. Evaluating the use of stimulus

Answers should include reference to how the experience will inform future projects. For example:

I managed requirements and constraints by consideration of the commissioning body (local authority) and target audience, as well as the purpose being to celebrate and entertain in relation to sport and the Olympics. I combined this information with the stimulus (theme of unity), thinking of ways that the two interconnect. For example, I considered what unity means to the wider public as well as what the Olympics means to people. I focused on key emotions such as pride, joy, hope and happiness. Using these as starting points for generating material was useful; I continually went back to the requirements and constraints to ensure I was on track. I considered whether my material was inclusive to all ages, whether the link to my stimulus was evident, whether it would be suitable as a local authority event and also if the purposes of celebration and entertainment had been successfully demonstrated. This will help me with future projects as I will give more consideration to elements such as target audience and be more focused on communicating my intention, including how this can be achieved.

Unit 7 Employment Opportunities in the Performing Arts

These answers are in no way prescriptive and are provided for guidance only.

120. Planning your preparation time

A plan based on the sample set task brief could look like this:

Week 1
- Analyse and research the brief
- Analyse my own skills and link them to the job
- Plan the professional portfolio
- Create the CV
- Arrange filming
- Record all of the footage
- Find all of the other evidence
- Type up notes

Week 2
- Edit all of the footage
- Get all of the evidence for the professional portfolio on a USB stick
- Check and review notes
- Print off notes
- Check everything

121. Organisational requirements

Vocalworks might look for employees with the following skills:
- good communication skills
- ability to work with the elderly
- time management skills

- singing skills
- leadership skills (for leading the workshops).

Learners' list of skills could include all or some of the skills identified above. They should be honest when evaluating their own skills.

122. The purpose of an organisation

Possible aims for Your World TIE company include:
- to broaden the minds of young adults
- to raise awareness of events in the news
- to perform exceptional and engaging theatre.

Possible objectives for Your World TIE company are:
- produce a new theatre piece each year that can be taken into schools
- perform in schools we have not yet visited
- find new ways to communicate complex themes and issues.

123. Vision, mission and values

The values could be any of the following:
- Creative collaboration comes first.
- Art is for all.
- Be innovative.
- No job is too big.
- Build strong relationships.

124. Intended audience and stakeholders

Answers could include the following:

Internal stakeholders:
- owners – to continue running as a business; to fulfil their mission
- managers – to make enough money for the organisation to continue; to make sure the workers do their job
- workers – to be happy at work; to be well paid

External stakeholders:
- customers – to get value for money; to have a good experience
- suppliers – to make a profit out of the purchasers; to maintain the contract
- the community – to be accessible to all and benefit everyone
- trade unions – to protect the rights of the workers; to make sure the workers get paid appropriately
- shareholders – to make a profit; for the company to be successful
- banks/creditors – for the company to be solvent; to make a profit
- pressure groups – that their beliefs are not offended or upheld

125. Scope

Answers could include the following:

Advantages of a **broad** scope:
- There are several different areas money can come from, so if one part of the business doesn't do well then the other income streams could compensate.
- Different customers can be drawn in from the different areas and become aware of the other aspects of the business.

Disadvantages of a **broad** scope:
- More money would be needed to begin the venture, and it could mean that the money is spread too thin.
- It could start off as a theatre space, but because another area makes more money (café, maybe) then the company might spend more time on the café than the theatre, which was not the original intention.

Advantages of a **narrow** scope:
- The business has one focus and can work really hard at developing it.
- It would be easier to stick to the mission without other distractions.

Disadvantages of a **narrow** scope:
- The business can be too reliant on one income stream, and if it is not successful the business might fail.

126. Types of legal constitutions

My group of friends and I would be best as an Unincorporated Association.

127. Types of organisational structures

Star Maker Academy would be more appropriate as a sole trader. It is cheaper, and a sole trader can still have employees. If the business grew substantially, a company limited by guarantee might be more appropriate.

128. Advantages and disadvantages of different organisational structures

Examples of types of organisations:
- sole trader – David Tennant (actor)
- unincorporated association – People Express, an arts organisation in Derbyshire, was an unincorporated association run by volunteers before it became a registered charity.
- community interest company – Arts First delivers music education opportunities at the Islington Music Education Hub.
- charity – Sadler's Wells Theatre is a registered charity.
- company limited by guarantee – Wac Arts is a performing arts venue in Hampstead Heath, London. It is both a registered charity and a company limited by guarantee. It offers classes, professional training and community activities.
- company limited by shares – Cameron Mackintosh Limited (West End Producer) is a company limited by shares.
- registered societies – PANDA (The Performing Arts Network and Development Agency) is a membership organisation that is registered with the Financial Conduct Authority. It supports venues, individuals and companies in the performing arts industry in the North of England.

129. Funding restrictions and opportunities

The following guides from Arts Council website would be useful.
- Payment conditions and Grants for the arts
- Public engagement and Grants for the arts
- Research and development, and Grants for the arts
You can find more useful guides in the Advice and Guidance section as well as the Funding Guidance section.

130. Public sector funding

1 A community project idea could be a dance workshop for children exploring the town's history, to tour local schools.
2 The Arts Council has a grants system. Individuals such as performers can apply. However, students cannot be funded for anything that is for their own courses – it has to be for the wider community. Going into local schools and delivering workshops to children is for the wider community. The Arts Council can fund education-related activity and touring work, among other things, which often includes performance work.

131. Private sector funding

Ideas to attract benefactors could include:
- first notification of ticket release
- free tickets to select performances
- a free drink or VIP room access
- meeting the performers after a performance
- invitations to watch a rehearsal.

132. Third sector funding

For example, DV8 Physical Theatre is funded by the Big Lottery Fund, the Arts Council England and via donations from the public.

133. Access to funding: grants and contracts

Examples of performing arts-related projects to tackle obesity: dance workshops based on Olympic sports; physical theatre workshops exploring how to be healthy

The idea most likely to receive tender would be the idea most developed to fit the requirements of the local authority. This could also be the most cost-effective project.

134. Fundraising and direct selling

Examples of fundraising ideas include:
- cake sales
- merchandising
- charity evening with ticket sales and variety performances
- donations tins
- bag-packing events in shopping centres.
The ideas most likely to generate income would be the charity evening with ticket sales, as long as the group could keep its expenses down.

135. Marketing, HR and finance

Examples of marketing ideas:
- radio advert
- newspaper press release
- posters placed in school/college
- leaflet distributing in the local town centre
- performing in the town centre.

136. Organisational operations

The RSC does not have a page dedicated to outreach, but education is an important focus for it. This includes all plays being broadcast live to classrooms free of charge, live lessons, school workshops and so on. It could possibly do more outreach to engage adults who are not really aware of Shakespeare. This could be with workshops for adult non-actors, projects taken into communities, and so on.

137. Education, creative and technical areas

Possible answers are: stage manager, assistant stage manager, lighting designer, lighting operator, sound designer, sound operator, costume designer and wardrobe manager.

138. Analysing information

Possible answers are:
- aim – to raise the profile of the company and the current performances
- objective – to provide high-quality training to children that would normally encounter barriers to participating in performing arts
- vision – to be a well-known company with close links with schools and clubs
- mission – to bring the work of the company to the wider community through workshops

139. Researching the organisation

The bottom of Candoco Dance Company's website shows logos for the Big Lottery Fund, Arts Council England, Esmée Fairbairn Foundation, British Council and Aspire. Funding bodies are the Big Lottery Fund, Arts Council England, Esmée Fairbairn Foundation, British Council and the Creative Europe Programme of the European Union. All of these bodies could potentially fund Breakin' Barriers.

140. Skills for professional practice

Evaluating written skills

Learners could identify difficulties in spelling certain words or their use of grammar. There could be issues with punctuation such as remembering to use full stops when they are typing or writing quickly. They could identify areas of strength, such as being able to structure essays well or knowing how to accurately spell the vocational terminology for performing arts.

How to develop areas for improvement

Learners can set themselves SMART targets to develop any areas for improvement. For example, 'I will improve my use of full stops by writing a little slower to give me a chance to finish sentences, and by accessing English exercises from the internet that test my ability to put the punctuation marks in the right places in sentences. I will do these exercises twice a week and measure my performance by proofreading my work and identifying how many corrections are needed.'

141. Experience for professional practice

Learner's own response, listing the skills learned at work. Here is a sample answer:

I spent my work experience in Year 10 at school at a reprographics business called Copy4U. This was mandatory work experience, but it was voluntary as I wasn't paid. During my two weeks I sat in the reception area, taking calls from customers, writing down orders using the company paperwork and then I was shown how to use the large copying machine for basic orders. The skills I needed for this included good communication and customer service skills, good writing skills so that I could write orders down easily, good reading skills to navigate the company's paperwork, and the ability to learn quickly when being trained to use the photocopying machine.

142. Effective communication skills

Learners can record themselves by using apps on their phones. When they listen back, they should think about whether they remove any consonants as they speak. Do they remove the Ts or Ds? Are they saying 'th' with clarity? Is their voice loud enough to be heard but not too loud that it becomes shouting? They can set themselves an action plan to improve their speaking.

143. Effective written communication skills

Learner's own response.

144. Pitching ideas

Here is a sample pitch:
My idea is to widen participation in drama by contacting lots of schools in the area, inviting them to participate in this project. We will go into the schools to reduce their travel costs and deliver a series of drama workshops based on devising work. The workshops will end in a final performance. I will hire the local theatre for a day. All of the participants will arrive for a technical/dress rehearsal in the day and then we will perform in the evening. Tickets will be sold to the parents, and in the programme there will be adverts for local drama clubs.

145. What is a promotional portfolio?

Here is a sample CV in note form:

```
James Smith
124 Wembrook Avenue
MT72 6LJ

Height: 5 foot 5 inches
Eye colour: Brown
Hair Colour: Brown
Training
2016–2018 Extended Diploma in Performing Arts
(predicted MMM)
2015–2016 BTEC Level 1/2 Diploma in Performing Arts
(Distinction)
Relevant experience
2016    Play    Dr Martin Dysart   Equus
College Theatre, West Midlands
2015    Play    Old Major         Animal Farm
College Theatre, West Midlands
```

146. Alternative portfolio formats

Learners should use search engines to check their online profile. They may want to amend their profile after thinking about how it might look like to a prospective employer.

147. Highlighting discipline and skills

Learner's own response.

148. Highlighting relevant skills

Here is a sample answer:
Skill – facial and bodily expression for dance.
Three performances that showcase these skills:
- 'Midnight' – A contemporary dance piece based on the painting *The Starry Night* by Vincent Van Gogh and the technique of Martha Graham. The piece showcases my ability to use contraction and release, and express the inner turmoil of the artist.
- 'Skidrow' – A musical theatre piece where I played a homeless person. I had a character and performed movement work while singing.
- 'Fosse' – A Jazz dance piece where I performed Fosse-style movement.

149. Understanding practical work

Here is a sample answer:
Unit 14: Choreography for Live Performance – I created a solo and a group dance. The end product shows my creativity skills, as well as reflecting how good I am at planning and preparing for a performance and having the sole responsibility for the outcome. I am able to work to deadlines, producing a final performance. I can adapt ideas to suit the capabilities of the dancers. I can create movement that answers the brief. I have good communication skills and I am able to liaise with people from other departments to negotiate the design elements of the final performance.

150. Selecting relevant video footage

Ideas for audition pieces:
- a song from a rock musical that demonstrates the same vocal abilities (maybe *Jesus Christ Superstar*)
- a suitable rock song that demonstrates the same vocal abilities
- a movement piece (evidence from a workshop or a solo).
The skills required would be singing, movement and acting through singing.

151. Promotional intent

Here is a sample answer:
In this video I am performing in 'Who's Afraid of Virginia Woolf?' by Edward Albee. It was performed at the School Theatre on 24 May 2016. It was an assessed piece for my training on the Level 3 National Extended Diploma course in Performing Arts. I played the role of Martha.

152. Are you right for the job?

Here is a sample answer:
Transferable skill: motivating people
Evidenced: in a reference from the Head of the Performing Arts Club where I teach at the weekends

153. Ensuring professionalism

Observations could include:
- The head shots look professional.
- They have the right lighting and are not selfies.
- All of the information is written well, with correct punctuation and grammar.
- The website is professional, with the name of the performer as the web address.

154. Relating the employment opportunity to your skills

Three possible funding sources for Breakin' Barriers are:
- the Big Lottery Fund
- Arts Council England
- trusts and charities.

155. Thinking of workshop ideas

Sample workshop idea based on *A Midsummer Night's Dream*: Explore the theme of magic through movement. Focus on Puck generating the fog to move the humans. Start with a warm-up, then a few exercises using arm swings. Then set some choreographic tasks where swinging movements shift other people around the space. The workshop could build physical skills such as co-ordination and stamina through the arm-swinging section, and agility when shifting around the space. There would also be team work as you need to be able to respond to someone else's movement.

156. Your performance skills

Additional skills could include juggling, gymnastics and martial arts, for example.

157. Writing about your performance skills

For example, gymnastics experience could enhance the fairy scenes, with use of tumbles and stunts. Juggling could be used by the Mechanicals when they rehearse the play Pyramus and Thisbe. Martial arts such as judo can inspire contact work to be used by the fairies.

158. Your employment skills

Sample answer:
1 Literacy skills include reading texts, using documents and writing. Past experiences where I have demonstrated this are when I have used books to research drama practitioners to inform my development.
2 My ability to write well means I can produce detailed reports on the outcome of my workshops.

159. Your communication skills

Here are some sample answers:
1 Listening skills – listening and responding to the director's instructions
Verbal skills – working in retail and speaking to customers
2 Listening skills – I will be able to listen and respond to the director of Breakin' Barriers. I will be able to listen to the expertise of the SEN team who can help me develop appropriate workshops. I will be able to listen to children in the workshops and respond to their needs.
Verbal skills – I will be able to speak to the SEN team, children, creative team, fellow cast members and production staff with courtesy and respect.

161. Planning your digital promotional portfolio

Example of a promotional portfolio plan:
1 My introduction – my name and short summary of who I am
2 My CV – adapted to include the Shakespeare work I have done and the workshops I have led in college
3 My head shot – black and white, head and shoulders
4 Video footage of my Shakespeare monologue – Oberon
5 Audio recording of me singing a folk song
6 Video footage of my performance in 'Surprise', a physical theatre piece (contact work section)
7 Video footage of me leading a vocal warm-up at college
8 My drama certificates
9 My GCSE certificate in English
10 A reference from my drama teacher
Video footage plan:
Video 1 – 2 minutes
Audio 1 – 2 minutes
Video 2 – 2 minutes
Video 3 – 1 minute
Video 4 – 1 minute
Video 5 – 2 minutes

162. Content of your digital promotional portfolio

Example of a completed video footage plan:
Video 1 – 2 minutes – Shakespearean monologue completed for a classical theatre unit
Audio 1 – 2 minutes – Solo song developed from singing unit
Video 2 – 2 minutes – Contemporary monologue from contemporary theatre unit
Video 3 – 1 minute – Leading a rehearsal in our physical theatre piece 'Shame'
Video 4 – 1 minute – Leading a warm-up for physical theatre piece 'Shame'
Video 5 – 2 minutes – Video footage from my role as Prospero in 'Return to the Forbidden Planet' at college

163. Creating your CV

Learner's own response, listing their own performance experience. The following important information should be included: the year, type of theatre role, production, company, director.

164. Preparing video evidence

When speaking to the camera, learners should speak directly to the camera lens. They can review recordings to see what can be done to improve delivery.

165. Selecting relevant video footage

This is a recording of me performing a monologue from 'Romeo and Juliet' (Act 3 scene 3). I play the role of Romeo when he has just received the news that he has been banished from the city. He is devastated because it means he won't be able to see his love, Juliet.

166. Planning your supervised assessment time

Learner's own response, taking personal strengths and weaknesses into account.

Notes

Notes

Notes

Notes

Notes

Notes

Published by Pearson Education Limited, 80 Strand, London, WC2R 0RL.

www.pearsonschoolsandfecolleges.co.uk

Copies of official specifications for all Pearson qualifications may be found on the website: qualifications.pearson.com

Text and illustrations © Pearson Education Limited 2017
Typeset and illustrated by Kamae Design
Produced by Out of House Publishing
Cover illustration by Miriam Sturdee

The rights of Emma Hindley and Heidi McEntee to be identified as authors of this work have been asserted by them in accordance with the Copyright, Designs and Patents Act 1988.

First published 2017

20 19 18 17
10 9 8 7 6 5 4 3 2 1

British Library Cataloguing in Publication Data
A catalogue record for this book is available from the British Library

ISBN 978 1 292 15040 6

Acknowledgements
We are grateful to the following for permission to reproduce copyright material:

Text
Extract on page 3 from *The Vision of Modern Dance*, (Brown, J.M., Mindlin, N., Woodford, C.H., Eds. 1998), quote from Martha Graham with permission from Princeton Book Company; Extract on page 12 from *The Life and Work of Martha Graham*, 1st Ed, Random House Inc (Agnes de Mille 1991) p.264, with permission from Random House Inc and Random House Group; Article on page 40 from Refugee crisis: Greek governor calls for state of emergency over thousands of people stranded on border, *Independent*, 05/03/2016 (Cendrowicz,L., Sandhu,S.), The Independent with permission; Quote on page 80 from Mandela, Nelson. Speech at the Inaugural Laureus Lifetime Achievement Award, Monaco 2000, Nelson Mandela Foundation (2000), with permission; Article in Answers, page 171 from UNHCR warns of imminent humanitarian crisis in Greece amid disarray in Europe over asylum, Edwards,A. 01/03/2016, UNHCR with permission; Links in Answers, page 171 © 2016 Discogs® Zink Media, Inc and WhoSampled.com.

Figures
Figure on page 54 from http://www.bloodpressureuk.org/BloodPressureandyou/Thebasics/Bloodpressurechart, Blood Pressure UK

Picture Credits
The publisher would like to thank the following for their kind permission to reproduce their photographs:

(Key: b-bottom; c-centre; l-left; r-right; t-top)

123RF.com: 96tl, Andrei Zaripov 60cl, Wavebreak Media Ltd 136br, wong yu liang 93tr; **Alamy Stock Photo:** A F Archive 150cl, AKP Photos 125tl, Annie Eagle 96cr, Cathy Yeulet 157b, Cattie Coyle 60cr, Cirque de Soleil / epa european pressphoto agency b.v. 121cl, Everett Collection Historical 3, 10br, 17bl, 19br, Cultura Creative (RF) 68cr, Dance by Beytan 55br, Danilo Moroni /:Anne Teresa De Keersmaeker / Rosas present Golden Hours (As You Like It) at Sadler's Wells Theatre 29cr, Dave And Les Jacobs / Blend Images 5br, Everett Collection, Inc 14cr, 26tr, EyeEm 1br, 35cr, Gato Desaparecido 165tr, Geraint Lewis 18br, 19tr, 30cl, 125cr, 150cr, Glyn Thomas 57tr, Granger Historical Picture Archive 20tc, Hill Street Studios / Blend Images 107cr, 144tr, 149br, Iris Friedrich / fStop Images GmbH 59br, James Boardman 42tr, Jon Legge 132br, Juergen Moers / vario images GmbH & Co.KG 59bl, Julio Calvo / Glasshouse Images 145br, Kathy deWitt 80tr, keith morris 64cr, 65c, keith morris 64cr, 65c, Keystone Pictures USA 19cl, Kiko Jimenez / Westend61 GmbH 109cr, Lordpice Collection 94tr, Lucianne Pashley / age fotostock 87c, Marc Hill 21bl, mikecranephotography.com 40cr, Nir Alon 148cl, Norma Jean Gargasz 42br, Paul Doyle 47br, pf 20tl, Pictorial Press Ltd 3br, Pictures Colour Library 127br, Roger Bacon / Reuters 46tl, Scott Campbell 122bl, theatrepix 25c, WENN Ltd 83cr, 84cr; **Arts Council England:** 125cl; **Ben Hodson at A Thin Place:** Luton Creates Project 82cr; **Bridgeman Art Library Ltd:** Bird in flight, plate 762 from 'Animal Locomotion', 1887 (b / w photo), Muybridge, Eadweard (1830-1904) / Private Collection / The Stapleton Collection 40tr, 54cl; **C-12 Dance Theatre:** Photo Credit Irven Lewis. Trolleys Choreographed by Shaun Parker, Performed by C-12 Dance Theatre. 47cr; **Camelot UK Lotteries Limited:** 130cl; **Fotolia.com:** bit24 140cl, Christian Robach 30br, dekART 94bl, drx 150bl, georgerudy 146cl, 164c, highwaystarz 162bl, hubb67 18cl, Kav 8tr, Lisa F. Young 93tl, Monkey Business 141tc, mwellis 73bc, olly 106cr, Piotr Marcinski 66tr, portokalis 41tr, Rawpixel.com 75br, 87tl, Roman Gorielov 45cr, Spectral-Design 109tr, stokkete 81cr, Victor Tongdee 94cr, Xavier Allard 16tr; **Getty Images:** Allan Tannenbaum / The LIFE Images Collection 13tl, Andreas Rentz 15cl, Chris Schmidt / E+ 8bl, Dave Bennett / Hulton Archive 22tr, iStockphoto 76cr, Jack Mitchell / Archive Photos 20tr, Joe Scarnici 79br, Laurie Cadevida in 'Miss Saigon' Sydney 103br, sturti / E+ 51b, Time Life Pictures / The LIFE Picture Collection 95bl; **Hull Truck Theatre:** Hull Truck Theatre Website 2016 52c; **Leeds City Council:** Courtesy of Academy of Northern Ballet Centre for Advanced Training 83tr; **Paul Blakemore:** 82tr; **Pearson Education Ltd:** Studio 8 102c, Ken Wilson-Max 5cr, 70br, 141tr; **Photoshot Holdings Limited:** LFI 56br; **Photostage Ltd:** Donald Cooper 44cr; **Rex Shutterstock:** Stephen Tompkinson in 'DCI Banks' Episode ' Aftermath' / ITV 46bl; **Saltmine Theatre Company:** 85tc; **Shutterstock.com:** AJP 62bl, Alexander Yakovlev 101c, Amble Design 91bl, Andresr 163tr, AoiTana 131bc, AYakovlev 161tl, BPTU 42bl, cobalt88 46bl/ (TV), ConstantinoZ 97cl, David Pereiras 142tr, Eduard Kyslynskyy 41bl, gorillaimages 43cl, kRie 143br, Ljupco Smokovski 42tl, Microstock Man 16bl, Nanette Grebe 67br, Narcis Parfenti 50cl, Rawpixel 87bc, Sylvie Bouchard 98c, TheFinalMiracle 41tl, William Perugini 80tl; **Siobhan Davies Dance:** Padi Naderi 84tr; **The Kobal Collection:** Sandra Bullock in 'Gravity' 2013 / WARNER BROS 96bl; **TopFoto:** Eleni Leoussi / ArenaPAL 17tr, Elliott Franks / Arenapal / www.arenapal.com: / TITS / TEETH by Wynne: 29cl, Nobby Clark / ArenaPAL / www.arenapal.com 50cr

All other images © Pearson Education

Notes from the publisher
1.
In order to ensure that this resource offers high-quality support for the associated Pearson qualification, it has been through a review process by the awarding body. This process confirms that this resource fully covers the teaching and learning content of the specification or part of a specification at which it is aimed. It also confirms that it demonstrates an appropriate balance between the development of subject skills, knowledge and understanding, in addition to preparation for assessment.

Endorsement does not cover any guidance on assessment activities or processes (e.g. practice questions or advice on how to answer assessment questions), included in the resource nor does it prescribe any particular approach to the teaching or delivery of a related course.

While the publishers have made every attempt to ensure that advice on the qualification and its assessment is accurate, the official specification and associated assessment guidance materials are the only authoritative source of information and should always be referred to for definitive guidance.

Pearson examiners have not contributed to any sections in this resource relevant to examination papers for which they have responsibility.

Examiners will not use endorsed resources as a source of material for any assessment set by Pearson.

Endorsement of a resource does not mean that the resource is required to achieve this Pearson qualification, nor does it mean that it is the only suitable material available to support the qualification, and any resource lists produced by the awarding body shall include this and other appropriate resources.

2.
Pearson has robust editorial processes, including answer and fact checks, to ensure the accuracy of the content in this publication, and every effort is made to ensure this publication is free of errors. We are, however, only human, and occasionally errors do occur. Pearson is not liable for any misunderstandings that arise as a result of errors in this publication, but it is our priority to ensure that the content is accurate. If you spot an error, please do contact us at resourcescorrections@pearson.com so we can make sure it is corrected.

Websites
Pearson Education Limited is not responsible for the content of any external internet sites. It is essential for tutors to preview each website before using it in class so as to ensure that the URL is still accurate, relevant and appropriate. We suggest that tutors bookmark useful websites and consider enabling students to access them through the school/college intranet.